Introduction to
TCP/IP
Internetworking

Patrick J. Bush, M.Ed, MCSE, MCT, MCP+I

VISIT US ON THE INTERNET
www.swep.com

South-Western Educational Publishing
an International Thomson Publishing company I(T)P®
www.thomson.com

Cincinnati • Albany, NY • Belmont, CA • Bonn • Boston • Detroit • Johannesburg • London • Madrid
Melbourne • Mexico City • New York • Paris • Singapore • Tokyo • Toronto • Washington

Team Leader: Karen Schmohe
Managing Editor: Carol Volz
Developmental Editor: Jean Findley
Marketing Manager: Larry Qualls
Development/Production Services: Shepherd, Inc.
Production Editor: Tricia Behnke
Technical Reviewers: Laura Schlegel, Jeff Beck
Cover Design: Joe Pagliaro

ISBN: 0-538-68870-X

Library of Congress Cataloging-in-Publication Data

Bush, Patrick.
   Introduction to TCP/IP Internetworking / by Patrick Bush.
      p.   cm.
   Includes index.
   ISBN 0–538–68870–X (alk. paper)
      1. TCP/IP (Computer network protocol)   2. Internetworking
(Telecommunication) I. Title.
TK105.585.B985   1999
004.6'2—dc21   99–26165
                                                            CIP

1 2 3 4 5 6 7 8 9 CK 02 01 00 99
Printed in the United States of America

International Thomson Publishing

South-Western Educational Publishing is a division of International Thomson Publishing, Inc.
The ITP trademark is used under license.

PREFACE

Congratulations on your decision to consider a career in Information Technology! You are about to embark upon a career full of challenges, rewards, and an almost endless pathway of opportunities and financial benefits. Your selection of TCP/IP as a Microsoft exam elective is an excellent one and will serve you well as a critical skill-set in this age of the Internet and wide-area network connectivity.

The topic of TCP/IP has long been reserved for the most advanced of computer engineers and "techno-jockies." Yet, the protocol suite called TCP/IP is really no more complicated or difficult to learn than any other computer protocol or application. In some ways, because the topic is specific, you may find the material easier to grasp than, say, Windows NT because of the focus on one particular topic rather than on a broad survey of operating systems and network interconnectivity. We will be specializing in TCP/IP and its function within the Windows NT environment for this course.

TCP/IP is a very robust protocol suite providing a great degree of customization ability to particular business requirements. As is the case with anything that offers this level of flexibility (operating systems, applications, or protocols), the more function in a product, the more complex it becomes. Yet, by taking the protocol suite one step at a time, you should easily grasp the concepts presented throughout this book.

This book is designed to demystify typically difficult TCP/IP topics including sub-netting, troubleshooting an IP network, DNS/WINS name resolution, and routing. While this book provides appropriate content for the 70-69 *Internetworking with Microsoft TCP/IP on Windows NT 4.0* exam, it is not focused solely on test success. It is my objective to prepare students with a *functional working knowledge* of the TCP/IP protocol as applied to the Windows NT operating system.

The TCP/IP exam is a popular elective in the MCSE (Microsoft Certified Systems Engineer) track and has the distinct reputation of being one of the more difficult examinations to pass. It is my goal as an author and instructor to provide you with the tools, terminology, and knowledge to successfully procure a "green bar" when you finish the Microsoft exam. To do this, the materials will be presented in a building block chapter format, providing a combination of theory, practice, and hands-on Windows NT configuration. Each chapter will have hands-on exercises as well as review questions that you should complete before proceeding.

To take this course, you should be thoroughly familiar with the Windows NT family of desktop and server operating systems as well as basic networking terminology. This is an advanced book focused on a particular implementation of a networking protocol and makes the assumption that you already fully understand the Windows NT 4.0 operating system, the function of a router and gateway, the OSI model, and network interconnectivity. If you feel uncomfortable with any of these topics, I strongly recommend that you review the materials before proceeding.

With that in mind, let us begin! I trust you will find this course to be as much fun to take as it was to write.

Patrick J. Bush, M.Ed, MCSE, MCT, MCP+I, A+ Certified Technician
March 1999

Microsoft Certified Professional Program

South-Western Educational Publishing is a participant in the Microsoft Independent Courseware Vendor program. Microsoft ICVs design, develop, and marked self-paced courseware, books, and other products that support Microsoft software and the Microsoft Certified Professional (MCP) program.

To be accepted into the Microsoft ICV program, an ICV must meet set criteria. Microsoft reviews and approves each ICV training product before permission is granted to use the Microsoft Certified Professional Approved Study Guide logo on that product. This logo assures the consumer that the product has passed the following Microsoft standards:

The course contains accurate product information.

The course includes labs and activities during which the student can apply knowledge and skills learned from the course.

The course teaches skills that help prepare the student to take corresponding MCP exams.

Why Get Microsoft Certified?

Certification gives you the credentials you need to make the most of your chosen career, grow in your present job, or move on to bigger and better things. It tells people you're computer literate, skilled, productive, and efficient. The Microsoft Certified Professional (MCP) program provides a means for technical professionals to demonstrate their proficiency in Microsoft BackOffice products. MCP certification is an industry-recognized standard for measuring a computer professional's ability to design, develop, support, and implement solutions with Microsoft products.

How Does It Work?

Once you have completed the necessary training using your South-Western courseware, you will be prepared to take the corresponding exam. Microsoft certification exams reflect real challenges found in the workplace and measure skills valued by organizations. The exam format may be objective-type questions or simulations, depending on the skill being tested.

For the most up-to-date certification information, visit the Microsoft Web site at http://www.microsoft.com/train_cert/

Step-by-Step Certification Procedures

Here are the specific steps to help you prepare for an exam:

1. **Choose your certification.** There are four basic MCP certifications.

   Microsoft Certified Systems Engineer (MCSE) Requirements:

   Microsoft Certified Systems Engineers are required to pass four operating system exams and two elective exams. The operating system exams require candidates to prove their expertise with desktop, server, and networking components. The elective exams require proof of expertise with Microsoft BackOffice products. MCSEs design, install, support, and troubleshoot information systems. MCSEs are network gurus, support technicians, and operating system experts.

   Microsoft Certified Solution Developer (MCSD) Requirements:

   Microsoft Certified Solution Developers are required to pass two core technology exams and two elective exams. The core technology exams require candidates to prove their understanding of Windows® 32-bit architecture, OLE, UI design, and Windows Open Services Architecture components. The elective exams require proof of expertise with Microsoft development tools. MCSDs use development tools and platforms to create business solutions.

   Microsoft Certified Product Specialist (MCPS) Requirements:

   Microsoft Certified Product Specialists are required to pass one operating system exam, proving their expertise with a current Microsoft Windows® desktop or server operating system. Some also specialize in other Microsoft products, development tools, or desktop applications.

   Microsoft Certified Trainer (MCT) Requirements:

   Microsoft Certified Trainers (MCTs) are trainers who teach Microsoft Official Curriculum courses at Microsoft Authorized Technical Education Centers. Once you have been approved as an MCT, your MCT credential will be accepted in all Microsoft education channels.

2. **Get an Exam Preparation Guide from the Microsoft Web site.** The exam preparation guide tells you the skills being measured by the exam.

3. **Complete your training.** Your South-Western courseware helps you prepare for a Microsoft certification exam.

4. **Apply your skills in a real-world environment.** It is necessary to have hands-on experience in the Microsoft product you are learning in order to pass an MCP exam.

5. **Get a Practice Test from the Microsoft Web site, and/or take the practice tests in your South-Western course.** Practice tests give you the

opportunity to answer questions that are similar to those on the certification exam. (Your score on a practice test doesn't necessarily indicate what your score will be on a certification exam.)

6. **Register for an Exam.** Call 1-800-755-EXAM (1-800-755-3926) to find a Sylvan Prometric testing center near you. Outside the United States and Canada, call your local Microsoft subsidiary. You will need to bring one photo ID and one other ID to the testing center when you go to take your exam.

Table of Contents

• •

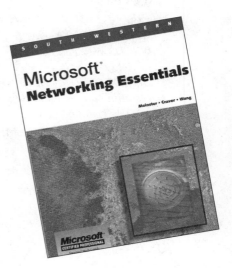
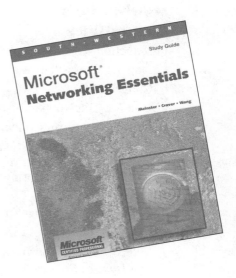

TCP/IP AT A GLANCE

OBJECTIVES

By the end of this chapter, you should be able to:

- Describe the origins and history of the TCP/IP Protocol Suite.

- Describe common Microsoft TCP/IP utilities provided with Windows NT Workstation and Server.

- Define and explain the purpose of a RFC (Request for Comment).

- Define the Internet Standards Process.

- Complete basic installation and configuration of Microsoft TCP/IP.

Introduction

This chapter provides a working foundation of terminology, history, and the logistics of the TCP/IP protocol suite. TCP/IP is a technically robust and flexible network protocol suite consisting of many utilities and programs to assist a computer user in performing common networking tasks such as file transfers, printing, viewing information, troubleshooting, and monitoring performance. We will be looking closely at some basic definitions of terminology, acronyms, the history of the protocol, the standards process, features and functions of the protocol, and basic TCP nomenclature as it relates to IP Addresses and subnet masks.

As we work through the chapter, we will also install and configure Microsoft TCP/IP on a Windows NT platform and discuss some of the installation options available to us when configuring the protocol. As we will see, Microsoft provides a full-featured implementation of TCP/IP that is tightly integrated into the Windows family of operating systems while maintaining adherence to generic TCP/IP standards. Microsoft is committed to providing network services using TCP/IP and will continue to further support, integrate, and enhance the protocol's implementation in its operating systems, product lines, and services.

Lesson 1.1 Acronyms and Terminology

Many of the terms presented in this chapter may be new to you as a student. Listed below are terminology and acronyms that we will be using throughout this chapter. You should be thoroughly familiar with each of these terms since they will be used throughout the rest of the book.

Protocol. Generally, a protocol consists of a set of rules and methods for communication. As applied in the computer networking field, it is any recognized and standardized method for computer communication. Examples of computer networking protocols include IPX/SPX, TCP/IP, and NetBEUI.

Suite. A suite is a grouping of related applications or protocols that are bundled together under one name. TCP/IP is a "protocol suite" consisting of many individual protocols. For example, TCP is a discrete protocol as is IP. Together, they are responsible for transmission and network access for the TCP/IP protocol suite.

TCP. Acronym for *Transmission Control Protocol*—A protocol within the TCP/IP suite responsible for the break-up of data messages into packets to be sent from a source computer via IP. It is also responsible for the subsequent reception and re-assembly of data on the target machine. TCP works at the transport layer of the OSI model and is known to be a method for "guaranteed" transport.

IP. Acronym for *Internet Protocol*. A protocol within TCP/IP suite that governs the sending and routing of data packets from sender to destination networks and stations. It is also responsible for the subsequent reception of data packets. IP then passes these packets to TCP for re-assembly into the original data message. IP corresponds to the network layer in the ISO/OSI model.

RFC. Acronym for *Request for Comment*—A document which contains a standard, a protocol, or other information pertaining to the operation of the Internet. The RFC is actually issued, under the control of the IAB, *after* discussion and serves as the standard. RFCs can be obtained from sources such as InterNIC.

DARPA. Acronym for *Defense Advanced Research Projects Agency*—The U.S. government agency that provided original support for the development of interconnected networks that later grew into the Internet.

ARPANET. A large wide-area network created in the 1960s by the U.S. Department of Defense Advanced Research Projects Agency (ARPA, renamed DARPA in the 1970s) for the free exchange of information between universities and research organizations, although the military also used this network for communications. In the 1980s, MILNET, a separate network, was spun off from ARPANET for use by the military. ARPANET was the network from which the Internet evolved.

MILNET. Acronym for *Military Network.* A wide-area network (WAN) that represents the military implementation of the original ARPANET. MILNET carries nonclassified U.S. military traffic and was created in the 1980s.

DOD. Acronym for United States *Department of Defense*—The military branch of the United States government. The Department of Defense developed ARPANET, the origin of today's Internet, and MILNET through its Advanced Research Projects Agency (ARPA).

NCT. Acronym for *Network Control Protocol*—A network protocol that was an early predecessor to TCP/IP. NCT was used by the ARPANET until 1981 when it was replaced by TCP/IP.

Telnet. A protocol that enables an Internet user to log on to, and enter commands on, a remote computer linked to the Internet, as if the user were using a text-based terminal directly attached to that computer. Telnet is commonly used for access to UNIX systems. Telnet is part of the TCP/IP suite of protocols.

FTP. Acronym for *File Transfer Protocol*—A protocol used for copying files to and from remote computer systems on a network using TCP/IP, such as the Internet. This protocol also allows users to use FTP commands to work with files, such as listing files and directories, on the remote system. FTP uses TCP for transport, assuring a guaranteed connection to and from the client and server.

DNS. Acronym for *Domain Name System*—A name resolution system by which hosts on the Internet have both fully-qualified domain name addresses (such as www.microsoft.com) and IP addresses (such as 192.17.3.4). The domain name address is used by human users and is automatically translated into the numeric IP address, which is used by packet-routing software. DNS uses a hierarchical database (very much like a directory tree) to resolve domain names to IP addresses. DNS is a "static" database. This means that all entries are added manually by a network administrator. DNS servers are also called *name servers.*

ISOC. Acronym for *Internet Society*—An international organization, comprising individuals, companies, foundations, and government agencies, that promotes the use, maintenance, and development of the Internet.

IAB. Acronym for *Internet Architecture Board*—The Internet Architecture Board (IAB) is a body within the Internet Society. The Internet Society publishes the *Internet Society News* and produces the annual INET conference.

InterNIC. A short name for NSFnet (*Internet*) *Network Information Center*. This organization is charged with registering domain names and IP addresses as well as distributing information about the Internet. InterNIC was formed in 1993 as a consortium involving the U.S. National Science Foundation, AT&T, General Atomics, and Network Solutions Inc. One of the consortium members (Network Solutions, Inc. in Herndon, VA) administers InterNIC Domain Name Registration Services, which assigns Internet names and addresses. InterNIC can be reached by e-mail at info@internic.net or on the Web at http://www.internic.net/.

PING. Acronym for *Packet Internet Groper*—A protocol in the TCP/IP suite used to test whether a particular computer or device (e.g., router) is connected (or "alive") to the Internet by sending a packet to its IP address and waiting for a response. Used in all TCP/IP suites, PING is a Windows NT command line application. The name originates from submarine active sonar, where a sound signal—called a "ping"—is broadcast, and surrounding objects are revealed by their reflections of the sound.

IPCONFIG. A TCP/IP utility used to troubleshoot local host TCP/IP configurations. IPCONFIG is a Windows NT command line utility that displays a computer's IP address, subnet mask, default gateway, and various other information that is useful when trying to determine the cause of TCP/IP configuration problems.

DHCP. Acronym for *Dynamic Host Configuration Protocol*—A TCP/IP protocol that enables a network connected to the Internet to assign a temporary IP address (also known as a leased address) to a host automatically when the host connects to the network. Microsoft Windows NT Server contains a DHCP server application that allows the network administrator to centrally manage IP configurations for a network. DHCP can also be used to configure many other TCP/IP configuration options, such as DNS server addresses, Default Gateways, and WINS server addresses/broadcast nodes, greatly easing a network administrator's workload.

UDP. Acronym for *User Datagram Protocol*—A connectionless protocol within the TCP/IP protocol suite that corresponds to the transport layer in the ISO/OSI model. From a functional perspective, TCP and UDP serve the same purpose: To convert data messages generated by an application into packets to be sent via IP. However, UDP does not verify that messages have been delivered correctly. This message conversion without verification is also known as "broadcasting". More efficient than TCP, but not as reliable, UDP is used for various transport protocols within the TCP/IP suite including TFTP (Trivial File Transfer Protocol) and SNMP (Simple Network Management Protocol).

IP Address. Acronym for *Internet Protocol Address*—A 32-bit (4-byte) binary number that uniquely identifies a host (computer) connected to the Internet to other Internet hosts for the purposes of communication through the transfer of packets. All ports on an IP network must have a unique IP address. An IP address is expressed in "dotted quad" format, consisting of the decimal values of its four bytes, separated with periods; for example, 127.0.0.1. Each number separated by a period is often referred to as an "octet" because of the relationship between the decimal number and the 8-component bits that make it up. The first one, two, or three bytes of the IP address identify the host network. The remaining bits identify the host itself.

Subnet Mask. A required (and very important) configuration option in a TCP/IP network that designates where a network address ends and where host addresses begin. A subnet mask is used to "mask" or hide a portion of the IP address so the computer can determine which part of the address is used for the network and which part is used for the host identification.

Subnet. A smaller network that is a component of a larger network typically connected by routers.

Lesson 1.2 What Is TCP/IP?

TCP/IP is a technically mature, robust, and extremely flexible suite of computer networking protocols and applications. It is *the* "Internet protocol" and in many ways is known to be the unilateral connectivity protocol common to all computers, manufacturers, and software vendors. TCP/IP is a general standard for communications. While each vendor has its own particular implementation of the protocol, they all adhere to the standards set forth by several governing bodies discussed later in this chapter. For instance, Microsoft's version of TCP/IP is slightly different than Novell's, Banyan's, or IBM's implementation. However, since all the vendors adhere to the basic rules for communicating established by a TCP/IP standards committee, these different implementations can effectively communicate.

TCP/IP is not a proprietary protocol like Novell's IPX/SPX or Microsoft's NetBEUI. The standards and architecture of the protocol are available to everyone (even yourself) for their use, review, and commentary. This, in part, stems from TCP/IP's origin as a government initiative. Even the standards board for TCP/IP is made up of a consortium of many companies, all of whom work together to see that the TCP/IP standards are generic and available for all to use. This makes TCP/IP the least common denominator (LCD) of protocols: It is truly a generic, all-purpose protocol. This is predominantly why it is often dubbed the "Internet Protocol."

TCP/IP Protocol Overview

TCP/IP often brings chills to those who are first exposed to the term. This is partly due to some misconceptions but also due to the fact that the protocol stack is riddled with acronyms and small modularized protocols and applications. This lesson will describe features and functions of the TCP/IP protocol suite. Many of the concepts, applications, and protocols presented in this section will be covered in far greater detail later in the book so don't worry if some of this information seems like gibberish at this point. It will all become clear, even easy, as you progress.

A Word on Protocol Stacks and Protocols

A protocol is nothing more than a set of rules governing behavior, conduct, and/or communications. Protocols find their use in our everyday lives as much as in the computer field. We have rules for almost everything we do: from conduct in school or society (these are most commonly known as laws) to how diplomats and politicians interact (these rules are known as protocols)! Computer networking protocols govern mechanisms for transport and reception of data across a network cable. Groups of these rules are known as protocol suites.

A particular protocol implementation is also often referred to as a "protocol stack". This term comes from the "stacking" of building blocks components that define the OSI model. The TCP/IP protocol stack consists of many component applications and protocols, some of which can be used interchangeably (and transparently) for network transport and delivery of data. All of these applications and protocols work together, allowing TCP/IP to provide a complete and comprehensive connectivity mechanism for network data transport.

Generic TCP/IP Features

While we will be focusing exclusively on Microsoft's TCP/IP protocol implementation, it is useful to note some general TCP/IP attributes that all implementations use. The nice thing about learning TCP/IP is that your knowledge is largely transferable to other platforms. This is not so with proprietary operating systems like Windows NT or Novell NetWare. They are very different operating systems with a whole different set of functions, commands, utilities, and considerations.

There may be some vendor-specific utilities or configuration anomalies within a particular TCP/IP implementation, but about 85% of what you learn in this course will be immediately applicable on whatever operating system or vendor implementation you work with. That is why TCP/IP is one of the more popular exams in the MCSE elective track. You get more "bang for your buck"! You would be easily able to transfer your knowledge to any vendor's TCP/IP implementation exam with what you will learn here.

Some of TCP/IP's general features and requirements are outlined here:

Routable. All TCP/IP implementations are routable. It is a routable protocol. You will remember from Networking Essentials that a routed network is usually a larger network that was "segmented" or divided into smaller networks. These smaller networks are called "subnets." Subnets are typically connected together by routers, brouters, and bridges. Routing is a very important feature in larger networks, allowing segmentation and better management of network performance. The Internet is nothing more than a huge routed network connected with routers!

Scalable. TCP/IP is a highly scalable protocol. It can effectively be used in the smallest of networks and yet is very suitable for use in the largest network in the world today—the Internet.

Connection-Oriented Communications. TCP/IP offers guaranteed, connection-oriented transport communications via TCP. In addition, broadcast-based transmissions are also supported through the use of UDP.

Industry Standard Protocol. TCP/IP is the de facto computer protocol standard. Every vendor supports it and it allows for unilateral access to any system anywhere in the world through the Internet.

Microsoft TCP/IP Features

Along with adhering to all the features and requirements listed above, Microsoft's implementation of TCP/IP offers several additional features and applications that are extremely useful to the network administrator. Microsoft packages a full-featured version of TCP/IP with both Windows NT and Windows95. We will be focusing on the Windows NT Server features of TCP/IP, which contain everything the client versions (Windows95 and Windows NT Workstation) have, plus several other useful services and utilities.

Microsoft is completely committed to the TCP/IP protocol. In fact, the Windows NT operating system was designed to include a full-featured version of TCP/IP supplied at no extra charge. In fact, Microsoft is so committed to TCP/IP, that with release 4.0 of Windows NT it is the default networking protocol installed.

Microsoft's implementation of the TCP/IP protocol includes the following protocols and utilities.

TABLE 1-1 THE MICROSOFT TCP/IP PROTOCOLS AND UTILITIES

ACRONYM	ACTUAL NAME	RESPONSIBLE FOR
TCP/IP Protocols		
TCP	Transmission Control Protocol	Providing guaranteed, error-correcting, and connection-oriented communications. TCP is a transport protocol.
IP	Internet Protocol	Delivering data packets to and from TCP/IP hosts. IP functions at the network layer of the OSI model.
ARP	Address Resolution Protocol	Mapping IP addresses to Media Access Control (MAC) network card addresses.
UDP	User Datagram Protocol	Providing nonguaranteed broadcast protocol used by several TCP utilities. UDP is a transport protocol.
ICMP	Internet Control Message Protocol	Reporting error and control messages for IP.
IGMP	Internet Group Management Protocol	Informing routers that hosts of a specific multicast (a type of TCP/IP broadcast communications) are available on a particular network.
TCP/IP Data Transfer Utilities		
TFTP	Trivial File Transfer Protocol	Providing file transfer capabilities. TFTP is actually an application as well as being considered a protocol in its own right. It uses UDP for its transport mechanism. TFTP functions at the Application and Session Layers of the OSI Model. It is faster than FTP but not as reliable.
FTP	File Transfer Protocol	Providing file transfer capabilities. FTP is actually an application as well as a protocol in its own right. It uses TCP for its transport mechanism. FTP functions at the application and session layers of the OSI model.
RCP	Remote Copy Protocol	Copying files between UNIX hosts and Windows NT computers.

TABLE 1-1 *CONTINUED*

ACRONYM	ACTUAL NAME	RESPONSIBLE FOR
TCP/IP Remote Access Utilities		
Telnet		Providing text-based terminal emulation when connecting to remote hosts (usually UNIX based machines).
REXEC	Remote Execution	Running processes on a remote host. (A process is similar to a service in Windows NT.) This command allows you to remotely start services on a UNIX host.
RSH	Remote Shell	Allowing users to run commands on a UNIX host from a Windows NT system.
Finger	None	Allowing a user to receive remote system information for another host, provided the host is running the TCP/IP finger service.
TCP/IP Diagnostic Utilities		
PING	Packet Internet Groper	Verifying that TCP/IP configurations are configured correctly on a local host by "pinging" either the TCP/IP loopback address (127.0.0.1) or a remote host on the network. Ping is similar to an echo.
NETSTAT	Network Statistics	Displaying TCP/IP network and protocol statistics. It also displays the current state of TCP/IP.
NBTSTAT	NetBIOS over TCP/IP Statistics	Displaying the status of NetBIOS over TCP/IP connections and a variety of other functions.
ROUTE	None	Displaying and editing local routing tables on local machines. Routes can be added that are static (always available) or temporary.
IPCONFIG	IP Configuration	Displays key TCP/IP configuration data for a local machine. Predominantly used as a troubleshooting tool in verifying a local workstation's configuration.
TRACERT	Trace Route	Tracing a route to a remote host displaying statistics on network performance.
HOSTNAME	Host Name Lookup	Providing a local computer's hostname for authentication purposes.
NSLOOKUP	Domain Name Server Lookup	Providing the ability to examine domain name entries in a DNS database that pertain to a particular domain or host.

Continued

TABLE 1-1 *CONTINUED*

ACRONYM	ACTUAL NAME	RESPONSIBLE FOR
TCP/IP Printing Utilities		
LPR	Line Printer Remote	Allowing printing to a remote host running the Line Printer Daemon Service.
LPD	Line Printer Daemon	A service that allows LPR requests and submission of print jobs. A daemon is a UNIX term similar to a service in Windows NT.
LPQ	Line Printer Queue	Obtaining the status of a print queue of a host running the LPD.

That's quite a list of functions! Do not despair . . . these basic TCP/IP protocols and utilities will all make more sense in just a few more chapters!

Microsoft also provides several address and name resolution applications with NT Server that warrant explanation. These are listed in Table 1-2 on the next page.

Lesson 1.3 The History of the TCP/IP Protocol

TCP/IP is one of the oldest network protocols in existence. The protocol stack has been around in some shape or form since the late 1960s. This lesson will provide a basic overview of the history of TCP/IP, why it was created, who created it, the evolutionary history of the protocol, and a high-level timeline tracing TCP/IP from its inception through present and future implementations of the protocol.

The DARPA, DOD, ARPANET, TCP/IP Connection

In 1969, the United States Department of Defense (DOD) commissioned the study of packet-switching networks and the establishment of a network

TABLE 1-2 MICROSOFT WINDOWS NT SERVER TCP/IP ADMINISTRATIVE APPLICATIONS

ACRONYM	ACTUAL NAME	FUNCTION
WINS	Windows Internet Naming Service	Allows NetBIOS names to be resolved to IP addresses. WINS is a *dynamic* database, meaning that updates are made automatically. NetBIOS names equate to computer names.
DNS	Domain Name System	Allows Fully Qualified Domain Names (FQDN) to be resolved to an IP address. DNS is a hierarchical *static* database, meaning that entries must be made manually. FQDN names equate to web addresses.
DHCP	Dynamic Host Configuration Protocol	Allows centralized and automatic TCP/IP address management. DHCP is a powerful tool that eliminates the need to configure TCP/IP manually on each workstation in a network. DHCP "leases" addresses and other configuration information to clients workstations.
Network Monitor	None	The Network Monitor application allows an administrator to gather protocol and statistics information on any number of protocols.
Performance Monitor	None	The Performance Monitor application allows an administrator to gather protocol and statistics information on a NT Server so that changes can be made to enhance performance. To enable the TCP/IP "counters," in Performance Monitor, you must install SNMP.
SNMP	Simple Network Management Protocol	SNMP is used to monitor performance of many TCP/IP devices through the use of a MIB (Management Information Base). NT Server can generate SNMP information but a third party utility must be used to display and use the data. SNMP is often used to monitor utilization on routers, bridges, and other network hardware.

where educational and military bodies could exchange information. To achieve these objectives, DOD created a new agency called DARPA. DARPA stands for the United States Department of Defense Advanced Research Projects Agency.

In 1970, DARPA created ARPANET (Advanced Research Project Agency Network) using a predecessor protocol to TCP/IP called NCT (Network Control Protocol). Higher education institutions were interconnected with the government to share technology and R&D (research and development) functions. Much of the development of TCP/IP and the inter-network occurred at educational institutions such as MIT (The Massachusetts Institute of Technology). NCT would continue to be the protocol of ARPANET until 1983 when it was replaced by TCP/IP.

Between 1970 and 1983, the TCP/IP protocol was under development and standards definition. Many of the utilities we discussed in the previous lesson were designed, standardized, and implemented during this period. The definition of the protocol surrounded a new group of standards procedures called RFCs or Requests for Comments. The next lesson further defines the RFC process.

The Telnet standard was defined in 1972 and submitted as RFC 318. As you will see in the next lesson, that means 317 RFCs were submitted between 1969 and 1972 before Telnet was defined. In 1973, the FTP protocol was defined as RFC 454, allowing file transfer capabilities across ARPANET as well as remote terminal session management. During 1974 the definition of TCP was established, and in 1981, IP was defined as RFC 791.

In 1981, the DCA (Defense Communications Agency) and ARPA established the TCP/IP protocol suite. Not long after this, the venerable NCT protocol was retired and replaced with TCP/IP for use on ARPANET. By then, a few hundred higher-education institutions and military installations were using ARPANET. While HOST file name resolution had been developed, it was quickly becoming difficult to maintain and update, so in 1984 DNS was introduced as a hierarchical name resolution database. (You will learn more on the HOST file and DNS in a later lesson).

The Relationship between TCP/IP, UNIX, and C

Closely coupled with ARPANET and TCP/IP development was the birth of UNIX and the C programming language. The operating system and programming language were being developed by Bell Labs under the direction of Brian Kernigan and Dennis Ritchie at roughly the same time DARPA was implementing the ARPANET network.

The C programming language also went through an evolutionary process. The first language was 'A' and the second iteration was named 'B'. C and

UNIX were developed to be "open" and very flexible in terms of platform independence and availability to the educational population. Eventually, much of the TCP/IP protocol would be programmed in C (as was the UNIX kernel). For a long time, TCP/IP would be exclusively associated with the UNIX operating system. This is why, even today, many people still associate TCP/IP almost exclusively with UNIX just as they associate IPX/SPX with Novell NetWare.

UNIX also carries much the same mystique as TCP/IP in terms of difficulty. As we will see, the more "open" and "flexible" a computer system or application is, the more difficult it seems to be to implement because of the variety of options available. This fact holds very true for both C and UNIX. The pair was written to be fast, compact, and extremely open in terms of architecture. However, once you know UNIX and C under one implementation, 85–90 percent of what you know is transferable across vendor-specific implementations of the operating system and programming language.

UNIX and C both use shorthand commands like 'tar' (UNIX command—short for Tape Archival and Restore), 'cd' (UNIX command for Change Directory), and 'printf' (C programming verb for printing to a variety of output devices) that are not terribly intuitive to the user. As a matter of fact, the commands look like an extra-terrestrial language! Furthermore, UNIX and C are case-sensitive. This means that a lower-case 'r' has a very different meaning than an upper case 'R'. In fact, they often do very different (and unexpected) things for a new user!

This flexibility and shorthand notation makes the operating system and programming language somewhat difficult to learn and use. Since UNIX used TCP/IP for network connectivity, the protocol also received the same difficult tag. Hopefully, by the end of this course, you will find that TCP/IP is no more difficult than anything else you have learned and the protocol will be demystified in your mind.

TCP/IP—Today and Tomorrow

TCP/IP usage grew through the 1980s to the point where well over 200 hosts existed by late 1988. Today, there are over 20–30 million hosts using the Internet at any time—and they all use TCP/IP for network connectivity. The explosive nature of Internet usage may cause the development of a new addressing standard since we are beginning to run out of unique addresses to assign users! Today, IP addresses are 32-bit numbers. When TCP/IP was developed, no person thought we would ever run out of addresses! In the future, the addressing scheme may change to a 64-bit algorithm effectively allowing every person in the world today to have 2 IP addresses for their use. That should keep us busy for a bit!

Lesson 1.4 RFCs and the Importance of Standards

What Is a RFC?

RFCs were briefly introduced in the last lesson. As we discovered, they are closely tied to the specifications for the TCP/IP protocol. In fact, they are the body of design and specification documents that define the entire TCP/IP protocol stack and Internet.

RFCs are developed by consensus. Any Internet Society member may submit a RFC for consideration as a standard. Usually the document undergoes scrutiny by technical experts, various panels, and/or the RFC editor for merit and appropriateness. The document is then assigned an RFC number and classification. There are five classifications a RFC can be assigned. Each of the following classifications relate to the status of a RFC as a standard:

Not Recommended. The document is not recommended for implementation.

Limited Use. The document is not intended for the general population's use.

Elective. The document's content may be implemented but is optional. Its implementation has been approved and agreed upon, but it never became widely used.

Recommended. The RFC is recommended for use by all TCP/IP hosts and gateways (routers) but is not required. Most recommended RFCs are implemented by vendors.

Required. The RFC must be implemented on all TCP/IP hosts and gateways for the TCP/IP implementation being created. The required rating means the RFC is a standard for implementing the protocol.

Once a RFC is considered for standardization, it also goes through an additional three-level document management process based on the maturity of the document. In fact, the three levels are actually known as *RFC maturity levels.*

Maturity Level 1: Proposed Standard. A proposed standard is generally considered stable, technically correct, and is fairly well understood by the evaluation body. This maturity level indicates that the evaluation body believes there is enough community interest for the RFC to be considered valuable.

Maturity Level 2: Draft Standard. A RFC must be well understood by the community and evaluation body and be technically stable to be considered for this maturity level. It is this RFC document that will be used as the basis for developing the actual standard.

Maturity Level 3: Internet Standard. This RFC designation indicates that the document has a high degree of technical maturity (in other words, it has been tested and used successfully in several different implementations), and that the service or protocol provides significant benefit to the Internet community.

Who Defines Internet Standards?

There are two key organizations that consolidate and evaluate submissions. These are briefly outlined below. We encourage you to read and research as much as possible about the technology you are implementing. It will differentiate you as an expert in your field.

The Internet Society. The first organization is known as the Internet Society (ISOC). This is a global group of member organizations including many businesses and educational institutions. Organized in 1992, it is primarily responsible for encouraging and developing the Internet. Part and parcel to this rather large charter, is the notion that they assist in developing additional standards and protocols that will meet their basic objectives.

The Internet Architecture Board. This board is actually part of the ISOC. Its duty is to evaluate and set Internet standards, publish and manage RFCs, and oversee the overall Internet standards process. The IAB also manages several supporting organizations that are responsible for the nuts-and-bolts implementation of each technical standard.

A Quick Note on RFC Document Precedence

The concept of document precedence is actually a legal term. What it means is that any new document associated with a prior version of a document becomes the new standard for the document—*and it supercedes all prior versions of the document.* This is a very important concept in the RFC process.

All documents submitted for evaluation to the standards body are assigned an RFC number. Subsequent revisions of the document are assigned a new number and the new RFC takes precedence over all previous versions of the document. As a RFC moves through the standardization process, there may be several different RFC numbers associated with a particular standard. It is very important that you have the latest copy of the standard.

These documents can be obtained from InterNic and several of the other Internet Standards organizations such as the Internet Society (ISOC) and Internet Architecture Board (IAB). The IAB publishes an IAB Official Protocol Standard that is very useful in determining the current RFC for a particular service or protocol. RFC standards are published in the public domain, which means they are available to any person connected to the Internet for review.

EXERCISE 1 READING A RFC

In this exercise, you will open and read through a RFC. The RFC you will be reading is RFC 768. Your instructor will provide this RFC for you.

This should be a challenging read—no RFC is easy to understand! They are usually fairly technical. However, you should get a good picture of the type of information and format a RFC takes. While you are reading the content, be aware how the RFC is organized, the different sections it contains, and its audience. When you have completed this exercise, you will be asked a few questions regarding the RFC's content.

The RFC is the backbone of the TCP/IP and Internet standards process. It is also a great place to learn the underlying technology of a particular protocol or standard. They are wonderful resources for additional knowledge beyond what this course will provide—and they are all at your fingertips. Have fun!

Q/A—RFC CONTENTS

Answer the following questions regarding the RFC:

1. What is the organization of the RFC?

2. What is the document like to read? Is it hard/easy? Why?

3. Who is the author of this particular document? When was it written?

4. Were any other RFC's replaced by this document?

5. In your own words, write a brief paragraph summarizing the contents of this RFC.

6. Is this RFC a standard? Can you tell what phase of review it is in?

7. Can you find any additonal places to read more about this RFC and its contents? If so, where?

8. What protocols/utilities use this RFC's transport mechanism at its publication? Now?

9. Do you think this particular RFC will be replaced through document precedence? Why or why not?

Lesson 1.5 Installing Microsoft TCP/IP 4.0

This lesson provides an introduction to the installation of Microsoft TCP/IP 4.0 on a Windows NT platform. Throughout this lesson, we will be discussing some key terminology related to successful configuration of the protocol as well as a few different methods for modifying, reinstalling, or removing the protocol should this be necessary. At the conclusion of this lesson, you will install the TCP/IP protocol as a lab and document several key options in a follow-on worksheet.

Default Windows NT Networking Installation

Windows NT is installed with TCP/IP as the default networking protocol. This is an important change for NT since previous versions of the software allowed the installation of TCP/IP but it was not the default choice. If you are wondering what the default choice originally was, the answer is the Microsoft-developed NetBEUI protocol.

Microsoft is committed to the Internet and TCP/IP, as shown by the fact that Windows NT 5.0 will base its enterprise directory services mechanism on Internet and TCP/IP connectivity features. TCP/IP is here to stay within the Microsoft NT family of operating systems and one could easily hypothesize that it will continue to become more deeply integrated within the framework of Windows NT in all future releases of the product.

What Is an IP Address, Subnet Mask, and Default Gateway?

Two key components necessary for the successful installation of the TCP/IP protocol are the IP address and the subnet mask. Together, these two configuration items provide the protocol with an address and network ID for the host computer. Without them (or with incorrectly configured options), the protocol would have no way of effectively communicating with other computers on the network. It would be sort of like sending a letter without a destination address or zip code. The Postal Service would have no way to deliver it!

IP Address. IP addresses are expressed in a "dotted-quad" decimal format separated by a period. A typical IP address might appear as follows:

10.216.5.1

These esoteric numbers provide key information to the TCP/IP protocol. Depending on the subnet mask, they determine the host and network ID for a computer. This is exactly like the address and zip code we use to send our mail.

Keeping with this analogy, every IP address must be unique (just like every street address must be unique). Otherwise, there would be no way for the data (or mail) to be sent or received by the host computer. We will see later that TCP/IP packets contain much the same information as a letter—each packet has a sender ID (the return address), a destination ID (the letter address), and data (the letter itself).

Subnet Mask. Subnet masks are also expressed in a "dotted-quad" decimal format separated by a period. A typical subnet mask might appear as follows:

255.255.0.0

The purpose of the subnet mask is to mask (or hide) a portion of the address so TCP/IP can determine which part of the IP address is the network ID (zip code) and which portion is the host ID (street address). The art of custom subnet masking usually causes great consternation among TCP/IP students. Yet, if you keep this illustration in mind it will simplify the whole process. Later in the book you will learn where those 0 and 255 values come from.

Default Gateway. The default gateway is not a required TCP/IP installation option. You can easily install TCP/IP on a local area network as long as you specify an IP and subnet mask address. In some installations, this might be the desired configuration. However, in most installations today, corporations want access to the Internet. If you remember, the Internet is nothing more that a huge network of interconnected smaller networks. Its not very different than our world—we live in the United States (one local network) but there are many other countries (each being a remote network).

Think of the default gateway as International Mail. There are many postal systems in the world (the United States being only one of many). Depending on the zip code assigned, the postmaster will deliver your mail to an address in the United States (on the local network) or it will forward it on to another country's system (the remote network). This is exactly what a default gateway address does.

Default gateways in TCP/IP are routers. By specifying a default gateway in TCP/IP, you are providing the protocol with a method of routing, or forwarding, the host information to a remote network. Without a default gateway address, you would be limited to communications on the local network your host computer was located (currently, the United States).

The default gateway is simply the IP address of a router that is connected to a remote network. Windows NT supports up to five default gateway addresses, allowing you to specify multiple paths to remote networks should one router be inoperative.

Static versus Dynamic IP Address Management

Prior to the Dynamic Host Configuration Protocol (DHCP), all TCP/IP configurations were done manually. Another word for this mode of installation is a **static** installation of TCP/IP. What this means is that if a network administrator had 150 users, they would have to go to each workstation and manually enter an IP, subnet mask, and possibly a default gateway. This could be very time consuming and the process was often wrought with errors (it's very easy to enter an incorrect address even if you know what you're doing—typographical errors cause more problems than you might think!) generating even more support calls.

DHCP allows for **dynamic** address management. This is a fancy way of saying address management is automatically managed. A server running a BootP or DHCP server can have all TCP/IP address, subnet, gateway, and other configuration information configured once and allow for automatic management across the network. This automatic system manages which hosts have a particular IP address, allows reservation of addresses for some hosts that require manual configuration, and allows for a single-point, centralized method of administering a TCP/IP network. It is the choice of administration for large enterprise TCP/IP installations.

Microsoft Windows NT Server comes with a DHCP Server option allowing the administrator to centrally manage their IP address pool and associated configuration settings. When you have a choice, use DHCP! It will make your life much simpler.

NOTE: *To install protocols and services, please remember that you must have administrative privileges or have been granted the user right to add and delete services and protocols by your system administrator.*

Basic Default TCP/IP Installation Using DHCP

Installing TCP/IP in Windows NT setup is really a snap. There are only a couple of questions that must be answered and these deal with whether your network is using a DHCP server or if you will be assigning a static IP address. For the purposes of this discussion, we will assume that the network has a DHCP server to automatically assign the IP address. This being the case (and the Microsoft default), you need only press the "Continue" button and TCP/IP will be installed! What could be simpler? So much for a difficult protocol installation. . . .

Windows NT will march along copying all the files required, start the network, and finish the installation without a hitch.

Basic TCP/IP Installation Using a Static IP Address

Installing TCP/IP using the "Configure TCP/IP manually" option is somewhat more complicated, requiring a minimum of two pieces of key information and a third if you wish to connect to a remote network like the Internet. To install TCP/IP manually, you **must** enter/have a valid and unique IP address and subnet mask. Additionally, if you wish to connect to a remote network, you must know the IP address of the default gateway (usually a router).

Once you enter these values correctly, the TCP/IP installation will continue copying all the files required, starting the network, and finishing the installation of NT successfully. *Correctly* is the key word here. If you make a mistake manually entering the addresses, the network will start, but depending on your error, you may not be able to see any other computers on the host subnet or on other subnets. This is why DHCP is such a useful tool. It eliminates a portion of the human error that can occur during installation and save a great deal of support calls. When you have the option, use DHCP!

NOTE: *To install certain TCP/IP administrative services such as DHCP, you must use the static IP address configuration option. This is required under Windows NT Server.*

Adding TCP/IP after Installation of Windows NT

Windows NT server requires that TCP/IP be installed in one of the two configurations listed above. The checkbox is grayed out on this installation forcing the administrator to manually enter this protocol for installation. However, Windows NT Workstation allows you to deselect TCP/IP and add another protocol of your choice (NetBEUI or NWLink).

What Gets Installed?

Many files are installed when your Windows NT installation is configured for use with TCP/IP. All of the basic services and utilities outlined earlier in this chapter are installed as part of the process. This includes all of the following:

TCP/IP Protocols	TCP/IP Data Transfer Utilities	TCP/IP Remote Access Utilities	TCP/IP Diagnostic Utilities
TCP	TFTP	Telnet	PING
IP	FTP	REXEC	NETSTAT
ARP	RCP	RSH	NBTSTAT
UDP			ROUTE
ICMP			IPCONFIG
IGMP			TRACERT
			Finger
			HOSTNAME
			NSLOOKUP

This is true under both Windows NT Workstation and Windows NT Server. However, some of the administrative services are not available under Windows NT Workstation. For instance, the WINS, DHCP, and DNS services are only available with Windows NT Server.

What Other Things Can I Install?

You can also install any or all of the additional services listed earlier in the chapter. However, not all the services are available to Windows NT Workstation. The following list presents the additional services available:

Utilities available in Windows NT Workstation *and* Windows NT Server:

- Microsoft SNMP Service

- Microsoft Performance Monitor (installed by default in both Windows NT configurations regardless of the protocol)

- Performance Monitor and Network Monitor TCP/IP Counters (only if SNMP is installed)

- Simple TCP/IP Printing

- Microsoft Network Monitor (not provided on the NT Workstation CD-ROM but can be installed if you meet appropriate licensing requirements)

Utilities available *only* with Windows NT Server:

- Microsoft WINS Server

- Microsoft DHCP Server

- Microsoft DNS Server

L A B

Installing the TCP/IP Protocol

● ●

This lab will allow you to configure your computer with the TCP/IP protocol suite in the event that you need to add TCP/IP after the initial Windows NT installation is complete. Before completing this lab be sure to discuss your individual classroom configuration and any questions about the dialogs or boxes presented with your instructor before you proceed!

Complete the following procedures to install Microsoft TCP/IP:

1. Open Control Panel and select the Network applet. An alternate method is to right-click on the desktop Network Neighborhood icon and click on the Properties menu option.

FIGURE 1-1
Control Panel: Network Applet.

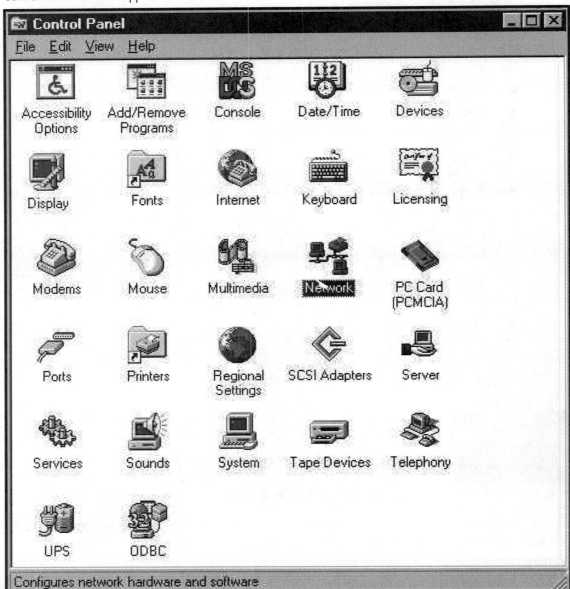

2. Select the Protocols Tab. Your screen should look something like the one below.

NOTE: *You will notice this figure already has TCP/IP added to this NT instal-* *lation. This is because the machine I will be using to demonstrate TCP/IP is a Windows NT Server. Assume TCP/IP has not been added for the rest of this procedure.*

FIGURE 1-2
Network Applet: Protocols Tab.

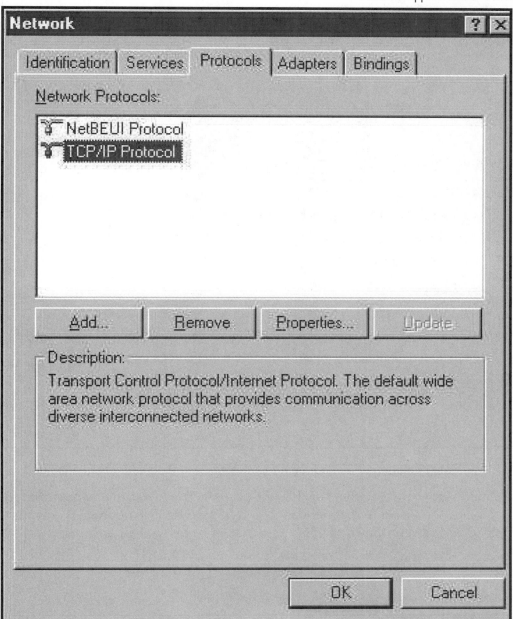

3. Click the Add Button. Scroll down the list of protocols until you find the "TCP/IP Protocol" selection. Click the OK button to add the protocol.

NOTE: *This installation will install Microsoft TCP/IP. If you were adding a* *third-party vendor's TCP/IP stack, you would click the "Have Disk" button and follow the instructions provided by that particular vendor's implementation. Make sure your third-party TCP/IP installation is for Windows NT!*

FIGURE 1-3
Protocol Tab: Add Button.

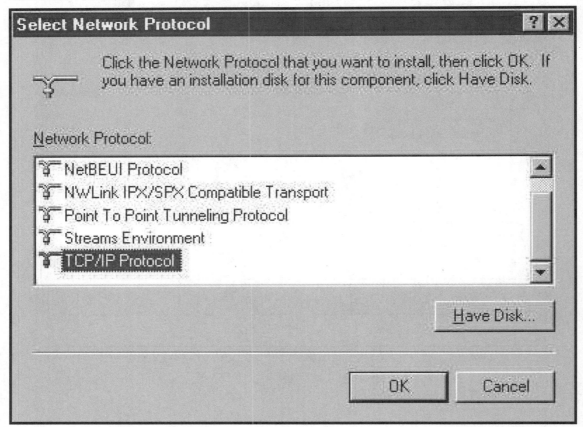

4. The installation program will then prompt the administrator to see if they wish to use DHCP. If you click "Yes," the installation will configure TCP/IP for DHCP use. If you select "No," you will be prompted to enter a static IP address (required), subnet mask (required), and default gateway (optional). The dialog box appears as follows.

FIGURE 1-4
TCP/IP Setup Dialog Box: Dynamic/Static Configuration.

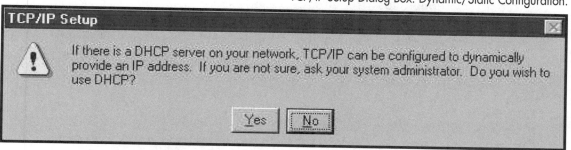

5. At this point, the installation program is ready to copy TCP/IP files and finish the protocol installation. The installation program will prompt you for a location to copy the files from. The default entry is wherever the original installation files were located for the first installation of Windows NT. This path can be changed and you may enter either a standard path (C:\NTSRVR) or a UNC path (\\PB01\NTSRVR) to a distribution server containing the Windows NT distribution files.

FIGURE 1-5
TCP/IP Setup Dialog Box: File Path.

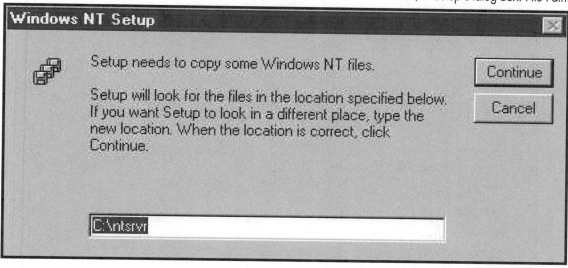

6. The installation program will then copy all required files, protocols, and applications to your Windows NT installation directory. Click the Close button and the protocol's network bindings will be configured.

If you selected DHCP, no further configuration will be required and you will be prompted to restart your computer. However, if you selected a static configuration, you will be provided another screen that allows you to enter the static IP address (required), subnet mask (required), and default gateway (optional). That screen will look something like figure 1-6 once it is completed.

NOTE: *Before entering static values for this lab, ask your instructor the proper configuration for your classroom TCP/IP installation. Remember, a mistake in this configuration dialog can render your network unavailable!*

FIGURE 1-6
TCP/IP Static Installation Configuration Dialog.

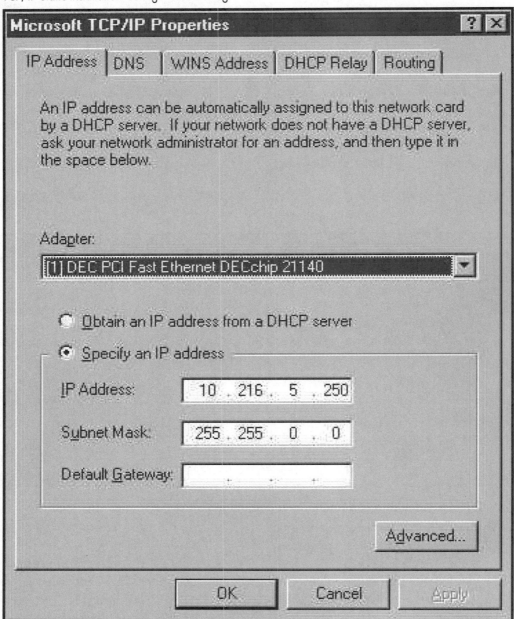

Once you have entered the specified values, click the OK button and TCP/IP bindings will be configured.

You will then be prompted to restart your computer with the following dialog box:

FIGURE 1-7
Network Settings Change Dialog Box.

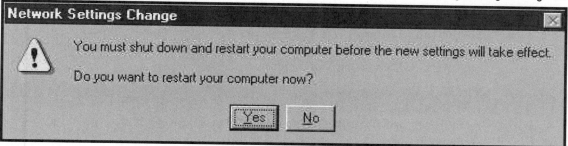

Congratulations! You have completed your first installation of Microsoft TCP/IP!

Exploratory Worksheet 1
TCP/IP Options

Prepare a Microsoft Excel Spreadsheet of the available configuration options available under each tab of the TCP/IP Protocol Properties. To get to this tab, you:

1. Right-click on the desktop Network Neighborhood icon and select the Properties menu option.

2. Click once on the Protocols tab.

3. Click once on the TCP/IP Protocol.

4. Click once on the Properties button.

Set your spreadsheet up in the following manner:

TCP/IP CONFIGURATION OPTIONS				
Tab	TCP/IP Option	Required Input	Default Value	Tab Function

If you do not know what each option or tab does, that's OK. Ask your instructor for a brief explanation or ask him/her to lead the class through the exercise.

When you have completed the spreadsheet, save the file as TCPIP Options. This will be a handy reference tool for your future work in this book as well as when you are working as a network administrator.

Summary

This chapter provided an introduction to the TCP/IP protocol suite. Topics covered in this chapter included:

- **Basic Terminology.** Vocabulary and acronyms needed to understand the balance of the chapter.

- **History and Origins of TCP/IP.** We discussed a number of topics relating to where TCP/IP came from, why it was created, and its relationship with the UNIX and C environments.

- **The RFC Process.** We discussed the importance of standards and how the RFC process incorporates standards into the TCP/IP Environment. Additionally, we had the opportunity to read a sample RFC to determine its content and form.

- **Installing Microsoft TCP/IP.** In this lesson, we looked at some key information and terminology required to configure and install Microsoft TCP/IP. We then took a quick look at the files that are installed, as well as utilities and services that are unique to Windows NT Workstation and Server.

● ● ● ● ● ● ● ● ● ● ● ● ● ●

Q & A

1. *Select all that apply.* What are the required configuration options for a static installation of TCP/IP?

   a. MAC address
   b. IP address
   c. Default gateway
   d. Subnet mask
   e. WINS address

2. *Select all that apply.* Which TCP/IP Administrative Utilities are only available in Windows NT Server?

   a. SNMP
   b. WINS
   c. DHCP
   d. ARP
   e. DNS
   f. Performance Monitor

3. *Select the best answer.* The main difference between TCP and UDP is

   a. TCP provides a broadcast message between a client and server while UDP provides a guaranteed connection-oriented mechanism for data transport.
   b. UDP is slower than TCP.
   c. TCP provides a guaranteed connection-oriented mechanism for data transport while UDP provides a broadcast-based message service between a client and server.
   d. TCP is used as the transport mechanism for the FTP protocol.
   e. UDP is used as the transport mechanism for the FTP protocol.

4. *Select all that apply.* Which of the following are true statements regarding an IP address, subnet mask, and default gateway?

   a. A gateway is usually associated with a router in TCP/IP.
   b. An IP address is not required to configure TCP/IP.
   c. A subnet mask is required to configure TCP/IP.
   d. A default gateway is not required to configure TCP/IP for access to a remote network.
   e. A subnet mask helps TCP/IP to determine which portion of the IP address is the host network and which portion of the IP address is the host computer ID.

5. *Select the best answer.* The purpose of DHCP is to

   a. resolve a MAC address to an IP address.
   b. resolve a NetBIOS name to an IP Address.
   c. automatically configure TCP/IP clients with key information.
   d. resolve a FQDN to an IP address.

6. *Select all that apply.* Which of the following are true of DNS?

    a. DNS is a static hierarchical database.
    b. DNS is a dynamic database.
    c. DNS is used to resolve NetBIOS names to IP addresses.
    d. DNS is used to resolve FQDNs to IP addresses.

7. *Select all that apply.* Which of the following are true of WINS?

    a. WINS is a static hierarchical database.
    b. WINS is a dynamic database.
    c. WINS is used to resolve NetBIOS names to IP addresses.
    d. WINS is used to resolve FQDNs to IP addresses.

8. *Select two answers.* Two common troubleshooting utilities that come with TCP/IP are

    a. IPConfig
    b. TFTP
    c. Telnet
    d. Finger
    e. Ping

9. *Select the best answer.* The relationship between the DOD and DARPA was

    a. DARPA commissioned DOD to create a network for information exchange.
    b. DOD commissioned DARPA to create a network for information exchange.
    c. There is no relationship between DOD and DARPA.
    d. None of the above.

10. *Select the best answer.* The purpose of a RFC is to

    a. Define standards for TCP/IP.
    b. Allow anyone to provide input into the standards process.
    c. Provide an audit trail for the evolution of a particular standard.
    d. Supply a documented and organized method for standards creation.
    e. All of the above.

11. *Select the best answer.* What is the difference between a protocol suite and protocol stack?

    a. There is no difference between a protocol stack and protocol suite.
    b. Protocol suites refer to groups of applications, protocols, and utilities associated with a network protocol while a protocol stack refers to the grouping of particular protocols mapped to the OSI model.
    c. Protocol stacks refer to groups of applications, protocols, and utilities associated with a network protocol while a protocol suite refers to the grouping of particular protocols mapped to the OSI model.
    d. None of the above.

12. Suppose the following situation exists:

John, a network administrator, needs to automate the process of IP address management for his network while also providing important configuration information to client TCP/IP machines. John also needs to be able to remotely monitor network server, router, and other network hardware devices.

Required Results:

■ Provide automatic lease and renewal of at least an IP and subnet mask for John's network.

■ Provide the ability to remotely monitor network performance statistics for various servers and network devices.

Optional Results:

■ Supply configuration information to clients for WINS and DNS servers located on the network.

■ Remotely view system information on a UNIX server located on the network.

Proposed Solution:

■ Install a Microsoft DHCP server on the network and configure clients to use DHCP for address management

■ Install the SNMP service on the Windows NT server.

a. The proposed solution meets both the required and optional results.
b. The proposed solution meets the required results and only one of the optional results.
c. The proposed solution meets the required results and none of the optional results.
d. The proposed solution does not meet required nor optional results.

13. *Select all that apply.* Jack wishes to provide name resolution services for both FQDN and NetBIOS names on his TCP/IP network. Which services should Jack install?

a. DHCP
b. ARP
c. Telnet
d. WINS
e. DNS

14. *Select the best answer.* Sue, a domain user, is attempting to add the TCP/IP protocol to her machine. However, she is unable to add the protocol. What is the most likely cause for this problem?

    a. Sue is attempting to configure a static installation of TCP/IP.

    b. Sue is attempting to configure a DHCP configuration of TCP/IP and there is no DHCP server on the network.

    c. Sue does not have administrative privileges and these permissions are required to add a protocol or network service to Windows NT.

    d. Sue has not entered the appropriate subnet mask for her network.

15. *Select the best answer.* Bob is trying to find a MAC address associated with a particular IP address. What TCP/IP protocol /utility should he be using?

    a. DNS

    b. WINS

    c. DHCP

    d. ARP

    e. RCP

TCP/IP TEST UTILITIES AND NAME RESOLUTION

OBJECTIVES

By the end of this chapter, you should be able to:

■ Describe the function, uses, and features of the IPCONFIG, ARP, PING, and TRACERT commands.

■ Effectively test your TCP/IP configuration and use common test utilities to gather information and verify network connectivity.

■ Define the reasons why name resolution is important to TCP/IP.

■ Define name resolution methods used by TCP/IP.

■ Conceptualize and demonstrate an understanding of how WINS and DNS operates.

■ Conceptualize and demonstrate an understanding of the relationship between HOSTS and LMHOSTS files to DNS and WINS.

■ Configure the HOSTS and LMHOSTS files for name resolution.

Introduction

Now that you have a basic understanding of the TCP/IP protocol suite, we will look more closely at some of the utilities provided with Windows NT to troubleshoot and gather information about a host installation of the protocol. This chapter takes a close look at several key utilities you will use throughout your tenure as a TCP/IP network administrator. We will define, use, and perform several tests using the IPCONFIG, PING, ART, and TRACERT utilities/protocols as part of this chapter. You will learn about the many switches associated with these commands and how you can customize each utility to perform tasks specific to a particular TCP/IP environment or installation.

We will also begin a preliminary discussion of the concept of name resolution, the applications used to help us resolve names, and why this concept is so important in a TCP/IP and Microsoft networking environment. We will introduce the concepts of NetBIOS name resolution using the LMHOSTS and WINS approaches as well as Fully Qualified Domain Name (FQDN) resolution using the HOSTS and DNS server tools. This chapter will supply a basic understanding of these concepts that will be built upon more fully in chapters 6 and 7 of the book.

Lesson 2.1 Testing Your TCP/IP Configuration

This lesson provides a look at several utilities that will be useful for you to test TCP/IP configurations. All of the utilities presented will provide invaluable information to you as a network administrator when it is time to troubleshoot a TCP/IP protocol problem. We will be covering the following utilities in this chapter:

- IPCONFIG
- PING
- TRACERT
- ARP

What Are the TCP/IP Test Utilities?

TCP/IP comes with a number of useful utilities to assist the network administrator in troubleshooting TCP/IP configuration and operational problems. We will be looking at the bread-and-butter tools for configuration troubleshooting in this section. If you will recall from Chapter 1, there are many other information gathering and troubleshooting utilities included with TCP/IP. However, we will be addressing them later in the book as they logically relate to a particular topic like WINS.

Most of the utilities discussed in this lesson were briefly defined in Chapter 1. We will be taking a much closer look at them in the following sections and will actually test and gather information on our newly installed TCP/IP configuration.

General Information about the TCP/IP Utilities Provided with Windows NT

The following paragraphs describe some common features of the TCP/IP utilities discussed in this section.

Character-Based Command-Line applications. All of the utilities in this section are character-based and require that you open a Windows NT

Command Window. To do this, you may either click on the Start menu, Programs, and select the Command Prompt application or you can click on Start menu, Run option and type **CMD** in the space provided. Both options will open a Windows NT Virtual DOS (NTVDM) session that will allow you to complete the exercises. The graphics below illustrate these two methods.

FIGURE 2-1
Start, Program, Command Prompt Method.

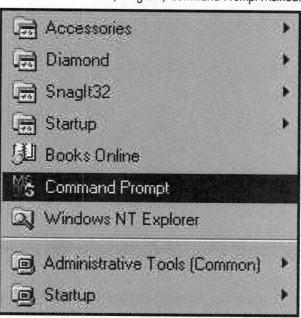

FIGURE 2-2
Start, Run Method.

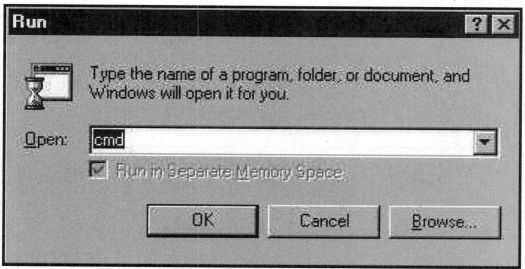

FIGURE 2-3
Windows NT Command Window.

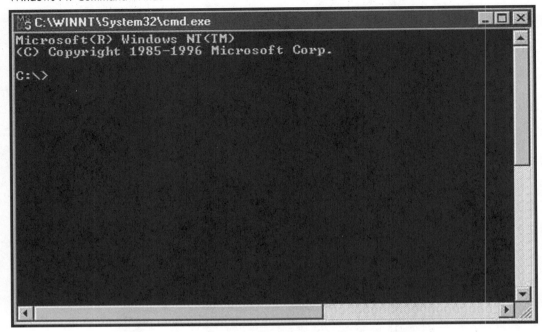

Case Sensitivity. Because TCP/IP is so closely linked to the UNIX operating system, many of the command switches are *case sensitive* meaning that a lower case 'a' does something very different from an upper case 'A'. It will be important that you pay close attention to these switches and options. The utilities will either use a – (dash) or a / (slash) to designate a switch. Two examples of how to enter a command and its output are shown below.

FIGURE 2-4
IPCONFIG/All Command Syntax and Output.

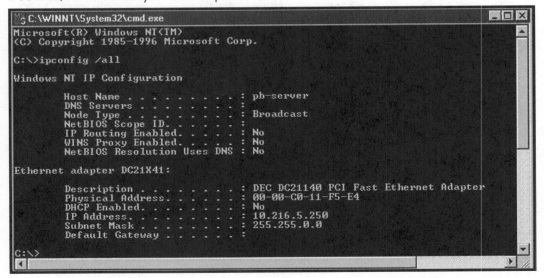

FIGURE 2-5
Arp –a Command Syntax and Output.

C:\WINNT\System32\cmd.exe
C:\>arp -a
Interface: 10.216.5.250 on Interface 2
Internet Address Physical Address Type
10.216.5.1 00-60-97-35-9c-12 dynamic
C:\>

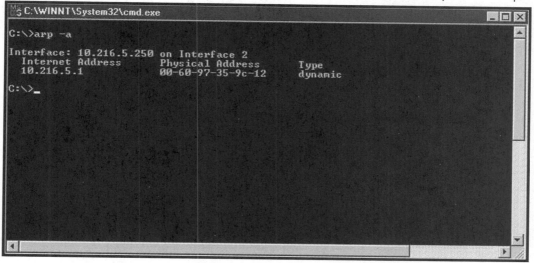

Getting Help. Help is available for every command we will discuss. However, this help is embedded in (another way of saying 'part of') the command.

Help on a particular command can be obtained in one of two ways (depending on the command). The first is with a common switch to most Windows NT and MS-DOS command line utilities: the **"/?"**. The second method is to simply type the command. These two methods of accessing help are mutually exclusive. In other words, one way or the other will work—but not both. Here is a sample request for help from the IPCONFIG command.

FIGURE 2-6
IPCONFIG Help Command Syntax and Output.

Microsoft(R) Windows NT(TM)
(C) Copyright 1985-1996 Microsoft Corp.
C:\>ipconfig /?
Windows NT IP Configuration
usage: ipconfig [/? | /all | /release [adapter] | /renew [adapter]]
/? Display this help message.
/all Display full configuration information.
/release Release the IP address for the specified adapter.
/renew Renew the IP address for the specified adapter.
The default is to display only the IP address, subnet mask and default gateway for each adapter bound to TCP/IP.
For Release and Renew, if no adapter name is specified, then the IP address leases for all adapters bound to TCP/IP will be released or renewed.
C:\>

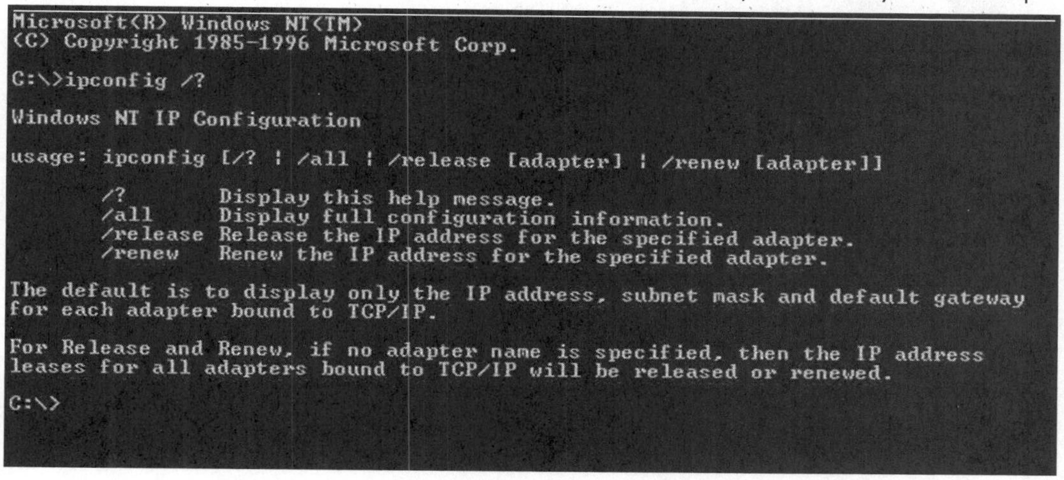

The IPCONFIG Command

IPCONFIG is an acronym for *IP Configuration.* As you may have guessed, this command is primarily used to display local TCP/IP configuration data for a client machine. It is very useful in troubleshooting problems related to IP address, subnet mask, default gateway, and several other parameters. One of the first utilities you should use if you suspect a configuration problem is the IPCONFIG utility.

Another very useful feature of this command is its ability to **Release** and **Renew** a DHCP server obtained address. DHCP leases an IP address to a client for a pre-determined period of time. It is possible that if changes are made to the DHCP configuration and a lease is still in effect, you might need to "release" the address from the client machine and then "renew" it to receive the updated information from the server.

IPCONFIG does not allow you to make any modifications to the client configuration; it simply displays the values the client machine is using. If there is a problem with the configuration, you would need to change settings located in the Network applet under the TCP/IP protocol tabs (similar to how we configured a static IP installation). Or you would issue the **/release** and **/renew** commands if you were using DHCP.

Listed below is a table of the information provided by IPCONFIG:

TABLE 2-1   IPCONFIG INFORMATION

INFORMATION	DESCRIPTION
Windows NT IP ConfigurationTCP/IP Grouping	**This section provides global information about the client configuration.**
Host Name	The current NetBIOS computer name of the client. The output will be text.
DNS Servers	Lists the currently configured DNS Server IP Addresses. The output will be one (or multiple) IP addresses for the configured DNS servers.
Node Type	Lists the method the NT client is using for NetBIOS name resolution (more on this later in the book). The output will be text.
NetBIOS Scope ID	Tells the current grouping of NetBIOS computers this client belongs to (more on this later in the book). The output will be a NetBIOS group name.
IP Routing Enabled	Tells whether IP Routing has been enabled on the client (more on this later in the book). This is a logical field—it will contain either a "Yes" or "No" value.
WINS Proxy Enabled	Tells whether this computer is configured as a "WINS Proxy" agent (more on this later in the book). This is a logical field—it will contain either a "Yes" or "No" value.
NetBIOS Resolution uses DNS	Tells whether NetBIOS names are being resolved using a special setting on the DNS Server (more on this later in the book). This is a logical field—it will contain either a "Yes" or "No" value.

TABLE 2-1 CONTINUED

INFORMATION	DESCRIPTION
Ethernet Adapter <Adapter Driver> Grouping	The client computer's adapter driver type(s) will be listed here. If you have multiple adapters or dial-up networking enabled there will be multiple sections for each adapter bound to TCP/IP.
Description	A longer description of the *Network Adapter Card* (also called Network Card or NIC).
Physical Address	The Media Access Control (MAC) address of the NIC.
DHCP Enabled	Tells whether DHCP is enabled for this *NIC*. This is a logical field—it will contain either a "Yes" or "No" value.
IP Address	The IP address associated with this NIC. It will be displayed in a dotted-quad decimal format (e.g., 10.216.5.250)
Subnet Mask	The subnet mask associated with this NIC. It will be displayed in a dotted-quad decimal format (e.g., 255.255.0.0)
Default Gateway	The default gateway(s) bound to this NIC. It will be displayed in a dotted-quad decimal format (e.g., 10.216.5.254). There can be up to five gateways configured for any adapter or none at all. If there are multiple gateways, they will all be listed.

As you can see, the utility provides a great deal of useful troubleshooting information. Some of the terms here have not been defined—if you don't understand them just yet, it's OK! By the end of the course, you will understand what each piece of information presented here is and how this one command can assist you in solving most configuration problems.

Let's take a quick look at the actual output of the Ipconfig /All command:

FIGURE 2-7
IPCONFIG/All Output.

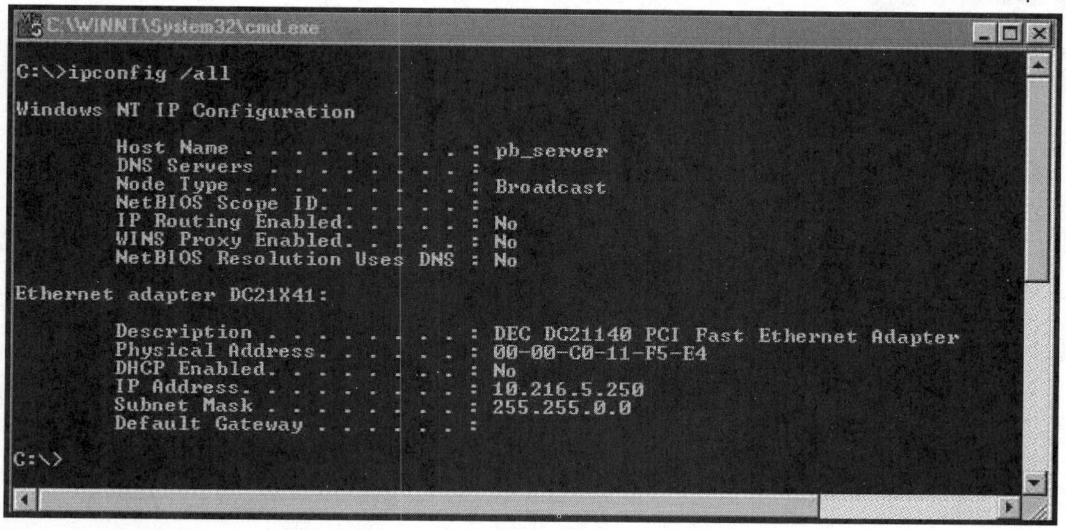

```
C:\>ipconfig /all

Windows NT IP Configuration

        Host Name . . . . . . . . . : pb_server
        DNS Servers . . . . . . . . :
        Node Type . . . . . . . . . : Broadcast
        NetBIOS Scope ID. . . . . . :
        IP Routing Enabled. . . . . : No
        WINS Proxy Enabled. . . . . : No
        NetBIOS Resolution Uses DNS : No

Ethernet adapter DC21X41:

        Description . . . . . . . . : DEC DC21140 PCI Fast Ethernet Adapter
        Physical Address. . . . . . : 00-00-C0-11-F5-E4
        DHCP Enabled. . . . . . . . : No
        IP Address. . . . . . . . . : 10.216.5.250
        Subnet Mask . . . . . . . . : 255.255.0.0
        Default Gateway . . . . . . :

C:\>
```

IPCONFIG Switches

Now that we have some idea of the information this command gives us, let's take a look at a few of the options available to us in terms of switches. The following command switches are valid for the IPCONFIG command.

IPCONFIG—No Switch. Displays the ethernet adapter, IP address, subnet mask, and default gateway for installed adapters. This is the short form if you think there may be a problem with the minimum required information for a client is incorrect.

IPCONFIG—/ALL Switch. Displays all information listed in Figures 2.8 and 2.9. This is the most commonly used switch to troubleshoot IP configurations on client machines.

IPCONFIG—/RELEASE Switch. If DHCP is enabled for the network adapter, this will send a Release request to the DHCP server asking the server to release the adapter's IP address to the pool. We will use this command later in the book when we cover DHCP in detail.

IPCONFIG—/RENEW Switch. If DHCP is enabled for the network adapter, this will issue a "renew" request to the DHCP address asking for a new IP address and configuration. We will use this command later in the book when we cover DHCP in detail.

IPCONFIG—/? Switch. Provides help for the IPCONFIG command.

LAB

2.1 Using IPCONFIG

• •

This lab will allow you to explore the IPCONFIG utility. To complete the lab, follow the directions below completing the table, any questions, and issuing all commands.

1. Open a Windows NT Command Window.

2. At the NT DOS prompt, enter **IPCONFIG** and record the configu-

ration information for your computer in the table provided.

3. At the NT DOS prompt, enter **IPCONFIG/ALL** and record the configuration information for your computer.

4. At the NT DOS prompt, enter **IPCONFIG/?** and record the options in your class notebook.

5. Optional—If your network is using a DHCP server for address management, release your IP lease by issuing the **IPCONFIG/RELEASE** command.

6. Optional— If your network is using a DHCP server for address management, renew your IP lease by issuing the **IPCONFIG/RENEW** command.

7. Close the NT DOS command window.

NOTE: *If you receive a "bad command or file name" error, contact your instructor. Additionally, if you receive IP address and subnet information of 0.0.0.0 and 0.0.0.0, your instructor will need to assist you with your configuration of TCP/IP.*

IP CONFIG COMMAND OUTPUT

INFORMATION

Windows NT IP Configuration

Host Name
DNS Servers
Node Type
NetBIOS Scope ID
IP Routing Enabled
WINS Proxy Enabled
NetBIOS Resolution uses DNS

Ethernet Adapter <Adapter Driver>

Description
Physical Address
DHCP Enabled
IP Address
Subnet Mask
Default Gateway

IPCONFIG INFORMATION FOR YOUR COMPUTER

The PING Command

The PING command is actually an acronym for *Packet Internet Groper.* This is a fancy way of saying the utility checks (or gropes) to see if a host exists on a TCP/IP network. The term actually comes from navy sonar where a "ping" is the reflected sound that is generated when the originally broadcast sound bounces off an object. The same concept holds true in TCP/IP. When you PING a host you are essentially sending out a message asking for a reply. A successful reply from the host will be acknowledged on the sending computer.

PING is one of the most popular tools in troubleshooting TCP/IP network connectivity. Next to IPCONFIG, this command will be one you use on a daily basis. PING is a relatively easy command to learn and use. There are several switches, but for the most part, the defaults work just fine. PING, like IPCON-FIG, is a command line utility and needs to be run in a NT DOS window. The basic syntax for the command is as follows:

PING <IP Address/NetBIOS Name/FQDN>

That's pretty simple. Let's take a look at the response we receive from a host we PING:

FIGURE 2-8
PING Command Response.

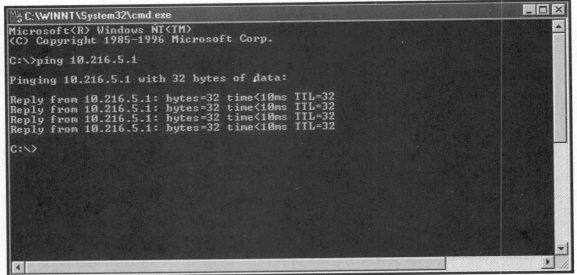

Notice the contents of the response. Let's define a few of the fields and acronyms we see above.

Reply From. This acknowledges that the host (10.216.5.1) has successfully replied to the client. This usually means TCP/IP is communicating properly for a particular situation. Notice that regardless of how you enter the command (using a NetBIOS name, FQDN, or IP Address), the reply value will always be in the form of a numeric IP address. This has to do with the way TCP/IP resolves names.

Bytes. This value will always be a number and indicates the number of bytes the PING message will transmit/receive. This value can be changed through a switch.

Time. This indicates the amount of time it took for the host to reply in thousandths of a second (milliseconds).

TTL. This is an acronym for something called *Time to Live*. TTL refers to a packet header field sent over the Internet indicating how long the packet should be held. In simpler terms, it defines a second count first and then the number of "hops" allowed across routers. Each time a TCP/IP PING packet crosses a router, its TTL value decrements (is reduced) by one. If the TTL expires either because the host did not reply in the specified time-frame or the number of router hops has been exceeded, the packet is discarded. This is also a value that can be modified using a switch.

HELP FOR THE PING COMMAND

PING Help is accessed simply by typing **PING** and pressing return. You will notice there are many additional switches associated with the command. Each has a specific use in a troubleshooting situation making the utility very flexible and powerful. However, in most instances, the default values should work fine in your situation.

127.0.0.1—THE SPECIAL IP ADDRESS

Although we have not covered IP address classes yet, there is one address that is used extensively in testing with PING and so we will introduce it at this point in our discussion. This IP address is 127.0.0.1. It is also commonly referred to as the *Loop-Back address*. It is reserved by the TCP/IP protocol for testing of the internal configuration of TCP/IP on a computer. If you ever suspect there is a problem with the actual drivers and internal workings of the TCP/IP protocol on a particular system you would use the command:

PING 127.0.0.1

If this returns an error, you will most likely need to reinstall the protocol. If it returns a reply as illustrated in Figure 2.9, the protocol is working correctly internally. This does *not* mean that anything else is configured correctly! It *only* means TCP/IP is installed properly on the client machine.

L A B

2.2   Using PING

This lab will allow you to explore the PING utility. To complete the lab, follow the directions below completing the table, any questions, and issuing all commands.

1. Open a Windows NT Command Window.

2. At the NT DOS prompt, enter **PING 127.0.0.1.** Did you receive a reply? How long did the response take? What does this reply mean in terms of troubleshooting?

3. At the NT DOS prompt, enter **PING <Instructor Workstation IP Address>.** Did you receive a reply? How long did the response take?

4. At the NT DOS prompt, enter **PING www.microsoft.com.** Did you receive a reply? How long did the response take? Was it longer than the response from your instructor's computer?

5. PING several of your classmate's workstations using both IP addresses and NetBIOS names. Did you find one way to be faster than another? Why do you think?

6. Display PING Help. Use the information from Help to try the optional exercises.

7. Optional—Try changing the value of the bytes field using the –l option. Were you successful? What changed when you issued the command?

8. Optional—Try using the –t switch. What happens when you use this command?

9. Optional—Try using the –n switch. What happens when you use this command?

10. Close the NT DOS command window.

ENRICHMENT ACTIVITY (OPTIONAL)

Research and document the function of the different PING options. Your instructor can help you find resources for each of the parameters and what they are used for.

The ARP Command

ARP is an acronym for *Address Resolution Protocol*. ARP's main function is to resolve IP addresses to MAC addresses. As a matter of fact, TCP/IP communications depend on ARP to answer the question, "Who is this IP Address and what is your hardware address?" before any communications occur.

ARP entries are also dynamic meaning, they will be stored only for a short time period before being flushed from the ARP Cache. This utility is typically used to see mappings between IP address and MAC address. Occasionally, it is also beneficial to add a static, or permanent, entry in the ARP cache. The ARP command allows you to do this as well. Please note though that the ARP cache disappears on reboot of a computer and all static entries will be lost.

Let's take a look at some of the most useful ARP commands:

To get Help on ARP type **ARP** at a Windows NT command prompt and press Return. Output from the command is listed below.

FIGURE 2-9
ARP Help.

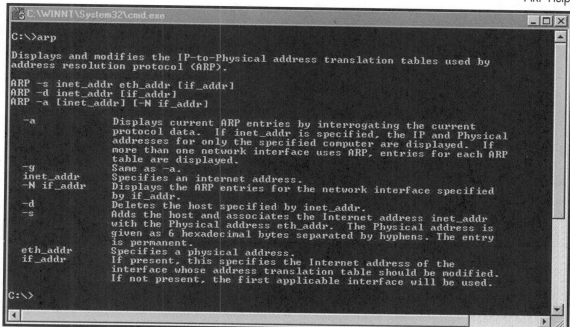

To see what information is currently stored in the ARP cache, use the –a switch. The output is defined below.

FIGURE 2-10
The ARP –a Switch.

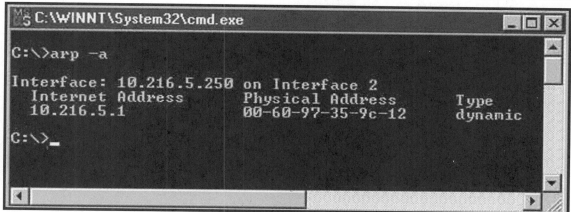

If you need to set up a static entry in ARP cache, you use the –s switch. For this command to work properly you must also enter the IP address and MAC address of the target host. Command syntax and output are provided below.

FIGURE 2-11
The ARP –s Switch.

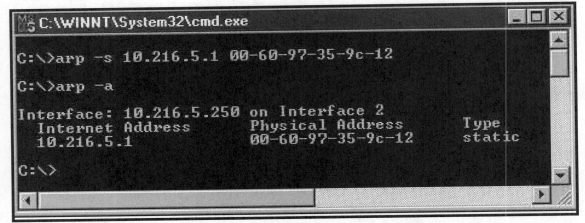

If you are having difficulty communicating with a host, ARP is a useful command to see what is stored in ARP cache. Remember, if there is no ARP entry for the host you are trying to contact, you will be unable to connect.

How Does ARP Resolve Addresses?

ARP uses two methods for resolution of addresses. One method is used for local subnet clients and the other is used for remote addresses. Each of these methods is briefly described as follows.

RESOLVING A LOCAL ADDRESS

1. Any time a host attempts to communicate with another local host, ARP first checks its internal cache to see if there is an entry.

2. If there is no entry and IP has determined that the address is local, an ARP broadcast request is made to all hosts on the local subnet.

3. Each host on the local subnet then processes the request. If there is no match on the local machine, the packet is discarded. If the destination host determines that the IP address is the same as its own, it sends a direct ARP reply to the sending host with its hardware address.

RESOLVING A REMOTE ADDRESS

1. Any time a host attempts to communicate with a remote host, ARP first checks the local routing table for a path to the destination network or host. If no entry is found, it then looks for the IP address of the default gateway.

2. If there is no entry and IP has determined that the address is remote, an ARP broadcast request is made to the default gateway. The gateway then sends its MAC address to the source computer and the source computer then sends the ARP packet to the router.

3. The router then determines whether the address is local or remote to the router and sends the ARP packet directly to the target host or another router.

4. Step 3 is repeated until the target computer (and MAC address) is found. The target host then replies to the source computer with its MAC address and ARP is updated.

RARP

RARP is an acronym for *Reverse Address Resolution Protocol*. RARP serves the same function as ARP except that the resolution occurs based on a known MAC address rather than an IP address. While RARP refers only to finding the IP address and ARP technically refers to the opposite procedure, ARP is commonly used for both functions. TCP/IP will automatically determine which method to use but it is helpful to understand that another protocol is used for this reverse situation.

LAB

2.3

Using ARP

● ●

This lab will allow you to explore the ARP utility. To complete the lab, follow the directions below completing the table, any questions, and issuing all commands.

1. Open a Windows NT Command Window.

2. At the NT DOS prompt, PING a computer in the classroom.

3. At the NT DOS prompt, enter **ARP -a.** What was the output of the command?

4. At the NT DOS prompt, enter **ARP -g.** What was the output of the command? Does this switch provide any other information not provided by the -a switch?

5. At the NT DOS prompt, enter **ARP –s.** What was the output of the command? Does this switch require any additional information to operate correctly? If so, what information is required?

6. Set-up a static mapping to the computer you PINGed in Step 1 using ARP.

7. Display the ARP command help by typing **ARP** and pressing Return.

8. Document the other options. Discuss possible uses of these options with your instructor.

9. Close the NT DOS command window.

The TRACERT Utility

TRACERT is an acronym for *Trace Route*. This command is useful in troubleshooting router and timing problems with TCP/IP packets. TRACERT allows you to trace the connectivity path a packet uses to go from the source computer to a target computer. Information provided from this command can be used to see if there is a bottleneck at a particular router or if slow communications are detected. It is also useful in seeing which networks are using a particular destination route. The syntax for the command is as follows:

TRACERT <switches/values> <Host Name/IP Address>

TRACERT displays each "hop" (or router crossed), the network the packet crossed, and the time it took to go across the router. There are several options and switches for TRACERT. Let's take a look at some of the more useful command line switches associated with TRACERT.

Help. TRACERT Help is accessed by simply typing the command **TRACERT** and pressing Return. All available options are displayed on the screen. Here is a sample of the screen output of TRACERT Help.

FIGURE 2-12
TRACERT Help.

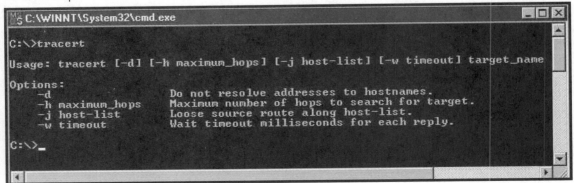

"Hop-Count" Switch (–h). One of the most useful switches for use with TRACERT is the "hop count" switch. By default, TRACERT will trace up to 30 hops, to a destination. If the packet has not reached its destination within 30 hops, the command will stop the trace. You can increase this hop count by using the –h switch. The command syntax and output are provided below.

FIGURE 2-13
TRACERT –h.

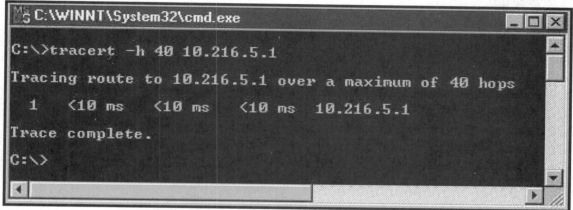

Timeout Switch (–w). Another useful option is the Timeout switch. This switch allows the user to configure a longer (or shorter) timeout value for TRACERT providing flexibility in identifying a slow router connection. The command syntax and output are provided below.

FIGURE 2-14
TRACERT –w.

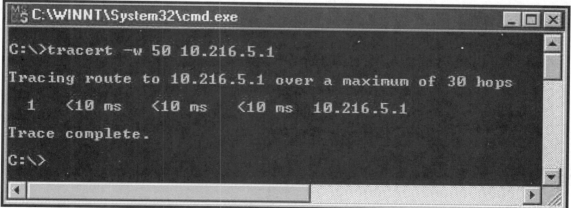

As you can see from the examples above, TRACERT requires that switches be used with a destination IP address or host name for the command to work properly. Switches used alone will generate an error message from the command.

2.4

Using TRACERT (Optional)

This lab will allow you to explore the TRACERT utility. To complete the lab, follow the directions below completing the table, any questions, and issuing all commands.

1. Open a Windows NT Command Window.

2. At the NT DOS prompt, enter **TRACERT** and press Return. What output is returned on your computer? Document the results.

3. At the NT DOS prompt, enter **TRACERT www.microsoft.com.** What was the output of the command? Document the results.

4. At the NT DOS prompt, enter **TRACERT <instructor computer**

name>. What was the output of the command? Document the results.

5. At the NT DOS prompt, enter **TRACERT <instructor IP Address>.** What was the output of the command? Document the results.

6. At the NT DOS prompt, enter **TRACERT –h 60 www.micro soft.com.** What was the output of the command? Document the results.

7. At the NT DOS prompt, enter **TRACERT –h 60 –w 60 www.microsoft.com.** What was the output of the command? Document the results.

8. Close the NT DOS command window.

Lesson 2.2 The Name Resolution Game

This lesson provides an overview of TCP/IP name resolution. This concept is very important in the implementation of TCP/IP. We will be looking at several methods of name resolution that are used within the Windows NT TCP/IP implementation. Some resolution methods will use an application while others will use flat text files. By the end of this lesson you will understand the following name resolution methods available through Microsoft's TCP/IP implementation:

- WINS Application
- DNS Application
- HOSTS File
- LMHOSTS File
- ARP/RARP

The TCP/IP Name Resolution Game

WHY NAME RESOLUTION?

At some level, all network protocols perform some level of name resolution. The concept of name resolution came about because of the arcane nature of most addressing schemes that a computer uses to reference and represent itself on the network. As you might recall, computers "talk" predominantly in the binary or hexi-decimal numbering systems. At a fundamental level, a computer's "language" of choice is in Base 2 since a computer really is only a series of complex switches (they are either off or on). Base 2 numbering is wonderful since there are only two numbers, **0** and **1.** Zero signifies an off state and one means the switch is on. When we look at subnet masks, memory dumps, MAC addresses, and network addressing schemes, we are actually seeing a higher-level of binary and hexi-decimal numbering at work.

When network transport occurs, it is actually these numbering systems that accomplish the transactions. However, for the human race, referencing binary or hexi-decimal addresses is like speaking a whole different language. Our numbering system (Base 10) and alphabet has little in common with the computer communication language. It is for this reason that name resolution is so important.

Many protocols insulate the user completely from name resolution. Net-BEUI is an excellent example of this—it completely takes care of name resolution. There is nothing for the user to configure at all. Name resolution is completely transparent—it just works. Unfortunately, TCP/IP is not quite so simple.

TCP/IP uses several methods to resolve high-level names humans understand like www.microsoft.com and INSTRUCTOR into IP addresses that TCP/IP understands and eventually a MAC address that the computer understands. As TCP/IP network administrators, one of our jobs is to manage this name resolution process. We have a great deal more flexibility with TCP/IP than NetBEUI but we also have more to worry about. These are the topics we will be discussing in this lesson.

NAME RESOLUTION OVERVIEW:

There are three types of name resolution we will be discussing throughout this book. A brief overview of each follows.

NetBIOS Name Resolution. NetBIOS computer names are the method Microsoft operating systems use to identify a computer on a network. NetBIOS names are most often called "Computer Names." They can consist of almost any alphanumeric characters but are limited to 15 in number. TCP/IP does not innately understand a NetBIOS name and so we need to form an equation that maps an IP address to the computer name. This is NetBIOS name resolution. The equation looks something like this:

$$\text{INSTRUCTOR} = 10.216.5.1$$

There are three methods of NetBIOS name resolution available in Microsoft Windows NT TCP/IP. These methods are:

WINS. The Windows Internet Naming Service is bundled with Windows NT Server. It is a Microsoft-developed database that maintains mappings very similar to the equation outlined above. WINS is dynamic, another word for automatic. Once installed and configured, WINS manages the entire process of resolution automatically and seamlessly to the user. Using a WINS server also provides better network optimization since broadcast transmissions typically associated with NetBIOS naming are minimized. All the name resolution activity occurs through the WINS server. WINS also keeps more information in its database than just simply computer names. Additional information maintained in the database includes workgroup and domain names, version numbers, and active status of the client computers.

LMHOSTS File. Before WINS was developed, NetBIOS name resolution still needed to occur between NetBIOS names and TCP/IP. The precursor to WINS was a flat-file (a standard ASCII text file) called the LMHOSTS file. LMHOSTS stands for *Logical Machine Hosts*. This file serves the same purpose as a WINS server except that all entries must be manually entered on each client computer—a very time-consuming and error-prone process. LMHOSTS files are still used in certain instances and continue to play an important role in the name resolution process. If a network is not using WINS, it is probably using a LMHOSTS file for resolution. The LMHOSTS file, when properly implemented, will also provide better network performance by reducing broadcast traffic on the network. However, they have been largely replaced by WINS.

NetBIOS Broadcasts. If WINS or LMHOSTS files are not in use on a Microsoft TCP/IP network, the only other method of name resolution available is the broadcast method. This works well in a small network but can cause unsatisfactory traffic on a larger network. Since there is no mapping database or file in use, the source computer broadcasts its name to all other computers on the network asking for a reply to the question: *"Are you the Instructor computer, and if you are, what is your IP address?"* Each computer on the network must process this question and either reply or discard the packet—a potentially significant drain on network resources in larger networks with many computers.

FQDN (Fully Qualified Domain Name) Name Resolution

When TCP/IP was first developed, Bill Gates and Paul Allen were teenagers! Microsoft Corporation was only a distant dream (if even conceived) at that point in time. The prior name-resolution method dealt specifically with TCP/IP name resolution as it applies to Microsoft networks. This section speaks to the original (and still very popular) TCP/IP name resolution method of using a FQDN and associating it with an IP Address.

All Internet URLs use this naming scheme for name resolution. As you may recall, a typical FQDN would be named as follows: www.microsoft.com. It is important to remember that a NetBIOS name and a FQDN serve exactly the same purpose, that is, to make it easier for a human being to remember the address of a target computer. Although they are implemented differently, their ultimate role is exactly the same!

TCP/IP does not innately understand a FQDN and so we need to form an equation that maps an IP address to the domain name. This is FQDN name resolution. The equation looks something like this:

$$\text{www.microsoft.com} = 10.216.5.1$$

There are two main methods of FQDN name resolution available in Microsoft Windows NT TCP/IP. These methods are outlined below:

DNS (Domain Name System). DNS is similar to WINS in its function: it maps names to IP addresses. However, DNS is very different in its implementation. Unlike WINS, DNS is a hierarchical database. Hierarchical means that DNS processes entries in a fashion similar to a directory tree. Further, DNS is a static database, meaning that all entries must be made manually to a DNS server. While this may seem cumbersome, it was a huge improvement over the other method for FQDN name resolution we will discuss shortly. If we take a quick look at a typical FQDN like www.microsoft.com we can see the hierarchy.

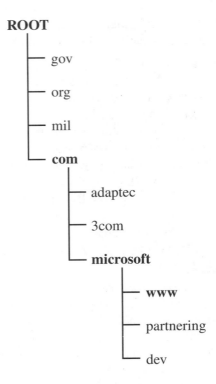

■ The **com** portion of the FQDN is a zone that contains all entries for companies. This DNS server is managed by InterNIC. You must register your name with InterNIC. When you do that they make an entry into their DNS servers with your organization's IP Address. There are many other zones besides com. You may have seen them before: *org* is an organization, *mil* is the United States military, *gov* is the United States government, and so on. This level is close to the Root directory of the Internet DNS tree.

■ The **microsoft** portion of the entry specifies the company's internal DNS servers. These servers may be located at the company (as is typically the case in larger companies) or managed by an ISP (*Internet Service Provider*). Every company that is on the Internet has an entry similar to this. This entry is underneath the com zone in the tree and is, therefore, inherently part of com.

■ The **www** portion of the entry is the lowest level (and most specific) in the DNS tree. It is part of the microsoft.com hierarchy. Entries such as these are typically related to specific site computers at a company and can again be managed by the company or an ISP. This entry is underneath the microsoft zone in the tree and is, therefore, inherently part of microsoft.

■ Each discrete zone, or level, will always be separated in a FQDN by a period (.). Entries are typically processed from the far right to the left with the rightmost entry being the most generic and the leftmost entry being the most specific. DNS trees can go very deep. As you can see this is a very flexible structure allowing for a great deal of growth.

HOSTS File. Prior to the creation of DNS, FQDN name resolution was managed using a flat-file called the HOSTS file. Just like the LMHOSTS file described earlier, the HOSTS file must be located on each client computer. HOSTS files are still used on many older systems or companies that do not use DNS.

If DNS or the HOSTS file is not used, the only way to connect to another machine using TCP/IP is to specify the target computer's IP address. This is why in the previous lesson you could use a NetBIOS name, FQDN, or IP address to run the utilities discussed. If you were observant, you probably noticed that whenever you used an FQDN or NetBIOS name, the computer returned the IP address in brackets on successful execution of the command.

TROUBLESHOOTING TIP: When troubleshooting name resolution always first try to use the NetBIOS or FQDN to PING, ARP, or TRACERT. If you get an error message using these names but do not get an error by using the IP address of the target computer, it means there is a problem with name resolution.

IP ADDRESS TO MAC ADDRESS

In the last lesson, we used the ARP utility to view and set up static entries in ARP cache. As you may have guessed, ARP is responsible for the last piece of the address resolution equation. It maps an IP address (which TCP/IP understands) to the Media Access Control (MAC) address of a target host (which the computer understands). The ARP equation looks like this:

$$10.216.5.1 = 00\text{-}60\text{-}97\text{-}35\text{-}9C\text{-}12$$

Notice that the MAC address is expressed in hexi-decimal format. This is what the computer is actually using to locate the target host. RARP performs the same function as ARP except that it takes the known MAC address and equates it to an IP address.

When all these name resolution methods are working correctly, we have what is called a transitive equation between the NetBIOS/FQDN, IP address, and MAC address that looks something like this:

$$A \qquad = \qquad B \qquad = \qquad C$$
$$\text{<NetBIOS/FQDN>} \ = \ \text{IP Address} \ = \ \text{MAC Address}$$

Transitive means that if $A = B$ and $B = C$ then $A = C$. This is how name resolution occurs in TCP/IP.

2.5 Locating and Viewing the HOSTS and LMHOSTS Files

• •

This lab will allow you to explore the HOSTS and LMHOSTS name resolution files. To complete the lab, follow the directions below, complete questions, and issue all commands. Share your work with the instructor when you are done.

1. Click on the Start button and open the Find Files applet.

2. Search for the file LMHOSTS.SAM. Did you find the file? Does the file have any entries in it? If so, what are they? Where is the location of the file on your hard disk? Document it.

3. Open LMHOSTS.SAM using the Notepad application. Read the LMHOSTS file sample and print the information out. You will need it later!

4. Edit the LMHOSTS file to provide a NetBIOS name mapping for the instructor's computer. Set up the mapping *exactly* as directed in the instructions. When you are done it should look something like this:

    <NetBIOS name of your Choice> <IP Address of Instructor Computer>

5. Save the LMHOSTS.SAM file as LMHOSTS.

6. Open a Windows NT Command Window.

7. PING the new NetBIOS name you just created for the instructor's computer. Did you get a response? Document your results.

8. Search for the file HOSTS. Did you find the file? Does the file have any entries in it? If so, what are they? Where is the location of the file on your hard disk? Document it.

9. Open the HOSTS file using the Notepad application. Read the HOSTS file sample and print the information out. You will need it later!

10. Edit the Hosts file to provide a FQDN name mapping for the instructor's computer. Set up the mapping *exactly* as directed in the instructions. When you are done it should look something like this:

   <FQDN name of your Choice> <IP Address of Instructor Computer>

11. Save the HOSTS file.

12. Close Notepad and the Find Files applet.

13. PING the new FQDN name you just created for the instructor's computer. Did you get a response? Document your results.

14. Have a partner try PINGING the instructor's computer using the same names you created on your machine. Were they successful? Why or Why not?

15. Discuss the results with your instructor.

16. Close the NT Command Window.

Summary

This chapter provided an introduction to several utilities useful in testing a TCP/IP configuration as well as a more detailed explanation of NetBIOS and FQDN name resolution. Topics covered in this chapter included:

■ **The IPCONFIG Utility.** We explored, documented, and tested the functions and importance of the IPCONFIG utility. IPCONFIG is very useful in troubleshooting problems related to IP address, subnet mask, default gateway, and several other parameters. We also discussed IPCONFIG's secondary function of "Releasing" and "Renewing" IP addresses from a DHCP server. Finally, we took a quick look at the limitations of the IPCONFIG command.

■ **The PING Utility.** PING is one of the most popular tools in troubleshooting TCP/IP network connectivity. Like IPCONFIG, PING is a command line utility and needs to be run in a DOS window for any OS. We discussed and tested the various switches used with PING and how they can be used to assist in verifying and troubleshooting a TCP/IP configuration. We also took a look at the special TCP/IP loop-back address 127.0.0.1, its uses, and its importance in verifying the local host's TCP/IP configuration.

■ **The ARP Protocol.** We discussed, tested, and explored the various functions of ARP in this lesson. We also took a detailed look at how ARP resolves a MAC address to an IP address. Further, we described the function of the RARP protocol and its relationship to ARP.

■ **The TRACERT Utility.** In this lesson, we explored, documented, and tested the trace route utility. TRACERT allows you to trace the connectivity path a packet uses to go from the source computer to a target computer. Information provided from this command can be used to see if there is a bottleneck at a particular router or if slow communications are detected.

■ **Name Resolution Methods.** We discussed the different methods of name resolution available in TCP/IP for both NetBIOS and FQDN name resolution. We also discussed the various files and applications that are used to accomplish these tasks within Windows NT. Particular emphasis in this lesson was placed on the rationale for having name resolution and the relationships between a high-level alphanumeric name, IP address, and MAC address.

● ● ● ● ● ● ● ● ● ● ● ●

1. *Select the best answer:* Which TCP/IP utility allows the user to test connectivity using the address 127.0.0.1?

   a. TRACERT
   b. IPCONFIG
   c. ARP
   d. RARP
   e. PING

2. *Select the best answer:* Which name resolution method uses a hierarchical database to process name requests?

   a. WINS
   b. DHCP
   c. LMHOSTS
   d. ARP
   e. DNS
   f. HOSTS

3. *Select the best answer:* The relationship between ARP and RARP can be defined as follows:

   a. ARP resolves a known FQDN to a MAC address, while RARP resolves a known MAC address to a FQDN.
   b. ARP resolves a known NetBios name to a MAC address, while RARP resolves a known MAC address to a NetBios name.
   c. ARP resolves a known IP address, to a MAC address, while RARP resolves a known MAC address to a IP address name.
   d. ARP resolves a known MAC address to a IP address, while RARP resolves a known IP address to a MAC address.
   e. None of the above.

4. *Select the best answer:* Release and Renewing an IP address are functions provided by which TCP/IP utility?

   a. ARP
   b. IPCONFIG
   c. TRACERT
   d. PING
   e. None of these utilities can perform this function

5. *Select all that apply:* How does a user access Help on command line TCP/IP utilities?

   a. Use the /h switch.
   b. Use the /? switch.
   c. Use the F1 key.
   d. Simply type the command with no arguments and press Enter.

6. *Select all that apply:* Which of the following are true of DNS?

    a. DNS is a static database.
    b. DNS is a dynamic database.
    c. DNS serves the same purpose as the HOSTS file.
    d. DNS is used to resolve FQDN's to IP addresses.

7. *Select all that apply:* Which of the following are true of MAC addresses?

    a. MAC addresses are always expressed in a dotted-quad decimal format.
    b. MAC addresses are always unique.
    c. MAC addresses are always expressed in a hexi-decimal format.
    d. MAC addresses are always associated with a Network Interface Card (NIC).

8. *Select the best answer:* What command and switch would you use to set up a static IP to MAC address in cache?

    a. IPCONFIG /A
    b. RARP –w
    c. ARP –s
    d. ARP –a
    e. TRACERT –s

9. *Select the best answer:* A user comes to you with a problem. They state that they are unable to connect to any hosts on their TCP/IP network using a computer name but they can connect to hosts by typing an IP address. What is the most likely cause of the problem?

    a. WINS name resolution is not working properly.
    b. The internal TCP/IP configuration is invalid.
    c. DHCP has not leased an address to the client.
    d. DNS name resolution is not configured properly.
    e. There is no problem. This is normal TCP/IP operation.

10. *Select the best answer:* Sara, a Windows 95 computer user on your network, cannot connect to any other computers on her network. The network uses only TCP/IP as a network transport protocol. You go to her workstation and use the PING command with the loop-back address and fail to get a response. What can you do to fix Sara's computer?

    a. Reinstall TCP/IP.
    b. Run the IPCONFIG utility to repair the installation.
    c. Configure the workstation to use DNS.
    d. Configure the workstation to use WINS.
    e. Configure the workstation to use DHCP.
    f. All of the above.

11. *Select the best answer:* You are the network administrator for a large TCP/IP networked installation of Windows NT Workstation computers. You have been charged with providing

an automated mechanism for allowing users to communicate using computer names and to reduce overall network traffic. What type of name resolution will meet these requirements?

a. Broadcast-Based Transmissions
b. A HOSTS file
c. A LMHOSTS file and WINS
d. DNS only
e. WINS only
f. None of the above.

12. *Suppose the following situation exists:*

Becky, a Windows NT Workstation computer user on your network, needs to access computers using FQDNs and NetBIOS names. However, your network is not currently running DNS and WINS servers. Management has asked you to provide an interim solution so Becky can access the resources she requires.

Required Results:
■ Provide NetBIOS name resolution on Becky's computer.
■ Provide FQDN name resolution on Becky's computer.

Optional Results:
■ Supply configuration information to clients for WINS and DNS servers located on the network.
■ Automate the name resolution update process on Becky's machine.
■ Provide an automatic mechanism for TCP/IP configuration to Becky's computer.

Proposed Solution:
■ Install a Microsoft DHCP server on the network and configure Becky's machine to use DHCP for address management.
■ Install and configure a LMHOSTS file on Becky's computer.
■ Configure Becky's computer as a Directory Replication Import partner with a NT server that has the master LMHOSTS file. Schedule the files to be updated at least once a day.

a. The proposed solution meets both the required and optional results.
b. The proposed solution meets the required results and only one of the optional results.
c. The proposed solution meets the required results and none of the optional results.
d. The proposed solution does not meet requirements nor optional results.

13. *Select all that apply.* Jack has modified his DHCP server information. He wants to see if clients are receiving the new lease information he has provided. How would Jack test a client configuration to see if his changes have taken place?

   a. Run PING –s on selected computers.
   b. Run ARP –a on selected computers.
   c. Run the IPCONFIG /All on selected computers.
   d. Run IPCONFIG /c on selected computers.
   e. Run IPCONFIG.
   f. None of the above.

14. *Select the best answer.* Sue, a domain user in Delaware, is attempting to access an Internet network host in California. She reports that she can only occasionally connect to the resource and it is very slow. What utility would you use to diagnose the performance problem?

   a. IPCONFIG /All
   b. PING
   c. FINGER
   d. ARP –s
   e. TRACERT

15. *Select the best answer.* Bob is trying to find a known MAC address associated with a particular IP address. What TCP/IP protocol/utility should he be using?

   a. DNS
   b. WINS
   c. DHCP
   d. ARP
   e. RARP

DIGGING DEEPER INTO MICROSOFT TCP/IP

CHAPTER *3*

OBJECTIVES

By the end of this chapter, you should be able to:

- Describe how Microsoft's TCP/IP implementation maps to the OSI model.

- Define and explain the function of intermediary layering products like TDI and NDIS 4.0.

- Define and explain how ICMP and IGMP service IP.

- Differentiate between a TCP/IP socket and port.

- Understand how TCP/IP works with RAS.

- Understand protocols available to configure a RAS TCP/IP implementation.

- Define and configure a multi-homed TCP/IP computer.

- Define and conceptualize the function of the Microsoft RIP for IP Router protocol.

- Define and conceptualize the concept of a TCP Sliding Window.

- Understand the TCP "handshaking" process.

Introduction

Up to this point in our discussion of TCP/IP, we have been focused on background, general concepts, and hands-on activities related to installing, testing, and performing some basic troubleshooting of a TCP/IP network. This chapter digs deeply into the OSI networking model surrounding general network transport and how specifically Microsoft's TCP/IP architecture maps to this conceptual framework. We will see that while TCP/IP loosely adheres to the seven layer OSI model, it adds function and segments layers differently than a standard OSI implementation. We will look at special tools and programmer interfaces provided by Microsoft to make access to the TCP/IP stack easier for vendors and see how the NDIS specification is mapped within the TCP/IP protocol.

As we work through this chapter, new concepts and protocols will be presented as they apply to TCP/IP. We will look at some of the more specialized protocols and architectural features of the protocol suite including ICMP, IGMP, ports, sliding windows, and TCP handshakes to illustrate how the many individual protocols and architectural designs of TCP/IP work together to provide guaranteed, connection-oriented communications. We will also take a look at how TCP/IP functions within a remote networking environment using RAS and dial-up networking and how we can extend the functions of a Windows NT server to create a dynamic router with a minimum of expense and time.

Lesson 3.1 Microsoft's Implementation of TCP/IP

This lesson discusses several of the generic and specific features of Microsoft's TCP/IP implementation. Within this lesson, we will be covering the following topics.

- Microsoft TCP/IP network transport overview

- RAS functions within Microsoft TCP/IP

- Multi-homed Windows NT computers

- Microsoft RIP for IP

- IP forwarding

- TCP windows

Much of the material in this lesson is conceptual and there are many new terms and definitions that we will be covering. You should take careful notes as you work through this lesson since many of the terms and concepts are very important to topics covered later in the book (and on your Microsoft exam). Your indepth understanding of these topics will make your job that much easier when we actually implement these concepts.

Microsoft TCP/IP Network Transport Overview

All protocols in one way or another map to the OSI model of network transport. In this lesson, we will take a look at how Microsoft's implementation of TCP/IP maps to the OSI model and further define several protocols and concepts related to how data is transported across the network in a Microsoft TCP/IP network. This section of the lesson is divided into two parts. The first section provides some terms and definitions that you must understand before we actually look at (and describe) the network model. The second part of this lesson looks closely at how Microsoft TCP/IP operates within the framework of the OSI model.

TERMINOLOGY AND CONCEPTS

ARP. See definition and protocol explanations in chapters 1 and 2.

ICMP. ICMP is an acronym for the *Internet Control Message Protocol.* ICMP is a network-layer Internet protocol that provides error correction and other information relevant to IP packet processing. ICMP works closely with the IP protocol. One of the functions of ICMP is to let IP software on one machine inform another machine about an unreachable destination. It is important to note that ICMP does not seek to make IP a reliable protocol. It is predominantly used only to report errors and specific conditions back to IP.

IGMP. IGMP is an acronym for the *Internet Group Management Protocol.* IGMP is a protocol used by IP hosts to report their host group memberships to routers that support a feature called multicasting. IGMP allows routers to pass information to other routers defining which multi-casting groups are available on a particular network.

IP. See definition and explanation provided in chapter 1.

ISO/OSI Model. An acronym for the *International Organization for Standardization Open Systems Interconnection* model. The OSI model is a layered network architecture map that standardizes levels of service and types of interaction for computers exchanging information on a computer network. The OSI model separates computer-to-computer communications into seven layers (or levels), each building upon the standards contained in the levels below it. The lowest of the seven layers deals solely with hardware links; the highest deals with software interactions at the application-program level.

NDIS 4.0. NDIS is an acronym for *Network Device Interface Specification.* Microsoft and 3COM originally developed the NDIS specification. All Microsoft operating systems use some version of the NDIS specification. Windows NT uses NDIS version 4.0. NDIS allows transport layers to call the NDIS driver, which then accesses the network card (Data Link layers and down). All n-network drivers shipped with Windows NT Server 4.0 and Workstation 4.0 are NDIS 4.0 compliant.

NBT. NBT is an acronym for *NetBIOS over TCP/IP*. NBT is a session layer protocol that performs name-to-IP address mapping for name resolution. NBT is automatically installed with any installation of Microsoft TCP/IP and works in concert with tools like WINS to perform name resolution on Microsoft networks.

TCP. See definition and explanation provided in chapter 1.

TCP/IP Port. A TCP/IP port is a number that enables IP packets to be sent to a particular process or service on a computer connected to the Internet. Some port numbers, called *well-known* ports are permanently assigned. For example, HTTP protocol data sent through a browser is sent to well-known port number 80 by default. 65,535 port numbers are individually available for both TCP and UDP.

TCP/IP Socket. A TCP/IP socket is a nomenclature identifier for a particular service or protocol and node on an IP network. The socket consists of a node (IP) address and a port number, which identifies the service. For example, port 21 on an Internet node indicates a FTP server. TCP/IP sockets are comprised of the IP address, FQDN, or NetBIOS name, and a port number separated by a colon. Typical TCP/IP socket nomenclature appears as follows:

10.216.5.1:8080

TDI. TDI is an acronym for *Transport Driver Interface*. The TDI is a Microsoft-developed software interface level allowing lower level networking components (Transport layer and down) to communicate with the Session (and higher) layers of the OSI model. It is loosely placed between the Session and Transport layers of the OSI model. The TDI is a common interface that allows developers to write generic source code without worrying about a particular protocol implementation. As long as they adhere to the TDI standards, the particular protocol implementation is transparent to the programmer.

UDP. See definition provided in chapter 1.

The Microsoft Network Model

This portion of the lesson provides an overview of the OSI model and how Microsoft TCP/IP maps to its various layers.

THE OSI MODEL

Microsoft's implementation of TCP/IP, like many third party vendors, does not map exactly to the seven layers of the OSI model. However, there is a loose mapping that can be established. Before we take a look at Microsoft's TCP/IP model, it will be helpful to take a quick look at the OSI model itself. The model is provided in Figure 3-1 with a brief description of each layer's function.

FIGURE 3-1
The OSI Model.

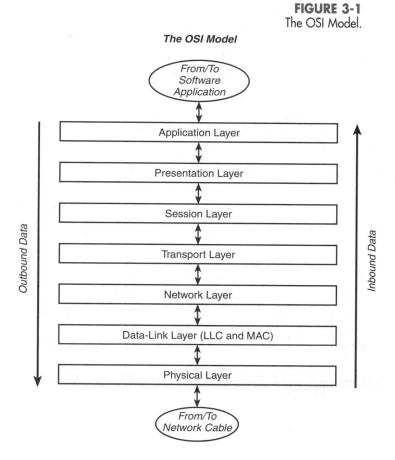

The OSI Model

The following paragraphs provide a brief summary of the function of each OSI layer:

Layer 7: Application Layer. The Application layer of the OSI model provides services that interact directly with a network-enabled application and serves as the entry point for an application to send data across a network. TCP/IP services and protocols like SNMP, FTP, Telnet, and SMTP function at this level. This level handles several functions including flow control, network access, and some components of error recovery.

Layer 6: Presentation Layer. The Presentation layer of the OSI model is also known as the Network Translator. Components at this level provide several primary functions, including translation of data into a generic intermediary format, compression, data translation, and encryption/decryption. The network redirector functions at this level. In Windows NT this represents both the Workstation and Server services.

Layer 5: Session Layer. The Session layer of the OSI model is responsible for establishing communications between two computers. Services and protocols in this layer are responsible for establishing contact, determining packet size, and timing for transmissions. In TCP/IP, the TCP protocol spans the Session and Transport layers.

Layer 4: Transport Layer. The Transport layer of the OSI model provides additional error checking and is responsible for assuring error-free transmissions between the client and server. In TCP/IP, the TCP protocol functions predominantly at this level.

Layer 3: Network Layer. The Network layer of the OSI model is responsible for determining paths to the destination computer, addressing messages, and translating logical addresses (like a NetBIOS or IP address) into physical addresses (MAC addresses). In TCP/IP, many protocols function in this level, including ARP, RARP, IP, IGMP and ICMP. Additionally, routers work extensively at this level.

Layer 2: Data Link Layer. The Data Link layer of the OSI model is responsible for creating a data frame containing the data to be sent across the network and for packaging the information into a format usable by the physical layer (a bitstream) for distribution across the network. Microsoft's NDIS and NDIS wrappers work at this level. Additionally, physical network devices such as bridges and NICS work at this level. Several IEEE standards function at this level. It is divided into the following two sublayers.

- **Logical Link Control (LLC) Sublayer.** This sublayer manages aspects of data-link communications and service access points. This sublayer was defined in the IEEE 802.2 standard.

- **MAC Sublayer.** The MAC sublayer actually spans the data link and physical layers. It is responsible for defining the transmission standards for network media. Its main purpose is to assure error-free data transmissions. Several standards are used at the MAC sublayer. IEEE 802.3 (CSMA/CD), 802.4 and 802.5 (Token Passing), and 802.12 (Demand Priority) access methods all function within this sublayer.

Layer 1: Physical Layer. The Physical layer of the OSI model allows data to be transmitted across the wiring medium. Transmission at this level is electronic, optical, or mechanical. The data transmitted is in the form of a raw bit-stream. NICS and other network hardware devices (ISDN Smart Cards, PADs, and ATM cards) that interface between the computer and the cable function at this level. Additionally, repeaters work at this level of the OSI model.

HOW MICROSOFT TCP/IP MAPS TO THE OSI MODEL

TCP/IP protocols follow a four-layer model that loosely maps to the OSI model. It is important to note that even though there are only four layers described

FIGURE 3-2
Microsoft TCP/IP Network Architecture

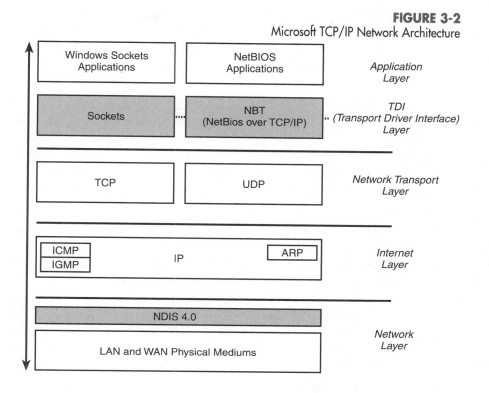

in this section, the network transport mechanism follows the OSI model in terms of modularity and function. The layers have simply been consolidated.

Figure 3-2 provides a graphical representation of the Microsoft TCP/IP protocol architecture. Take a look at this architecture. After you have reviewed the diagram, an explanation and mapping describes the functions and terminology provided.

Level 4: Application Layer. The Application layer in the standard TCP/IP model encompasses functions of the Application, Presentation, and Session layers of the OSI model. In Microsoft's implementation (as in the OSI model), TCP/IP utilities and protocols such SNMP, SMTP, FTP, TFTP, and Telnet operate here. Additionally, Microsoft provides two additional services: the Windows Sockets and NetBIOS Application Interface. A brief explanation of the function of these two additional services is provided here.

■ **Windows Sockets Interface.** For routable protocols like TCP/IP and IPX, Microsoft has provided a standard programming interface (called an API) that allows applications to use the services of Microsoft TCP/IP. This simplifies development efforts for programmers with a predefined set of functions that help to insulate the programmer from the lower levels of the model.

- **NetBIOS Application Interface.** For NetBIOS-based applications, Microsoft provides a similar interface that allows applications using NetBIOS naming conventions and transport mechanisms to communicate using the services of TCP/IP. Applications written for TCP/IP and NetBEUI use this interface to communicate.

Additionally, Microsoft's implementation adds another modular interface to the lower levels of the model. This layer is known as the Transport Device Interface or TDI. The TDI is a Microsoft-developed software interface that allows lower level networking components (Network Transport layer and down) to communicate with the application layer of the TCP/IP model. The TDI provides for NetBIOS over TCP/IP (NBT) services as well as Sockets.

Level 3: Network Transport Layer. The Network Transport layer is concerned with establishing communications between computers. TCP/IP implementations use either TCP for guaranteed connection-oriented communications or UDP for connectionless, nonguaranteed broadcastlike communications. The determination of which transport protocol to use is made by the services and protocols that reside in the application layer. For instance, FTP uses TCP for transport. TFTP and SNMP use UDP for their transport mechanism. This layer maps to the Session and Transport layers of the OSI model.

Level 2: Internet Layer. The Internet layer is concerned with routing of data, preparation of data for transmission into a datagram (a fancy name for a message), and sending/receiving frames of data. Five protocols work at this level: ARP, RARP, ICMP, IGMP and IP. These protocols are briefly described here.

- **IP.** IP's main responsibility is to route and address packets between a host and the network. It works closely with ARP, RARP, ICMP, and IGMP. Information from these protocols provide IP with the information it needs to transmit the data to the destination computer and network.

- **ARP/RARP.** These two protocols are responsible for mapping IP addresses to MAC addresses. Review chapter 2 for a complete description of these protocol functions.

- **ICMP.** ICMP reports errors and feedback on various states of a packet's transmission status to IP. For example, on a busy network where there is a great deal of traffic, a router can send what is called an ICMP Source Quench request asking the sending computer to slow down.

- **IGMP.** IGMP is responsible for transmitting group information for computers that can accept something called a multicast transmission. A multicast is nothing more than a "push" of information that uses the full bandwidth of a host computer's network from a source computer to a group of other computers. It is not really a directed transmission and resembles a broadcast of sorts. The only difference is that a multicast is destined for groups of computers, not just computers on a single network like a broadcast. For IGMP to function, the specific router must have this feature and it must be enabled. IGMP information is passed between routers and makes the router aware of the groups that can accept multicast transmissions on a specific subnet. The Internet layer maps to the Network and portions of the Data Link layers of the OSI model.

Level 1: Network Layer. The Network layer is responsible for the creation and sending/reception of data frames on the network medium. This layer correlates with portions of the Data Link and Physical layers of the OSI model.

TCP/IP PORTS AND SOCKETS DEFINED

As you may recall from chapter 1, TCP/IP clients use an IP address to distinguish themselves with a host network and unique identifier. This covers the client component of transmissions but leaves unanswered the question, "How does TCP/IP know what service or protocol to use on the target computer?" By this point, we have seen that there are many different protocols and services associated with the implementation of TCP/IP. This section of the lesson discusses the concept of a TCP/IP socket and port, how these two mechanisms work together, and why they are important in TCP/IP communications.

Any Port in a Storm . . . Every TCP/IP node acting as a server has a port for communications with a particular service or protocol within TCP/IP. A port is analogous to a port for a ship. It is a predefined place where a session, service, protocol, or process can be bound from an inbound TCP/IP connection (the ship).

TCP/IP has 65,535 ports available for TCP connections and another 65,535 ports available for UDP connections. When a client attempts to connect using one of the transport protocols, TCP/IP connects to a server resource using a port. There are two main types of ports available in TCP/IP. These are defined below:

Well-Known Ports. A well-known port port is simply a default communication channel used for a particular protocol or service. All TCP/IP protocols and processes connect using a port. A table of some of the well-known ports for protocols and services we have discussed are provided in Table 3-1.

If you would like to see all the well-known ports, open the SERVICES file located in the \WINNT\System32\drivers\etc directory. You can also review the ports by connecting to the InterNIC website and opening RFC 1700.

User-Defined Ports. A user-defined port is not actually defined by the client user. A network administrator most commonly configures this port.

TABLE 3-1 SOME TCP WELL-KNOWN PORTS

TCP PORT	PROCESS/PROTOCOL NAME	DESCRIPTION
1	TCPMUX	TCP Port Multi-Plexer
5	RJE	Remote Job Entry
20	FTP-DATA	FTP Protocol Data Transfer
21	FTP-CONTROL	FTP Protocol Control Transfer
23	TELNET	TelNet Protocol Connection Port
25	SMTP	SMTP Protocol Connection Port
42	NAMESERV	Host Name Server Port
49	LOGIN	Login Host Protocol Port
53	DOMAIN	DNS Connection Port
69	TFTP	TFTP Protocol Connection Port
70	GOPHER	Gopher Protocol Connection Port
80	HTTP	HTTP (Browser) Protocol Connection Port
103	X.400	X.400 (E-Mail) Protocol Connection Port
110	POP3	Post Office Protocol Connection Port
138	NETBIOS – NS	NetBIOS Name Service Connection Port
139	NETBIOS – DG	NetBIOS DataGram Connection Port
156	NETBIOS – SS	NetBIOS Session Service Connection Port
179	SQLSRV	SQL Server Connection Port

It allows specific services, protocols, and processes to be mapped to another TCP or UDP port of the user's choosing, thereby changing access for the modified protocol.

User-defined ports usually start above port 1023. Ports below this are reserved for server-side applications like those described Table 3-1.

TCP/IP Sockets. The purpose of a well-known port is actually twofold. The first objective of the well-known port is to provide a standard across systems to communicate with TCP/IP processes, services, and protocols. TCP/IP would be a real mess if each protocol (like FTP) in every implementation was configured to use a different default port.

The second objective of the well-known port is to provide easier nomenclature for an end-user to connect to a standard TCP/IP resource. For instance, when you connect to a web address on the Internet, you are using the HTTP (Hypertext Transfer Protocol). To connect you need only type the web address. Because HTTP uses a well-known port of "80", TCP/IP knows, by default, where to connect. If this was not the case, you would be forced to specify the actual port number for TCP/IP to use.

In some cases, this specification is required so we have a need to understand the function of a TCP/IP socket. This section describes the components and nomenclature for a host to use a socket to communicate with a TCP/IP server.

What Makes Up a TCP/IP Socket? A socket is comprised of two main pieces of information. The first is the IP address of the destination server. If you recall, every IP address is comprised of two pieces of information: the host network and host network ID. These are specified within the IP address and delineated through the use of a subnet mask. The second piece of information that defines a socket concerns the port TCP/IP should use to connect.

The default well-known values are automatically handled by TCP/IP, based on the protocol, service, or process being used. That is why you are able to simply type http://www.instructor.com/ and connect to your resource. TCP/IP automatically knows that since you are using the HTTP protocol, it should attempt to connect to the destination server using port 80. If the port were not 80, you would be unable to connect to the resource without providing the actual port number. This is why we need to understand a TCP/IP socket.

TCP/IP Socket Nomenclature. To specify a TCP/IP socket you enter the FQDN or IP address of a resource *and* the port number to be used in the following formats.

http://www.instructor.com:8080
http://10.216.5.1:8080

This tells TCP/IP to connect using the HTTP protocol at port 8080. Notice the protocol is the first item specified, then the IP address of the destination computer, and finally the port to be used for a connection. The IP address and port are always separated by a colon (:). If you were attempting to connect to a FTP or gopher server on a different port than the default, the socket would look something like this:

ftp://ftp.instructor.com:2000
gopher://gopher.instructor.com:2100

Common Uses for a TCP/IP Socket. Sockets are most often specified for two reasons: security and custom application development. User-defined ports can provide an additional level of security for a particular protocol, process, or service since a client must know the port number and provide it in the form of a TCP/IP socket address (discussed below) to connect to the server resource. In addition, custom developed client software applications that use TCP/IP for transport also need a port. The developer usually selects a user-defined port for connectivity to the server.

● ●

This lab allows you run and test a TCP Socket connection. To complete this lab, follow all instructions, issue any commands, and answer all questions.

1. Open your Internet browser.

2. Ask your instructor for the IP address of his/her computer.

3. Type a command similar to: http://<IPAddress/.

4. Did you receive a HTML page from the instructor's computer? Why, do you think? Why not?

5. Ask your instructor for the port number they have assigned to the HTTP Service in Internet Information Server.

6. Type a command similar to: http://<IPAddress/:8080.

7. Did you receive a HTML page from the instructor's computer? Why, do you think? Why not?

8. Close your browser.

NOTE: *For this lab to operate correctly, your instructor must be running Internet Information Server and have changed the default port setting for the HTTP service on his/her machine to 8080.*

Lesson 3.2 Remote Access and Microsoft TCP/IP

Windows NT Remote Access Server (RAS) allows a remote host to connect, authenticate, and gain access to a Windows NT network. RAS and dial-up networking have very different meanings in Windows NT. This section of chapter 3 discusses the methods for using RAS and dial-up networking with TCP/IP, the protocols involved in establishing communications using the PSTN, a private network, or the Internet and some security concerns surrounding the use of remote networking.

What Is the Difference between Dial-Up Networking and RAS?

While it may first seem that the two terms Dial-Upand RAS are the same, they actually designate very different functions in Windows NT. A brief explanation of remote networking functions in Windows NT follows.

Dial-Up Networking. In Windows NT, dial-up networking surrounds *Outbound* connections to another server or network. In other words, the host computer is "dialing out" to another computer. It is important to note that it makes no difference whether the computer is a Windows NT Workstation or Server. Both operating systems have dial-up or dial out capabilities.

RAS. RAS provides the function that allows a remote host to dial-in to a Windows NT network. RAS allows a Windows NT computer to be a dial-in server. Windows NT Servers and Workstations both have RAS capabilities. Their implementations are, however, slightly different. In a Windows NT Workstation, there can only be one inbound connection. Windows NT Server can accept up to 256 simultaneous inbound connections.

Dial-Up and RAS Protocols

RAS and dial-up networking both use the same set of protocols for the initial communications link between a remote computer and server. Before computers can gain access to a remote network, they must connect and validate user information. This section briefly discusses the protocols that are responsible for this initial contact.

SLIP. SLIP is an acronym for *Serial Line Internet Protocol.* The SLIP protocol was the first type of connection protocol used for remote networking. It was, for a very long time, the predominant method for communications using TCP/IP and is typically associated with the UNIX operating system. The compressed version of this protocol is known as CSLIP. SLIP is very fast and efficient protocol but requires a significant amount of manual configuration to operate properly. SLIP uses a text script to pass information for a particular client and server configuration. SLIP passes information across the connection in Clear Text form, meaning information like usernames and passwords are in a readable, nonsecure ASCII text format.

Windows NT supports the SLIP protocol *only on outbound dial-up connections.* Windows NT cannot be a SLIP server. It can only be a SLIP client.

PPP. PPP is an acronym for *Point-to-Point Protocol.* PPP has become the standard communications protocol for dial-up and RAS networking. Windows NT RAS servers (remember this can be either a NT Workstation or Server) accept *only* PPP connections from their clients. PPP offers many additional features not found in SLIP like data compression, user ID and password encryption, and automatic IP client address management (DHCP).

Windows NT supports the PPP protocol on *both* outbound dial-up and inbound RAS connections.

Remote Network Physical Connection Methods

Windows NT supports several different modes of physical connectivity. The methods can be broken out into three basic types outlined here. Each is associated with the *type of network* the client uses to connect to a host.

PSTN. PSTN is an acronym for *Public Switched Telephone Network.* A more common name for this type of connection is your phone. Modems are used to establish connections using a PSTN. This is by far the most popular and widely used method for establishing Windows NT RAS connections.

Private Network. Any network that is private (owned or leased by an individual or company). This includes, but is not limited to, X.25, ISDN, ATM, Frame Relay, T1, T3, or FDDI networks. These connections are commonly known as *dedicated* or *leased* lines. Windows NT supports ISDN and X.25 connections "out-of-the-box." Other hardware interface devices are supported from various manufacturers.

PPTP. PPTP is an acronym for *Point-to-Point Tunneling Protocol.* This connectivity method is new to Windows NT 4.0. PPTP is not really a physical connection although it uses the Internet as its network. PPTP "tunnels" through the Internet using all the existing lines to establish RAS connections from a workstation to a host. PPTP supports data and user encryption and compression. For PPTP to operate, the workstation or ISP server and the Windows NT server must have PPTP enabled.

PPTP requires that a RAS server be directly connected to the Internet and a company network. This can introduce a security risk that the network administrator must anticipate. To address this issue, Microsoft implemented a feature called PPTP filtering. When PPTP filtering is enabled, all protocols other than PPTP will be disabled on a selected network adapter. This will allow only PPTP protocol connections through the link.

RAS and TCP/IP

RAS fully supports TCP/IP connectivity and serves as a router for inbound TCP/IP remote connections. Microsoft's TCP/IP RAS server implementation provides a PPP connection, integrated Windows NT security, and several different logon validation schemes. In terms of troubleshooting and managing TCP/IP RAS connections, you should use the same mechanisms we discussed (and will discuss) throughout the balance of this book. All of the information presented about subnet masking, troubleshooting, and configuration applies to RAS connections as well as to a dedicated LAN or WAN. The only additional layer of troubleshooting that is required deals with the actual remote connection and hardware.

Lesson 3.3 More on TCP/IP Features

This section provides an introduction to some of the more advanced features of Microsoft's TCP/IP implementation under Windows NT. In this section, we will describe a routed Windows NT computer, IP forwarding, and the RIP for IP protocol. These topics are covered in greater detail in chapter 5.

Multi-Homed Computers Introduced

A multi-homed in Microsoft terminology is defined as any computer having more than one network card installed in it. When Windows NT is configured in this manner it is acting as a router. This additional functionality allows a network administrator to quickly segment network traffic without the expense of installing a physical router. It is possible to install several network cards into a Windows NT system—you are only limited by the hardware and available IRQS and IO addresses. However, each card must have its own unique IP address and is usually connected to a different subnet. Multi-homed computers work using a concept called IP forwarding. There is no special setting to make a computer multi-homed. If you install an additional NIC in a machine it is by default multi-homed.

IP Forwarding Introduced

When multiple network cards are installed in a Windows NT computer, a special option in the Windows NT TCP/IP properties is available for use. On the Routing Tab, the IP forwarding check box allows packets to be forwarded between network cards in a multi-homed computer either statically (by making a manual entry in a route table) or automatically (using the RIP for IP protocol). This tab is provided in Figure 3-3.

RIP for IP Introduced

Microsoft Windows NT originally shipped with the ability to act as a static IP router. Static routing usually works well for small networks and remote sites. In a static routing situation, you must manually edit the route tables of each multi-homed computer and router on the network with all the possible paths for a remote connection. This can be very time consuming and error prone to implement in a large network. To help address this issue, Windows NT Server 4.0 now has the ability to be a dynamic IP router using the RIP for IP routing protocol. Windows NT Workstation and Server implement the RIP (Routing Information Protocol) for IP protocol. This protocol was actually developed for physical routers and uses an algorithm (another name

FIGURE 3-3
Routing/IP Forwarding Tab.

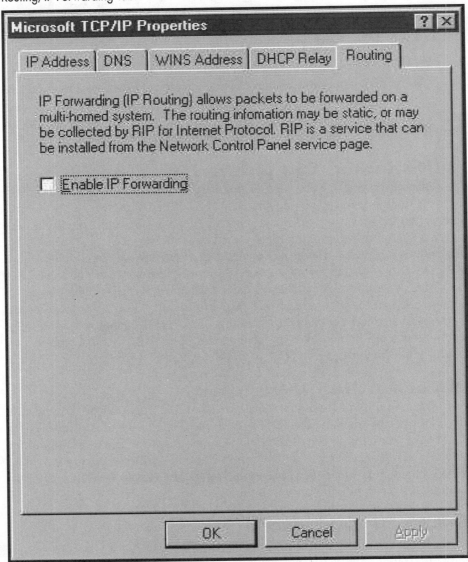

for a formula) to populate a table found on each router with all the available paths to other routers on the network. RIP for IP is a distance vector-routing protocol that allows routers to exchange gateway information on an IP network. While simple and relatively well supported in the industry, RIP for IP suffers from several problems. It is provided with Windows NT for use in small to medium-size networks with a relatively small number of routers. If you are implementing Windows NT in an Enterprise environment, use of physical routers (like those from Cisco or Bay Networks) running a routing protocol like OSPF should be considered instead of a multi-homed Windows NT/RIP for IP routing solution.

LAB

3.2 Locating the IP Forwarding and RIP for IP Functions

This lab allows you explore the Routing tab and Add protocol function of the TCP/IP Protocol. To complete this lab, follow all instructions, issue any commands, and answer all questions.

1. Open the Network Control Panel.

2. Click on the Protocols tab.

3. Select TCP/IP and Click on the Properties button.

4. Locate the Routing tab. Click on this tab.

5. Is the IP Forwarding checkbox available or grayed out on your computer? Why or why not?

6. Is the multi-homed computer serving as the classroom router using IP forwarding?

7. Ask the instructor to demonstrate the effects of unclicking the IP Forwarding checkbox on the classroom router. Can you PING other subnets in the classroom? Document your results and describe why you believe this works or does not. Share your responses with the instructor.

8. Click Cancel on your machine. This should bring you back to the Protocols Tab.

9. Click the Add button. Locate the RIP for IP protocol. Are there any other routing protocols available to be installed? If so, what are they? What do you think they are used for? Document them and discuss your findings with the instructor.

10. Click Cancel twice. This should close the Network Control Panel.

TCP/IP Security

Windows NT implements something known as packet filtering within its TCP/IP stack. Packet filtering allows you to protect your computer by limiting the ports and protocols that can be used to connect to your computer. This ability provides a basic level of security for the type of network traffic that will be allowed on the computer. This feature is only available in Windows NT Workstation and Server.

Packet and protocol filtering works by either "permitting" or "denying" access to any specified port. By default, TCP/IP allows all protocols to be used for communications. Depending on the type of protocol, the security features of TCP/IP will do the following.

- If the Permit All button is checked, all inbound communications will be allowed on valid ports for the TCP, UDP, and IP protocols. This means anybody can connect to your machine using these protocols.

- For UDP and IP ports, if a specific port is denied, the packet will simply be dropped and discarded.

- For TCP connection requests to denied ports, the request is answered with a connection reset. This generates a bit of traffic but no actual connection is created.

To access TCP/IP security features, you must click on the Advanced button on the IP Address tab and then click the "Enable Security" checkbox at the bottom of that screen. The Advanced TCP/IP properties box is shown in Figure 3-4.

The actual Security dialog is accessed by clicking on the Configure button in the lower lefthand corner of the screen. Figure 3-5 shows the Security dialog.

The security implemented at this level is fairly basic. It is however, nice to have these methods available right out of the box. There are many other Microsoft products (like Internet Information Server 4.0 and Proxy Server 2.0) that supply far more security control over TCP/IP connectivity. If security is important, you should consider implementing either a third-party fire-wall or Microsoft product implementation with additional security monitoring, logging, and filtering.

FIGURE 3-4
Advanced IP Addressing Dialog.

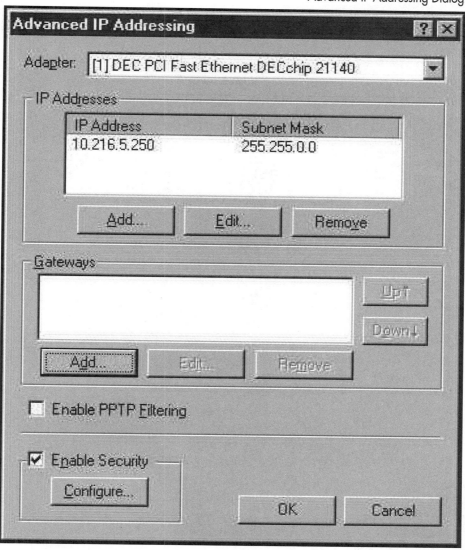

FIGURE 3-5
TCP/IP Security Dialog.

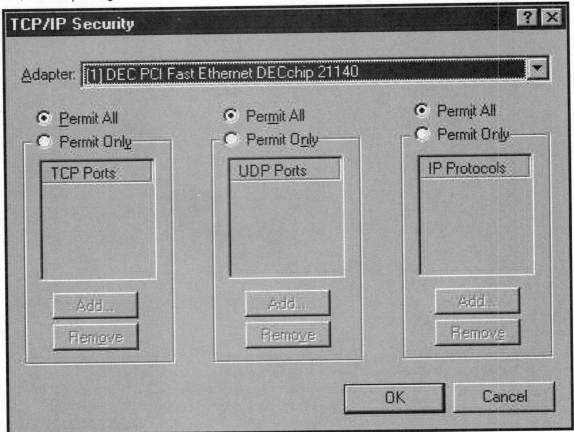

3.3 Accessing and Viewing Microsoft TCP/IP Security

● ●

This lab allows you to explore the Advanced tab of the TCP/IP Protocol Configuration box. To complete this lab, follow all instructions, issue any commands, and answer all questions.

1. Open the Network Control Panel.

2. Click on the Protocols tab.

3. Select TCP/IP and click on the Properties button.

4. Locate the IP Addressing tab (It should be the default as you open the TCP/IP properties).

5. Click on the Advanced button in the bottom righthand of the dialog.

6. Document the information and options that can be exercised here. What are the defaults? Verify this information with your instructor. Did you find some of the features discussed previously in this chapter? What are they and why do you think they were placed on this menu?

7. Check the Enable Security box. Then click on the Configure button.

8. What are the defaults? Document the process of adding security. What is required? Verify this with the instructor. DO NOT IMPLEMENT ANY SECURITY AT THIS TIME!

9. Click the Cancel button four times. This should close the network control panel.

Lesson 3.4 TCP Windows and Handshaking

Communication with TCP is a rather involved process consisting of two subprocesses. This section of the chapter takes a quick look at the concept of a TCP Window and the TCP Handshake process for establishing and transmitting data.

What's a TCP Handshake?

As you will recall, TCP provides guaranteed communications. To accomplish this, it uses a three-step process to communicate that is known as a *handshake*. When an application wishes to communicate with another application these steps are followed.

1. The client who wishes to initiate communications sends a packet off to the destination host. This packet states that it wishes to establish a connection.

2. The destination host replies to the client with an acknowledgement (or ACK) and several pieces of information that set up the transmission.

3. The client then sends verification information in another packet back to the destination host.

4. The data is then transmitted based on this information.

Handshaking assures that both the sender and receiver establish all the parameters required for successful transmission of data. This is why TCP is said to offer a "guaranteed" connection. The same handshake process occurs when the sender and receiver have completed their transaction. This assures that the port is closed and verifies that the information was successfully transmitted.

This is all well and good, but one might also ask how the data is actually transmitted. The following section discusses TCP's main method for transport—a sliding window.

What's a TCP Sliding Window?

TCP transmits packets of data through the use of sliding windows. A sliding window is nothing more than a buffer space that holds a series of packets. In TCP, there are two windows. One is called the Send window (this one is on the sending computer) and the other is called the Receive Window (on the receiving computer). These windows send and receive the packets of information and verify that the packets were transmitted correctly with no errors. This is really the purpose of the sliding window.

As packets are transmitted from a sending workstation, the computer buffers this data until it receives a response from the receiving computer that the packet was successfully transmitted. If it is, the window "slides" forward and allows additional packets to be sent. If it is not, the packet is retransmitted. In actuality, both computers have a Send and Receive window since they are constantly transmitting data back and forth.

Setting a TCP Sliding Window

The size of TCP window is set in kilobytes (KB). Windows NT automatically manages the size of your TCP windows and optimizes them as required. Microsoft recommends (and so do I!) that you **not** modify these values as it could impact performance significantly.

It should be noted that the typical size is different between Token Ring and Ethernet networks. Typically, Ethernet windows are 8KB; Token Ring windows, on the other hand, are usually 16KB. The implication of this is that there will always be some delay when passing packets between these two network implementations. It will take longer for Token Ring packets to be processed on an Ethernet network (since one Token Ring packet needs to be broken into two Ethernet packets by a router) than it will take an Ethernet packet to reach a Token Ring host (the exact opposite applies in this case).

Summary

This lesson discussed several of the generic and specific features of Microsoft's TCP/IP implementation. Within this lesson, we covered the following.

- **Microsoft TCP/IP Network Transport Overview.** In this section, we did a quick review of the OSI model and took a look at how TCP/IP maps to this network standard. We defined some terms and looked at how Microsoft's TCP/IP networking model fits into both the generic TCP/IP and OSI models.

- **RAS Functions within Microsoft TCP/IP.** In this section, we reviewed the differences between dial-up networking and RAS, discussed the methods and protocols used to establish communications in a dial-up network, reviewed the major network types that Windows NT RAS supports, and took a brief look at how TCP/IP and RAS work together.

- **Multi-Homed Windows NT computers.** In this section, we defined what a multi-homed computer is and how one is configured.

- **Microsoft RIP for IP.** We took a quick look at the function and purpose of the Routing Information Protocol (RIP) for IP provided with Windows NT and looked briefly at its benefits and limitations.

- **IP Forwarding.** We defined and explained the concept of IP forwarding, where this is located, how to configure it, and why it is important in multi-homed Windows NT computers.

- **TCP/IP Security.** In this section, we took a look at some of the built-in security functions that come with Windows NT TCP/IP.

- **TCP Windows and Handshaking.** In this section, we defined the communication processes used by TCP to "guarantee" error-free communications between sender and receiver. We discussed how TCP establishes a connection, and additionally, how the data is transmitted using TCP Send and Receive windows.

● ● ● ● ● ● ● ● ● ● ● ● ● ●

1. *Select all that apply.* Which of the following illustrate correct nomenclature for a TCP/IP socket?

    a. ftp:\\10.216.5.1:8080
    b. http://www.instructor.com/tests:65000
    c. gopher://10.216.5.1:3800
    d. http:\\jackrabbit.com/master/docs:80
    e. ftp://ftp.files.com

2. *Select two.* What are the well-known port numbers for FTP communications?

    a. 80
    b. 69
    c. 20
    d. 21
    e. 23

3. *Select all that apply.* Which of the following are true statements regarding RAS and dial-up networking communications?

    a. SLIP and PPP can be used as communication protocols on inbound and outbound communications.
    b. SLIP is faster than PPP.
    c. Windows NT can be a SLIP client but not a SLIP server.
    d. PPP is faster than SLIP.
    e. Both SLIP and PPP offer data encryption and compression.

4 *Select the best answer.* Which of the following protocols is responsible for handling multi-cast transmissions?

    a. IP
    b. TCP
    c. ICMP
    d. IGMP
    e. None of the listed protocols can perform this function.

5. *Select the best answer.* What is the purpose of PPTP?

    a. To provide packet filtering for TCP/IP.
    b. To provide RAS authenticated security.
    c. To allow RAS communications across the Internet.
    d. To supply RAS communications across X.25 networks.

6. *Select all that apply.* John wants to use his Windows NT server as a static router. What must John install to accomplish this objective?

   a. Install another network card in the server.
   b. Install RIP for IP.
   c. Enable IP Forwarding.
   d. Enable Packet Routing.
   e. Assign a different IP address to each NIC.

7. *Select the best answer.* Jack wants to restrict certain TCP ports from being accessed on his Windows NT Workstation. What function will Jack have to use to accomplish this?

   a. PPTP filtering.
   b. No changes are required. TCP/IP automatically manages security.
   c. TCP port security in the Windows NT protocol configuration.
   d. This cannot be accomplished without third party add on software.
   e. None of the above.

8. *Select the best answer.* Which layers of the OSI model does the Network layer of a generic TCP/IP implementation map to? (Select the best answer)

   a. Application and Presentation.
   b. Session and Transport.
   c. Transport and Network.
   d. Network and Data Link.
   e. Data Link and Physical.

9. *Select all that apply.* Susan, a network administrator, would like to implement a multi-homed Windows NT computer. What must she do?

   a. Install at least three network cards in the machine.
   b. Install at least two network cards in the machine.
   c. Implement RIP for IP.
   d. Enable IP Forwarding.
   e. Implement RIP for IPX.

10. *Select the best answer.* Bob, a network technician, reports that two developers have reported poor performance on their machines. The developers have been working on a sockets-based application using TCP to communicate. What is the most likely cause of this problem?

   a. The developers have implemented TCP/IP security limiting access to a particular port.
   b. The developers have manually configured the TCP Sliding Windows values.
   c. There is a router bottleneck on the network.
   d. PPTP filtering has been applied to the workstations.
   e. ICMP is not forwarding response messages to TCP.
   f. None of the above.

11. *Select all that apply.* Which of the following are true statements regarding the use of Windows NT routing?

    a. Use of RIP for IP and a Windows NT router is advisable in an enterprise environment.
    b. RIP for IP is a distance-vector protocol.
    c. IP Forwarding must be enabled for a Windows NT computer to act as a router.
    d. RIP for IP allows for a static router implementation.
    e. Use of RIP for IP and a Windows NT router is not advisable in a small-to-medium LAN.

12. Suppose the following situation exists:

Harry, a crack network administrator, has been monitoring network performance. He has noted that there is a great deal of traffic on a particular subnet that houses 100 Windows NT computers and a SQL Server. Harry has reported these statistics to his management and they have asked for an inexpensive solution that maximizes existing resources and solves the probem.

Required Results:
-   Reduce network traffic by 50%.
-   Improve performance for the workstations and the SQL Server.

Optional Results:
-   Supply automatic routing information to other routers on the network.
-   Provide automatic IP management for the network.
-   Allow for growth in the routed environment.

Proposed Solution:
-   Configure the Windows NT file server as a multi-homed Windows NT computer implementing DNS.
-   Assign the SQL Server to a separate subnet from the workstations.
-   Implement IP Forwarding and RIP for IP.

    a. The proposed solution meets both the required and optional results.
    b. The proposed solution meets the required results and two of the optional results.
    c. The proposed solution meets the required results and only one of the optional results.
    d. The proposed solution meets the required results and none of the optional results.
    e. The proposed solution does not meet requirements nor optional results.

13. *Select the best answer.* Which of the following statements is true concerning TCP and UDP ports?

    a. TCP and UDP share 65,535 ports.
    b. TCP and UDP each have 65,535 ports available for well-known connections.
    c. Well-known ports are limited to those above port 1023.
    d. User-defined ports are limited to those below port 1023.
    e. There is no physical limit on the number of ports available to TCP and UDP.
    f. None of the above.

14. *Select the best answer.* The main differences between dial-up networking and RAS is:

    a. RAS deals only with outbound connections.
    b. Dial-up networking only deals with inbound connections.
    c. Dial-up networking can use PPP and SLIP to communicate.
    d. RAS can use only SLIP for communications.
    e. None of the above.

15. *Select all that apply.* Which types of networks are suitable for RAS and Dial-Up networking communications?

    a. X.25
    b. ISDN
    c. PSTN
    d. ATM
    e. Frame Relay

IP ADDRESSING AND TCP/IP SUBNETTING DEMYSTIFIED

OBJECTIVES

By the end of this chapter, you should be able to:

- Describe the difference between a network identifier and a host identifier.

- Define and explain the different IP address classes available in TCP/IP.

- Define and explain the purpose of a subnet mask and its relationship to an IP address.

- Convert Base 2 (binary) numbering to Base 10 (decimal) notation.

- Define and explain the concept of an octet and its relationship to the dotted-quad format of IP addresses.

- Define and explain the difference between a custom subnet and supernet.

- Calculate custom subnet masks based on host and network variables.

- Calculate IP Address ranges for a specific subnet mask based on requirements.

- Solve subnetting problems based on particular business situation.

Introduction

This chapter explores the composition of IP Addresses, their relationship to network identifiers, and how these terms relate to a subnet mask. We will look at several different methods for "segmenting" or dividing a TCP/IP network based on an available network ID (a process known as custom subnetting).

This chapter provides instruction on what is often considered to be one of the most difficult topics you will encounter in TCP/IP. This topic is so difficult that all of my students were able to custom subnet mask with ease and complete accuracy within a period of three days—and they all passed their TCP/IP exams on the first attempt! The art of determining subnet masks based on a set of business criteria is not all that difficult if we take a structured and metered approach to the problem. I hope that you will find this chapter as demystifying and easy as my students.

Within this chapter, we will take a close look at all the components and concepts required to calculate a custom subnet mask and a range of host ids. We will do this from a "building block" approach—looking at each concept discretely and then building and combining concepts and mathematics to implement a working solution. It is very important that you fully understand all concepts and skills taught in this chapter since many of the topics later in the book demand a full understanding of this chapter. Moreover, if you are planning to certify in other Microsoft web-based products like Internet Information Server or Proxy Server, a solid understanding of custom subnetting is essential prerequisite knowledge.

The approach used to teach these materials is the same method used in my classroom to instruct high school students in this difficult topic. My approach to subnetting is functional, not theoretical, so we will calculate masks with a minimum of confusing binary math and theory and a maximum of problem-solving practice.

Lesson 4.1 Defining IP Addresses and Subnet Masks

IP Addresses, Subnets, and Default Gateways Revisited

We briefly discussed the concept of an IP address, subnet mask and default gateway in chapter 1. As a point of review, let's take a quick look back and expand the definitions for these terms again before diving into a more detailed discussion of each component.

WHAT IS AN IP ADDRESS AND DO I REALLY NEED ONE?

As you will recall an IP address provides two key pieces of information to TCP/IP. The definition of these two terms are as follows.

Network Identifier. The network identifier (also known as a network ID) tells TCP/IP what network segment a computer is located on. A network segment is simply a component of a larger network. Large networks are often subdivided into smaller segments to improve performance. In TCP/IP, a network segment is referred to as a subnet.

Host Identifier. The host identifier (also known as a host ID) is a unique number that identifies a computer on a TCP/IP network. The host ID serves the same purpose as a NetBIOS computer name. Every TCP/IP host must have a unique host ID just as every computer on a Microsoft network must have a unique NetBIOS computer name. Hosts are defined as any port used by a device on a network. They are not limited to computers. Every router, bridge, printer (or anything else) attached to TCP/IP network *must* have a host ID.

Together, these two components comprise an IP address. IP Addresses are understood by a computer as a binary number (more on this later) and are separated by a period (.). This notation is known as a dotted-quad display format because an IP address will always be comprised of four numbers (the quad portion) that are separated by periods (the dotted portion). A typical IP address will look as follows:

10.216.5.1

Each number shown in the IP address is referred to as an *octet. Oct* is Latin for eight. While we only see a Base 10 decimal number like "216" in the IP address, that number is actually comprised of a series of eight binary bits that the computer uses—the octet. Bits are expressed in Base 2 or the Binary numbering system so they are either a 0 (off) or a 1 (on). Remember, a computer is nothing more than a sophisticated system of switches!

So, here we are again converting from a computer's language to a human's language (it seems like we are always doing that!). Decimal notation is what humans understand; Binary is what a computer understands. Later in this chapter we will actually do the conversions between the two numbering systems and see how those decimal numbers are generated.

WHAT IS A SUBNET MASK AND WHY IS IT IMPORTANT?

The purpose of the subnet mask is to mask (or hide) a portion of the IP address so TCP/IP can determine which part of the IP address is the network ID and which portion is the host ID. Without a subnet mask, TCP/IP could never distinguish between the two key pieces of information the IP Address contains.

Subnet masks are also expressed in a dotted-quad decimal format separated by a period. A typical subnet mask might appear as follows:

255.0.0.0

The subnet mask is crucial to TCP/IP communications. TCP/IP's first job in transmission is to determine whether the destination host is on the local or a remote network. An incorrect subnet mask causes TCP/IP to get (and then try to transmit) information to the destination host erroneously.

WHAT'S UP WITH THE DEFAULT GATEWAY?

Default gateways in TCP/IP are routers. By specifying a default gateway in TCP/IP, you are providing the protocol with a method of "routing" or "forwarding" the host information to a remote network. The default gateway is *not* a required TCP/IP installation option.

You can easily install TCP/IP on a local area network without a default gateway as long as IP and subnet mask addresses are specified. However, communications will be limited to the local network segment (or subnet) where the computers are located. No remote transmissions will be allowed. It is important to note that remote does not necessarily mean far away. If two computers are separated by a router in the same room, they are on remote subnets! If a gateway is not specified on both computers, they will be unable to communicate!

WHAT IS A CUSTOM SUBNET MASK?

This chapter is dedicated to computing custom subnet masks so it is important to understand why we would want to accomplish this task! Before we actually talk about what a custom subnet mask is, it will be helpful to understand how a network number is allocated.

The InterNIC Connection. As previously stated, every host ID must be unique. In addition, every network ID must be unique. When an organization wishes to become part of the Internet, they must get a unique network ID. These IDs are managed by the InterNIC organization. InterNIC's responsibility is to assign and manage Internet network IDs. A company applies for a network ID based on its size and the number of hosts that will be using the connection. InterNIC then determines the class (more on classes in just a bit) of network ID the organization requires and provides a network number and default subnet mask to the organization looking something like this:

Network ID: 151.131.0.0
Default Subnet Mask: 255.255.0.0

What has been provided is ONE logical network for the entire organization. It is then the responsibility of the owning organization to divide and manage its internal structure with this network ID. This is why organizations develop custom subnets.

Robbing Peter to Pay Paul—Custom Subnetting. The concept of custom subnetting is really not that difficult to understand. What we are really doing when we create a custom subnet is stealing host IDs to make more networks. If we consider our host ID to be "Peter" and our network ID to be "Paul," then we are robbing Peter to pay Paul, allowing us to create additional networks without adding another network ID through InterNIC. Actually, we're not really stealing; just permanently borrowing some bits from an adjacent octet. Its OK if you don't quite understand the mechanics of this as long as you understand the general concept. This concept will be detailed later in the chapter.

Custom subnetting arises from a network administrator's need to break their internal network up into logical (and smaller) segments for security and performance reasons. The implications of a mistake in this area are obvious: If an organization has an incorrect subnet mask, TCP/IP communications simply cannot occur properly—the protocol will be unable to discriminate where to send packets and transmissions will fail. This is a real disaster for a TCP/IP network administrator and it is why it is such an important concept to understand!

Robbing Paul to Pay Peter—Supernetting. The reverse of subnetting is called supernetting. In this situation, we are stealing network ID bits from an adjacent octet to create additional hosts. The supernetting process is exactly the same as creating a custom subnet. However, to implement this type of network management, special router hardware is required.

If we consider our host ID to be "Peter" and our network ID to be "Paul," then we are robbing Paul to pay Peter, allowing us to create additional hosts without adding another network ID through InterNIC. We will be exclusively focusing on how to create a custom subnet in this book. By default, if you understand custom subnetting you understand the process of supernetting. It is, however, helpful to understand what supernetting is and its function in a TCP/IP network.

What Do I Need to Know to Calculate a Custom Subnet Mask? Since we are dealing with networks and hosts, it should come as no surprise that we will need to know something about these two variables to calculate our custom subnet.

Every problem you will see in this chapter and on the Microsoft exam that requires you to calculate a custom subnet will have to provide you with either the number of networks and/or the number of hosts required for a particular situation. So, in essence, we must solve an equation based on either one or two variables. That's not so hard now, is it?

THE BINARY AND DECIMAL NUMBERING SYSTEMS

As we have mentioned throughout the book thus far, computers function using the Binary numbering system; humans use the Decimal numbering system. This section will take a quick look at the relationship between the two numbering systems we will be using throughout this chapter.

Base 2 (Binary) System. *Binary* means 2 and another term for binary numbering is Base 2 numbering. In this numbering system there are only two numbers: 0 and 1. All mathematical calculations are performed with these two numbers. Computers use the binary numbering system to perform their functions.

Base 10 (Decimal) System. The decimal numbering system is based on numbers from 0 through 9. If we count (and include) 0, this provides us with 10 numbers to work with. This is the numbering system humans typically use for their calculations. I think it is because we have ten fingers but that's just a hypothesis!

So What? If you asked yourself that question, here's the answer! When we are working with IP addresses and subnet masks, we are working with a combination of the binary and decimal numbering systems. The decimal numbers we see as part of an IP address or subnet mask actually come from the binary values of the eight bits that make up each of the four numbers in the address. If we do the math, we can now see why IP addressing in TCP/IP uses 32 bits.

4 Decimal Numbers × 8 Bits in each number = 32 Bits of information

Now that we understand that concept, let's look at how those decimal numbers are created. Let's take one octet of information from the following IP Address:

10.216.5.**5**

We will be working with octet 4 (the number is highlighted in the IP address above) and the decimal number 5. How do we get that 5 out of the eight bits that make it up? That is the question we will answer next.

The Binary to Decimal Calculator. To calculate the decimal value 5 from the binary numbering system requires us to complete a conversion process. Base 2 numbering is expressed in powers of 2 in Table 4-1. By simply calculating the appropriate bit value to the power under it, we have converted the number to decimal.

To calculate the decimal number 5 in binary we look at the Table 4-1 and put a "1" under the corresponding bits that will add up to 5. All the other bits will have a 0 value. When complete our binary equivalent for decimal 5 is 00000101 as shown below. **Memorize this table—it will save you on the exam and we will be using it throughout the chapter!**

Let's try a few calculations and conversions using the table.

TABLE 4-1 THE BINARY TO DECIMAL CONVERTER

OCTET 4

Bit Number:	Bit 8	Bit 7	Bit 6	Bit 5	Bit 4	Bit 3	Bit 2	Bit 1
Binary Equivalent:	2^7	2^6	2^5	2^4	2^3	2^2	2^1	2^0
Decimal Equivalent:	128	64	32	16	8	4	2	1
Binary Number:	0	0	0	0	0	1	0	1

In this example we have been asked to convert decimal 5 to binary.

1. To solve this problem we look at our 8 bits and decided which combination will produce a value of 5.
2. We notice that if we add Bit 3 (4) + Bit 1 (1) we will get 5.
3. Place a 1 under these bits. (Anything we add gets a placeholder of 1.)
4. All the other bits get a 0 value (since they're not being used).
5. So our Binary equivalent for decimal 5 is 00000101. Got it? Good.

L A B

4.1

Binary/Decimal Conversions

Part 1

Convert the following Binary numbers to their decimal equivalents. An example is provided:

00010110 = 22

Explanation: Take all the bits that have a 1 and add them up using Table 4-1 to see the decimal result.

Bit 5 (16) + Bit 3 (4) + Bit 2 (2) = 22

1. 00000111

2. 00101010

3. 11000000

4. 10101010

5. 01010101

6. 11110000

7. 11100000

8. 10000011

9. 10000000

10. 00001111

Part 2

Convert the following Decimal numbers to their binary equivalents. An example is provided.

35 = 00100011

Explanation: Create the table. Determine what combination of numbers will add up to 35. Place a 1 under each bit that is required. Then place 0 in every other placeholder. The answer is as follows:

Bit 6 (32) + Bit 2 (2) + Bit 1 (1) = 35; all other bits are 0 so the answer is 00100011

1. 12

2. 230

3. 27

4. 154

5. 224

6. 240

7. 193

8. 100

9. 253

10. 9

EXERCISE 4.1 TERMINOLOGY REVIEW

Define and answer the following questions regarding this lesson in your own words. Share your work with the instructor after you have completed this exercise.

1. Define the relationship between an IP address, subnet mask, and default gateway.

2. What is the difference between a network segment and a subnet?

3. How are subnets divided in a TCP/IP network?

4. What is a dotted-quad format?

5. What is the difference between a subnet and a supernet?

6. What is a custom subnet and what is its purpose?

7. What two pieces of information are required to solve any custom subnetting question?

8. What is an octet? Why is it important in our discussion of subnet masking and IP addressing?

9. Define the Base 2 and Base 10 numbering systems and why they are important in TCP/IP.

10. What happens if a TCP/IP network does not have a default gateway specified?

Lesson 4.2 IP Address Classes

What Is an IP Address Class?

Put simply, the IP address class defines the number of networks and IP addresses that are available for an organization to use. Remember from our previous discussion that an IP address is comprised of 32 bits (4 octets) of information. Also recall that the IP address is working with two pieces of information: the network ID and the host ID. If we look at our table again and label all the bits instead of just octet 4 we get the following master tables:

BINARY TO DECIMAL MASTER TABLES

OCTET 4

Bit Number:	Bit 8	Bit 7	Bit 6	Bit 5	Bit 4	Bit 3	Bit 2	Bit 1
Binary Equivalent:	2^7	2^6	2^5	2^4	2^3	2^2	2^1	2^0
Decimal Equivalent:	128	64	32	16	8	4	2	1

OCTET 3

Bit Number:	Bit 16	Bit 15	Bit 14	Bit 13	Bit 12	Bit 11	Bit 10	Bit 9
Binary Equivalent:	2^{15}	2^{14}	2^{13}	2^{12}	2^{11}	2^{10}	2^9	2^8
Decimal Equivalent:	32,768	16,384	8,192	4,096	2,048	1,024	512	256

OCTET 2

Bit Number:	Bit 24	Bit 23	Bit 22	Bit 21	Bit 20	Bit 19	Bit 18	Bit 17
Binary Equivalent:	2^{23}	2^{22}	2^{21}	2^{20}	2^{19}	2^{18}	2^{17}	2^{16}
Decimal Equivalent:	8,388,608	4,194,304	2,097,152	1,048,576	524,288	262,144	131,072	65,536

OCTET 1 (REALLY BIG)

Bit Number:	Bit 32	Bit 31	Bit 30	Bit 29	Bit 28	Bit 27	Bit 26	Bit 25
Binary Equivalent:	2^{31}	2^{30}	2^{29}	2^{28}	2^{27}	2^{26}	2^{25}	2^{24}
Decimal Equivalent:	2.14×10^9	1.07×10^9	5.36×10^8	2.68×10^8	1.34×10^8	6.71×10^7	3.35×10^7	16,777,216

These tables in an actual IP address look like this:

Octet 1 . Octet 2 . Octet 3 . Octet 4

As you can see, the further to the left we go, the bigger the numbers (and they really get big in octets 1 and 2!). In actuality, we will never be working in octet 1 and rarely in octet 2. Most of our computations and custom subnets will be performed in octets 3 and 4. As you can see, these numbers are much easier to deal with!

TABLE 4-2 THE IP CLASSES

IP ADDRESS CLASS	NUMBER RANGE	NUMBER OF NETWORKS	NUMBER OF HOSTS	DEFAULT SUBNET MASK
A	0–127	128 (2 Unusable)	16.7 Million	255.0.0.0
B	128–191	16,384	65,536	255.255.0.0
C	192–223	2,097,152	256	255.255.255.0
D (Multicast)	224–239	N/A	N/A	N/A
E (Experimental)	240 and up	N/A	N/A	N/A

THE IP ADDRESS CLASSES

Things are going to get a little tricky in this section in terms of how the math and numbers are calculated for various IP classes. Hang in there though, we have almost worked our way through the worst of this topic!

First, take a look at the table 4-2. These are the IP Address classes used in TCP/IP. We will describe each in more depth in just a bit but let's see if we can draw some conclusions about what organizations would use what classes.

There are only a certain number of total host/network address combinations available no matter how we look at the situation—our Peter and Paul relationship at work! As you increase the number of networks, you decrease the number of hosts. On the other side of the equation, as we increase the number of hosts, we decrease the number of networks. This is known as an *inverse relationship*.

The Address Classes. *Class A* addresses are for the largest organizations. Just look at the number of hosts that can be on a network! Notice though that there are only a relatively small number of networks available for use. In fact, there are no Class A network addresses available today. They have all been used.

Class B addresses have a good deal of networks available and a smaller amount of hosts. Class B addresses are used for large organizations as well. All the Class B addresses are also used.

Class C addresses have a large number of networks available, but not that many hosts on each network. These addresses are used for smaller organizations. There are still many Class C addresses available, but they are going fast! When we run out of Class C addresses, we will have to change the TCP/IP addressing system. At this point it looks like TCP/IP will probably move from a 32- to 64-bit addressing system.

Class D addresses are associated with multicasting and are not used in IP Addressing. Class D addresses range from 224 to 239. Because of the way they are used, Class D addresses do not have a network number. Additionally, the address does not specify a particular computer, it specifies a group that is intended to receive the multicast. Microsoft uses Class D addresses with WINS and Net-Show to allow certain computers to tune in to a TCP/IP multicast broadcast.

Class E addresses are experimental and not available for use. Addresses above 240 fall into this class. They are reserved for development and testing.

So Where Do the Network Numbers Come From? To understand the IP Address Class table, we must understand where the numbers in the tables come from and their relationship to the octets. It is at this point that the subnet mask comes into play.

NOTE: *When we are looking at the following information, keep in mind that 0 is included as a valid number for a range of addresses. Therefore, when we say a range spans from* n *to* n *there are actually* n + *1 addresses. For example, if we say the range runs from 0–255 there are actually 256 available numbers. This is why the total number of bits in an octet equals 256.*

Class A Addresses. All Class A addresses use the first octet (octet 1) for their network ID. This can be seen from the default subnet mask of 255.0.0.0. That 255 in the subnet mask means the first octet is masked as a network ID. Therefore, we can only assign Network IDs in a Class A address using 8 bits. The other 24 bits are used for host IDs.

Bit 8 Value	$\times$	Octet 1 Total Bits Used	= Number of Networks
128	$\times$	1	= 128 Possible Networks

Class A addresses are identified by high-order bit 8 being "off". Network IDs start at 0 in a Class A address because of the following formula:

Bit 8	=	Start Address for Class A
0	=	0

Therefore, the range for Class A network IDs work forward from 0 (0–127). Two of the IDs are unusable in Class A networks. By definition, 0 is invalid as a Network ID (more on this later) and network ID 127 is reserved for testing (remember that loopback address 127.0.0.1 from chapter 2?). This means there are only 126 usable network IDs in the Class A address pool. Hence the range of valid networks for Class A is as follows:

Class A Start	Class A End
1.0.0.0	126.0.0.0

Any IP address that begins with 1 through 126 in octet 1 will always be a Class A address.

Class B Addresses. All Class B addresses use the first two octets (octets 1 and 2) for their network ID. This can be seen from the default subnet mask of 255.255.0.0. Those 255s in the subnet mask mean the first two octets are masked as a network ID. Therefore, we can only assign network IDs in a Class B address using 16 bits. The other 16 bits are used for host IDs.

Bit 7 Value	$\times$	Octet 1 Total Bits Used	= Number of Networks
64	$\times$	256	= Number of Networks
64	$\times$	256	= 16,384 Possible Networks

Class B addresses are identified by high-order bit 7 being "off" and bit 8 being "on." Bit 8 is, as you recall, 128 in decimal and bit 7 has a decimal value of 64. Network IDs start at 128 because of the following formula:

Bit 8	+	**Bit 7**	=	**Start Address for Class B**
128	+	**0**	=	**128**

Therefore, the range for Class B network IDs work forward from 128 in octet 1 (128–191). Hence the range of valid networks for Class B is as follows:

Class B Start	**Class B End**
128.0.0.0	**191.255.0.0**

Any IP address that begins with 128 through 191 in octet 1 will always be a Class B address.

Class C Addresses. All Class C addresses use the first three octets (octets 1, 2 and 3) for their network ID. This can be seen from the default subnet mask of 255.255.255.0. Those 255s in the subnet mask mean the first three octets are masked as a network ID. Therefore, we can only assign network IDs in a Class C address using 24 bits. The other 8 bits are used for host IDs.

Bit 6 Value	×	**(Octet 1 Bits Used * Octet 2 Bits Used)**	= **# of Networks**
32	×	**(256 * 256)**	= **# of Networks**
32	×	**65,536**	= **2,097,152**
			Possible
			Networks

Class C addresses are identified by high-order bits 7 and 8 being "on" and bit 6 being "off." Bit 8 is, as you recall, 128 in decimal and bit 7 has a decimal value of 64. Bit 6 is 32 in decimal. Network IDs start at 192 because of the following formula:

Bit 8	+	**Bit 7**	+	**Bit 6**	=	**Start Address for Class C**
128	+	**64**	+	**0**	=	**192**

Therefore, the range for Class C network IDs work forward from the 192 in octet 1 (192–223). Hence the range of valid networks in a Class C is as follows:

Start Address	**End Address**
192.0.0.0	**223.255.255.0**

Any IP address that begins with 192 through 223 in octet 1 will always be a Class C address.

Whew! Feeling just a bit confused? Do not feel like you have missed the boat here. This is tough material for just about everyone. It may be a good idea to let this sink in just a bit. . . then try the exercise below and reread this section.

EXERCISE 4–2 DETERMINING THE CLASS OF AN IP ADDRESS

From the following IP addresses, determine the IP class for each of the following items. (*Hint:* Refer to Table 4-1 to see the ranges for each class.)

DETERMINING IP ADDRESS CLASSES

IP ADDRESS	IP NETWORK CLASS (A, B, OR C)
208.200.155.0	
151.131.0.41	
5.0.1.1	
9.0.5.25	
194.167.230.220	
138.192.220.224	
100.220.160.1	
206.220.255.210	
12.3.1.1	
200.200.250.210	

But What About the Number of Hosts? Thankfully, calculating the number of hosts is far easier than the network IDs. This is where the magic of the table can be applied. There is one rule that we must consider before we begin.

NOTE: *By definition, no host ID can have all its bits set to all zeroes or all ones. 00000000 has a special meaning to TCP/IP—it says "This Network Only." Likewise, 11111111 has a special meaning—a broadcast address. So, these two values will never be included as part of the host ID pool of addresses. This is why the number of addresses is always decremented by 2.*

Let's look at how Class C hosts are computed using the table with just one modification.

Class C Address.

CALCULATING CLASS C HOSTS

	OCTET 4							
Bit Number:	Bit 8	Bit 7	Bit 6	Bit 5	Bit 4	Bit 3	Bit 2	Bit 1
Binary Equivalent:	2^7	2^6	2^5	2^4	2^3	2^2	2^1	2^0
Decimal Equiv./ # of Hosts:	128	64	32	16	8	4	2	1

Notice that the decimal equivalent line also tells us how many hosts will be on each network. If you add all the decimal values in octet 4 you will arrive at the number 255 (but remember we have to add one number for 0 so we actually end up with 256).

$$128 + 64 + 32 + 16 + 8 + 4 + 2 + 1 + (1) = 256$$

Since all Class C addresses use octet 4 for their host numbers, we have 256 available addresses we can use. But wait, we can't have any addresses with all zeroes or ones! So in a Class C situation, there can only be 254 hosts on one network. **Every Class C network address has a maximum of 254 hosts!**

Class B Addresses. For a Class B address we are using octets 3 and 4 for host IDs. The principle is exactly the same as above. We take the 256 addresses in octet 4 and add the "Decimal Equivalent/# of Hosts line in octet 3 together to arrive with 65,534 available addresses as follows:

CALCULATING CLASS B HOSTS

OCTET 4

Bit Number:	Bit 8	Bit 7	Bit 6	Bit 5	Bit 4	Bit 3	Bit 2	Bit 1
Binary Equivalent:	2^7	2^6	2^5	2^4	2^3	2^2	2^1	2^0
Decimal Equiv./ # of Hosts:	128	64	32	16	8	4	2	1

OCTET 3

Bit Number:	Bit 16	Bit 15	Bit 14	Bit 13	Bit 12	Bit 11	Bit 10	Bit 9
Binary Equivalent:	2^{15}	2^{14}	2^{13}	2^{12}	2^{11}	2^{10}	2^9	2^8
Decimal Equiv./ # of Hosts:	32,768	16,384	8,192	4,096	2,048	1,024	512	256

Octet 4 Available Addresses = 256

Octet 3 Available Addresses = 32,768 + 16,384 + 8,192 + 4,096 + 2,048 + 1,024 + 512 + 256
= 65,280

Octet 3 (65,280) + Octet 4 (256) = 65,536 available addresses. But wait, we can't have any addresses with all zeroes or ones! So in a Class B situation, there can only be 65,534 hosts on one network. **Every Class B network address has a maximum of 65,534 hosts!**

Class A Addresses. Class A host IDs work exactly the same except we're using those really big numbers in octet 2 (plus everything in octets 3 and 4).

CALCULATING CLASS A HOSTS

OCTET 4

Bit Number:	Bit 8	Bit 7	Bit 6	Bit 5	Bit 4	Bit 3	Bit 2	Bit 1
Binary Equivalent:	2^7	2^6	2^5	2^4	2^3	2^2	2^1	2^0
Decimal Equiv./ # of Hosts:	128	64	32	16	8	4	2	1

OCTET 3

Bit Number:	Bit 16	Bit 15	Bit 14	Bit 13	Bit 12	Bit 11	Bit 10	Bit 9
Binary Equiv./ # of Hosts:	2^{15}	2^{14}	2^{13}	2^{12}	2^{11}	2^{10}	2^9	2^8
Decimal Equivalent:	32,768	16,384	8,192	4,096	2,048	1,024	512	256

OCTET 2

Bit Number:	Bit 24	Bit 23	Bit 22	Bit 21	Bit 20	Bit 19	Bit 18	Bit 17
Binary Equivalent:	2^{23}	2^{22}	2^{21}	2^{20}	2^{19}	2^{18}	2^{17}	2^{16}
Decimal Equiv./ # of Hosts:	8,388,608	4,194,304	2,097,152	1,048,576	524,288	262,144	131,072	65,536

Octet 4 Available Addresses = 256

Octet 3 Available Addresses = 65,280

Octet 2 Available Addresses = 8,388,608 + 4,194,304 + 2,097,152 + 1,048,576 + 524,288 + 262,144 + 131,072 + 65,536 = 16,711,680

Octet 2 (16,711,680) + Octet 3 (65,280) + Octet 4 (256) = 16,777,216 available addresses. But wait, we can't have any addresses with all zeroes or all ones! So in a Class A situation, there can only be 16,777,214 hosts on one network. **Every Class A network address has a maximum of 16,777,214 hosts!**

And that is how host and network IDs are computed. That really wasn't all that bad now was it? Now that you have all that theory under your belt, what is really important about this discussion is that you know the starting and ending ranges for each class and the number of hosts in each! This will tell you the default subnet mask, number of hosts, and class of IP address. The numbers will always fall within the ranges provided. For practical purposes, Table 4-1 is what you will need to memorize.

Rules of IP Addressing Summarized. This lesson provides a summary of the three rules of addressing. These rules have all been provided as part of our discussion of IP classes but placing them here is a nice place to bring this all together before we embark on custom subnetting. Make sure you understand the following rules or you will have trouble with the next section.

Rule 1. The network portion of an IP address can neither be all 1s (value of 255) or all 0s (value of 0). These values have special meanings to TCP/IP. For example, in a Class A address, 0.34.234.5 is *not* valid because the entire network ID is 0. However, a Class C address of 204.0.5.250 *is* valid because only a portion of the network ID is zero.

Rule 2. The host portion of an IP address cannot be all 1s (value of 255) or all 0s (value of 0). 00000000 has a special meaning to TCP/IP—it says "This Network Only". Likewise, 11111111 has a special meaning—a broadcast address. So, these two values will never be included as part of the host ID pool of addresses. This is why the number of addresses is always decremented by 2.

Rule 3. All host IDs must be unique on their network. This means that no two machines can share the same IP address. If they do, communication problems will result. Remember, every device that is physically connected to a TCP/IP network *requires* a host ID. This includes computers, printers, routers, bridges, switches, and any other device!

Lesson 4.3 Custom Subnet Masking

Now that we have a solid understanding of IP addressing and classes, it is time to use that information to compute the "dreaded" custom subnet mask. This is really not difficult at all. Most of the time, this becomes a really difficult topic because folks try to explain all the gory theory behind the process. For our purposes, I will only explain at a very high level what is transpiring within TCP/IP. We will take for granted that all that "stuff" is working and just focus on how to solve subnetting problems—*the easy way!*

Custom Subnetting at a Glance

When we custom subnet we are taking bits away from the available host ids in an adjacent octet to make more sub-networks within an organization. This is the "Peter—Paul" principle we discussed earlier. There is really nothing more to the concept!

If we take a Class B address we already know that, by default, the network ID takes the first 16 bits (octets 1 and 2). What we will be doing is stealing some bits from octet 3 to make more networks without having to go to InterNIC for another IP network number.

BUT WHY?

Well, take a look at a Class A network ID. We have ONE network with 16.7 million hosts! Yikes!!! This sort of thing sends shivers down a network administrator's spine. If we tried to implement this default network, we could be fairly certain that the network bandwidth would be completely overutilized and users would have a real problem communicating. Subnetting, as you will recall, is done mainly to segment (or isolate) users on different networks in an effort to improve performance and security.

Think of it this way: If you are going to (and watching) a rock concert and you want to really hear the music (and get home in a reasonable amount of time), wouldn't it be better to have 1,000 people in a small concert hall rather than 16.7 million screaming fans in a stadium? Unless you like lots of chatter, rotten traffic going to and from the concert, and the inability to get most anything accomplished in a timely fashion, you would probably select the 1,000 person option. Things are no different on a network. Our job is to make sure that communications are efficient and that the network is running efficiently. This is why we sometimes have the need to create custom subnets.

SUBNET MASKS BRIEFLY REVISITED

As you will recall, one of the main functions of a subnet mask is to "hide" the network portion of an IP address from the host portion of the address. The other main function of the mask helps TCP/IP determine whether the destination host is on the local network or on a remote network. Without going through an advanced binary math sermon, what happens is this:

1. TCP/IP looks at the network ID and subnet mask of the sending and destination hosts.

2. It then compares the subnet masks using a process called binary ANDing.

3. If the host is local, ARP follows one path for resolving the address. If it is not, the packet is sent to a default gateway and ARP uses another process to resolve the IP address to a MAC address. (If you need a refresher on this concept, review the ARP command in chapter 2).

That's it in a nutshell. You can see why an incorrect subnet mask could be a real problem on an IP network—if it is incorrect, TCP/IP will not forward the packet correctly and communications will fail. That is why this is such an important topic for us to understand.

Getting into the Meat of the Matter

When you are presented with a custom subnetting problem, you will always be provided with at least two, and sometimes three or four, basic pieces of information. Let's take a look at what we can expect to see.

1. **IP Address.** You will always be presented with an IP address or network ID number. It will be your job to determine the class of this address and its default subnet mask. This is why it is important to understand IP address classes.

2. **Number of Hosts.** You may be provided with a number of hosts that need to be placed on each subnet to be created. The number of Hosts line in the earlier tables provide you with the *minimum* number of hosts on each subnet. The actual value is the preceding (next left) bit value minus 2. For example, if we used a subnet value of 255.255.224.0 and looked at the table, we would see 8,192 hosts. This is the minimum number of hosts supported on the subnet. The maximum value is in bit 7 (16,384–2) or 16,382.

3. **Number of Networks.** You may be provided with the number of networks that need to be created to meet the requirements in the problem.

4. **Both Hosts and Networks.** Sometimes you will be given both the Number of Hosts and Number of Networks and you will have to figure out whether the presented solution will work.

NOTE: *You will always be provided with either the number of hosts or number of networks (Items 2, 3, or 4). It would be impossible for you to answer the question without this minimum level of information.*

In almost all custom subnetting questions, you will be asked to select the correct custom subnet mask from a series of answers. To do this you must know what class of address you are working with, the default subnet mask for that class of address, and what octet you will be working on. This is really not hard at all as is illustrated below:

IP ADDRESS CLASS/CUSTOM SUBNET MATRIX

IP ADDRESS CLASS	DEFAULT SUBNET	OCTET TO SUBNET
Class A	255.0.0.0	2
Class B	255.255.0.0	3
Class C	255.255.255.0	4

In general, the next to last octet that is part of the default subnet mask is the one that you will be working with. As stated earlier, what we are doing when we subnet, using bits allocated for host IDs for networks. This has the effect of reducing the number of available host IDs while increasing the number of network IDs. Custom subnets always work from right to left meaning we take bits from the high-order first (bit 8) and then work towards the low-order bits as required.

CALCULATING A CUSTOM SUBNET MASK

To calculate a custom subnet mask, we will be using the tables created in the previous lesson with a couple of modifications. Additionally, we will be using our trusty binary to decimal converter. Before we actually work through the three types of problems, let's look at our toolkit:

NOTE: *You must be able to create these tables and the binary/decimal converter on the fly. It is better to know and understand them than to simply memorize. There will be little or no time on your exam to be fiddling with calculators—know these tables and the following sections and you will breeze through custom subnetting questions!*

TOOL NUMBER 1 THE IP ADDRESS AND CLASS TABLE

You will notice this is the short version of Figure 4-1 presented earlier in this chapter. Make sure you can create this table on the fly or better yet "just know it".

IP ADDRESS CLASSES

IP ADDRESS CLASS	NUMBER RANGE	DEFAULT SUBNET MASK
A	0–127	255.0.0.0
B	128–191	255.255.0.0
C	192–223	255.255.255.0

TOOL NUMBER 2 THE "WORKING" BINARY/DECIMAL CALCULATOR

Use this tool whenever you are presented with a "number of networks" problem. You will use this tool to determine how bits in a particular octet will be used to create the custom subnet mask. Essentially, you will convert whatever the required decimal number of networks are provided in the question into binary and count all the total number of bits.

BINARY TO DECIMAL CONVERTER

Bit Number:	Bit 8	Bit 7	Bit 6	Bit 5	Bit 4	Bit 3	Bit 2	Bit 1
Binary Equivalent:	2^7	2^6	2^5	2^4	2^3	2^2	2^1	2^0
Decimal Equivalent:	128	64	32	16	8	4	2	1
Binary Number:								

TOOL NUMBER 3 THE SUBNETTING MASTER TABLES

You will need to create two tables similar to our calculator with one new line the custom subnet number. One of the tables is for octet 3 (this will be for any Class B subnetting problems) and the other is for octet 4 (this will be for any Class C subnetting problems). If a Class A subnetting problem pops up you will need to create that table as well. Class C and B tables are provided.

SUBNETTING MASTER TABLES

OCTET 4 (CLASS C PROBLEMS)

Bit Number:	Bit 8	Bit 7	Bit 6	Bit 5	Bit 4	Bit 3	Bit 2	Bit 1
Binary Equivalent:	2^7	2^6	2^5	2^4	2^3	2^2	2^1	2^0
Decimal Equiv/ #of Hosts:	128	64	32	16	8	4	2	1
Custom Subnet Bits Required:	128	192	224	240	248	252	254	255

OCTET 3 (CLASS B PROBLEMS)

Bit Number:	Bit 8	Bit 7	Bit 6	Bit 5	Bit 4	Bit 3	Bit 2	Bit 1
Binary Equivalent:	2^{15}	2^{14}	2^{13}	2^{12}	2^{11}	2^{10}	2^9	2^8
Decimal Equiv/ # of Hosts:	32,768	16,384	8,192	4,096	2,048	1,024	512	256
Custom Subnet Bits Required:	128	192	224	240	248	252	254	255

Building the Tables. The best way to build these tables is to understand how they are constructed. The first two lines in the table are the only ones you must memorize. The rest of the table can be easily built. To build line three, raise 2 to the appropriate power to get your result. Or, you may have noticed, we double each value as we move from right to left. The new line, Custom Subnet, is the same in all octets. To build this line, simply add each bit to its predecessor. For instance, to calculate Bit 6 you would add the decimal equivalent of Bits 8 and 7 and 6 (128 + 64 + 32) to arrive at the custom subnet of 224. This means all three bits are "on" or 1s.

The Three Types of Problems

The best way to learn this concept is to actually do it. So, we will work through each type of problem together.

PROBLEM TYPE 1: NUMBER OF ADDITIONAL NETWORKS PROVIDED

Select the best answer. John, a network administrator, needs to subnet his IP network so that there are five additional networks. The network ID provided by InterNIC is 204.175.220.0. Which of the following custom subnet masks will accomplish John's objective?

a. 255.255.255.128

b. 255.255.128.0

c. 255.255.255.192

d. 255.255.255.224

e. 255.255.255.240

Step 1: Extract the pertinent information.
Network ID: 204.175.220.0
Number of Networks Required: 5
What is the correct custom subnet mask?

Step 2: Determine the class of address you are subnetting.
In this example we have been provided with a network ID number of 204.175.220.0. We know this is a Class C address and that the default subnet mask is 255.255.255.0. We also know this Class C network has a maximum of 254 hosts available on one network.

Step 3: Determine whether you are calculating the custom subnet based on the number of networks.
John has been asked to create an additional five networks using this Class C network ID. This is a number of networks problem. We will have to calculate a custom subnet mask in octet 4 since the other three octets are already being used for networks.

Step 4: Use the Binary Calculator to determine the number of bits required to make the additional networks.
If we use our binary converter, the decimal number 5 equates to 00000101 binary. Notice that the 1 bits are positioned at bits 3 and 1 with bit 2 being 0. This means we will need 3 bits of octet 4 to create the custom subnet.

WORKING TABLE/CALCULATOR

Bit Number:	Bit 8	Bit 7	Bit 6	Bit 5	Bit 4	Bit 3	Bit 2	Bit 1
Binary Equivalent:	2^7	2^6	2^5	2^4	2^3	2^2	2^1	2^0
Decimal Equiv./ # of Hosts:	128	64	32	16	8	4	2	1
Binary Number:	0	0	0	0	0	**1**	**0**	**1**

Step 5: Swap the low-order bits to high-order. Take the three low-order bits and move them to bits 8, 7, and 6, and change the values to all 1s. The table now looks like this:

WORKING TABLE/CALCULATOR

Bit Number:	Bit 8	Bit 7	Bit 6	Bit 5	Bit 4	Bit 3	Bit 2	Bit 1
Binary Equivalent:	2^7	2^6	2^5	2^4	2^3	2^2	2^1	2^0
Decimal Equiv/ # of Hosts:	128	64	32	16	8	4	2	1
Binary Number:	**1**	**1**	**1**	0	0	0	0	0

Step 6: Look at the Master Table in octet 4 to see the correct subnet number for this question.

MASTER SUBNET TABLE—OCTET 4

Bit Number:	Bit 8	Bit 7	Bit 6	Bit 5	Bit 4	Bit 3	Bit 2	Bit 1
Binary Equivalent:	2^7	2^6	2^5	2^4	2^3	2^2	2^1	2^0
Decimal Equiv./ # of Hosts:	128	64	32	16	8	4	2	1
Custom Subnet:	128	192	**224**	240	248	252	254	255
Bits Required:	**1**	**1**	**1**	0	0	0	0	0

The correct subnet number is 224. Therefore, our correct custom subnet mask is **255.255.255.224** or answer D. That's all there is to it!

PROBLEM TYPE 2: NUMBER OF HOSTS ON EACH SUBNET PROVIDED

Select the best answer. Sara, a network administrator, needs to subnet her IP network so that there are 12 hosts per network. The network ID provided by InterNIC is 199.175.190.0. Which of the following custom subnet masks will accomplish Sara's objective?

a. 255.255.255.128

b. 255.255.128.0

c. 255.255.255.192

d. 255.255.255.224

e. 255.255.255.240

Step 1: Extract the pertinent information.
Network ID: 199.175.190.0
Number of Hosts Required on each Subnet: 12
What is the correct custom subnet mask?

Step 2: Determine the class of address you are subnetting.
In this example, we have been provided with a network ID number of 199.175.190.0. We know this is a Class C address and that the default subnet mask is 255.255.255.0. We also know this Class C network has a maximum of 254 hosts available on One network.

Step 3: Look at the Decimal Equiv./Number of Hosts line in the Master Table.
Look at that line and find the value that corresponds to the *Minimum* number of hosts per subnet. In this problem, we have been asked to assure that there are 12 hosts per subnet. Looking at the table we see that the closest we come to 12 is in Bit 5—16. The minimum number we can use is 16.

MASTER SUBNET TABLE—OCTET 4

Bit Number:	Bit 8	Bit 7	Bit 6	Bit 5	Bit 4	Bit 3	Bit 2	Bit 1
Binary Equivalent:	2^7	2^6	2^5	2^4	2^3	2^2	2^1	2^0
Decimal Equiv./ # of Hosts:	128	64	32	**16**	8	4	2	1
Custom Subnet:	128	192	224	240	248	252	254	255

Step 4: Look at the Master Table in the appropriate octet (4 for this problem) to see the correct custom subnet number for this question.

MASTER SUBNET TABLE—OCTET 4								
Bit Number:	Bit 8	Bit 7	Bit 6	Bit 5	Bit 4	Bit 3	Bit 2	Bit 1
Binary Equivalent:	2^7	2^6	2^5	2^4	2^3	2^2	2^1	2^0
Decimal Equiv./ # of Hosts:	128	64	32	16	8	4	2	1
Custom Subnet:	128	192	224	**240**	248	252	254	255

The correct subnet number is 240. This will provide 16 hosts per subnet meeting and exceeding the requirements for the question. Therefore our correct custom subnet mask is **255.255.255.240** or answer E. That's all there is to it!

PROBLEM TYPE 3: NUMBER OF REQUIRED HOSTS AND NUMBER OF NETWORKS PROVIDED

Select the best answer. Jack, a network administrator, needs to subnet his IP network so that there are a *minimum* of 3,000 hosts per network. There also needs to be 12 available subnets. The network ID provided by InterNIC is 129.150.0.0. Which of the following custom subnet masks will accomplish Jack's objective?

a. 255.255.128.0

b. 255.255.224.0

c. 255.255.192.0

d. 255.255.240.0

e. 255.255.248.0

Step 1: Extract the pertinent information.

Network ID: 129.150.0.0
Number of Hosts Required on each Subnet: 3,000
Number of Networks Required: 12
What is the correct custom subnet mask?

Step 2: Determine the class of address you are subnetting. In this example we have been provided with a network ID number of 129.150.0.0. We know this is a Class B address and that the default subnet mask is 255.255.0.0. We also know this Class B network has a maximum of 65,534 hosts available on one network.

Step 3: Determine whether you are calculating the custom subnet based on the number of networks. Jack has been asked to create an additional 12 networks using this Class B network ID. This is a number of networks problem. We will have to calculate a custom subnet mask in octet 3 since the other two octets are already being used for the network ID.

Step 4: Use the Binary Calculator to determine the number of bits required to make the additional networks. If we use our binary converter, the decimal number 12 equates to 00001100 binary. Notice that the 1 bits are positioned at bits 4 and 3 with bits 2 and 1 being 0. This means we will need four bits to create the custom subnet.

WORKING TABLE/CALCULATOR

Bit Number:	Bit 8	Bit 7	Bit 6	Bit 5	Bit 4	Bit 3	Bit 2	Bit 1
Binary Equivalent:	2^7	2^6	2^5	2^4	2^3	2^2	2^1	2^0
Decimal Equiv./ # of Hosts:	128	64	32	16	8	4	2	1
Binary Number:	0	0	0	0	**1**	**1**	**0**	**0**

Step 5: Swap the low-order bits to high-order. Take the four low order bits and move them to bits 8, 7, 6, and 5. Then change the values to all 1s. The table now looks like this:

WORKING TABLE/CALCULATOR

Bit Number:	Bit 8	Bit 7	Bit 6	Bit 5	Bit 4	Bit 3	Bit 2	Bit 1
Binary Equivalent:	2^7	2^6	2^5	2^4	2^3	2^2	2^1	2^0
Decimal Equiv/ # of Hosts:	128	64	32	16	8	4	2	1
Binary Number:	**1**	**1**	**1**	**1**	0	0	0	0

Step 6: Look at the Master Table in octet 4 to see the correct subnet number for this question.

MASTER SUBNET TABLE—OCTET 4								
Bit Number:	Bit 8	Bit 7	Bit 6	Bit 5	Bit 4	Bit 3	Bit 2	Bit 1
Binary Equivalent:	2^7	2^6	2^5	2^4	2^3	2^2	2^1	2^0
Decimal Equiv./ # of Hosts:	128	64	32	**16**	8	4	2	1
Custom Subnet:	128	192	224	**240**	248	252	254	255
Bits Required:	**1**	**1**	**1**	**1**	0	0	0	0

The correct subnet number is 240. We meet the requirement of 12 subnets. Therefore our correct custom subnet mask is **255.255.240.0.** That takes care of the network portion of the question. Now we have to evaluate whether this subnet mask will provide ample hosts on each subnet.

Step 7: Look at the Decimal Equiv./Number of Hosts Line in the Master Table. Look at that line and find the value that corresponds to the *minimum* number of hosts per subnet. In this problem, we have been asked to assure that there are 3,000 hosts per subnet. Looking at the table we see that our mask of 255.255.240.0 will provide us with a minimum of 4,096 hosts on each network. Therefore, this custom subnet mask meets both requirements. That's it!

MASTER SUBNET TABLE—OCTET 3								
Bit Number:	Bit 8	Bit 7	Bit 6	Bit 5	Bit 4	Bit 3	Bit 2	Bit 1
Binary Equivalent:	2^7	2^6	2^5	2^4	2^3	2^2	2^1	2^0
Decimal Equiv./ # of Hosts:	32,768	16,384	8,192	**4,096**	2,048	1,024	512	256
Custom Subnet:	128	192	224	**240**	248	252	254	255

LAB

4.3 Custom Subnetting

● ●

The only way to get good with subnetting is to actually work problems and practice. Work the following problems out and discuss the answers with your instructor when you have completed them. Remember, every problem will be one of the three types we discussed in this lesson.

1. *Select the best answer.* Bob was recently assigned a network address of 221.200.150.0. Due to traffic generated on his network, he needs to divide his network into six subnets. Which of the following custom subnet masks will accomplish Bob's objective?
   a. 255.255.255.224
   b. 255.255.255.240
   c. 255.255.255.192
   d. 255.255.255.248
   e. 255.255.255.252

2. *Select the best answer.* Heather is concerned about security between the human resources department and the rest of the company. She knows that by subnetting her network she can isolate the human resources department. The human resources department has 275 employees and is expected to grow to over 500 in the next two years. Heather has a network ID of 151.180.0.0. Which of the following custom subnet masks will meet

Heather's requirements and provide ample growth for her network?
   a. 255.255.192.0
   b. 255.255.224.0
   c. 255.255.240.0
   d. 255.255.248.0
   e. 255.255.252.0

3. *Select the best answer.* Dan works with a large TCP/IP network ID of 129.170.0.0 that already has 24 subnets . Dan needs to further expand his network to allow for an additional six subnets while assuring there are still at least 512 users on each network. What subnet mask should Dan use to accomplish his objective.
   a. 255.255.192.0
   b. 255.255.224.0
   c. 255.255.240.0
   d. 255.255.248.0
   e. 255.255.252.0

4. *Select the best answer.* Marty has been assigned a network ID of 202.199.199.0. He needs to divide his existing network to provide 13 hosts on each subnet he creates. What is the correct subnet mask Marty should use?
   a. 255.255.255.192
   b. 255.255.255.224
   c. 255.255.255.240
   d. 255.255.255.248
   e. 255.255.255.252

5. *Select the best answer.* Ira has been assigned a network ID of 204.200. 192.0. He has an Exchange and SQL server that need to be isolated on their own subnets away from the users due to the traffic they produce. Ira has already divided the network into four subnets. He needs to increase this number to six subnets. What is the correct custom subnet mask Ira should use?

a. 255.255.255.128
b. 255.255.255.192
c. 255.255.255.224
d. 255.255.255.240
e. 255.255.255.248

Lesson 4.4 Calculating Subnet Address Ranges

Now that we have a handle on how to custom subnet, we have one more task that must be accomplished: We must decide which IP addresses to use for each subnet. As with subnet masking, this is another topic which seems to cause students a great deal of consternation and difficulty. Again, if we use our trusty tables and remember our basic rules, this becomes a rather easy exercise. So, let's take a look at what we need to do to calculate these IP ranges.

What Is a Subnet IP Range?

When we custom subnet, we are actually dividing the network into different segments connected by routers. Remember, when InterNIC assigns a Class C network ID we only have *one* network with 254 usable hosts. Once we have custom subnetted, these addresses have been divided between the additional networks we have created. This is not a haphazard process! Only certain IP addresses can be associated with a particular subnet. This is also known as the *range* of IP addresses.

One More Rule . . .

The very first subnet (Subnet 0) and the very last subnets (Subnet 7) in the following example is not used when addressing. Therefore, in our examples there really would only be six usable subnets. This is because of the "0/1" rule—we cannot have all 0s or 1s in any address. No matter what combination of networks you create, the first and last subnets will be unusable! Keep this in mind as you construct custom subnets! It is possible to use these ranges if all the network hardware in your organization supports the first (all 0s) and last (all 1s) subnets but it is not advisable to do this.

How Do We Contruct the Address Ranges?

Once a custom subnet is established, ranges of IP addresses are divided into their respective subnets. Subnets are logically ordered starting with 0 and working forward. Let's take a look at an example from one of the custom subnetting problems we completed in the last section:

Select the best answer. John, a network administrator, needs to subnet his IP network so that there are five additional networks. The network ID provided by InterNic is 204.175.220.0. Which of the following custom subnet masks will accomplish John's objective?

a. 255.255.255.128

b. 255.255.128.0

c. 255.255.255.192

d. 255.255.255.224

e. 255.255.255.240

As you recall, the correct subnet mask to use in this situation is answer D, 255.255.255.224. To calculate the range of IP addresses for this particular situation, we use our handy working calculator again. This is what it looks like for this problem:

WORKING TABLE/CALCULATOR

Bit Number:	Bit 8	Bit 7	Bit 6	Bit 5	Bit 4	Bit 3	Bit 2	Bit 1
Binary Equivalent:	2^7	2^6	2^5	2^4	2^3	2^2	2^1	2^0
Decimal Equiv/ # of Hosts:	128	64	**32**	16	8	4	2	1
Binary Number:	1	1	**1**	0	0	0	0	0
Subnet Mask:	128	192	**224**	240	248	252	254	255

Line 3 tells us the information we need to construct the range of IP addresses on each subnet. We see that there will be a minimum of 32 hosts on each Class C network using a mask of 255.255.255.224. To construct our IP address assignments, we build a table as follows:

ASSIGNING SUBNET ADDRESS RANGES

SUBNET	START ADDRESS	END ADDRESS	ADDRESS RANGE
Subnet 0	Unusable	Unusable	N/A
Subnet 1	32	63	204.175.220.(32–63)
Subnet 2	64	95	204.175.220.(64–95)
Subnet 3	96	127	204.175.220.(96–127)
Subnet 4	128	159	204.175.220.(128–159)
Subnet 5	160	191	204.175.220.(160–191)
Subnet 6	192	223	204.175.220.(192–223)
Subnet 7	Unusable	Unusable	N/A

Notice that the problem requirement was for five networks. We actually create eight networks using a 255.255.255.224 subnet mask. All we did to construct the address assignments was add 32 to the Start Address column (since this is the number of hosts). The End Address column simply is Start Address – 1 for each range. Also, notice that the first and last subnet ranges, "Subnet 0" and "Subnet 7," have been omitted from the ranges—remember our rule from the previous lessons—No all 0s or 1s in the network or IP address; they have special meanings to TCP/IP. That's all there is to it!

LAB

4.4   Calculating Host Subnet Ranges

Calculate the subnet address ranges for the following masks. Discuss the results of your calculations with your instructor.

1. 255.255.255.254

2. 255.255.255.128

3. 255.255.255.240

4. 255.255.255.252

5. 255.255.255.192

6. 255.255.128.0

7. 255.255.255.248

8. 255.255.225.224

9. 255.255.254.0

10. 255.255.224.0

Summary

This chapter explored the composition of IP Addresses, their relationship to network identifiers, and how these terms relate to a subnet mask. We looked at several different methods for segmenting, or dividing, a TCP/IP network based on an available network ID and how to assign addresses to a particular subnet.

Within this chapter, we covered the following material:

- **The difference between a network identifier and a host identifier.**

- **The different IP address classes available in TCP/IP.** We learned that there are five classes or IP addresses—A through E. Only classes A through C are available for use in addressing. Class D is used for multicast transmissions and Class E addresses are used for experimental purposes.

- **The purpose of a subnet mask and its relationship to an IP Address.** We reviewed the concept of a subnet mask, its purpose, and a brief description of what TCP/IP does if a host is local or remote.

- **Conversion of Base 2 (binary) numbering to Base 10 (decimal) notation.** We learned how to convert binary numbers into decimal and its importance in subnet masking.

- **Explanation of an octet and its relationship to the dotted-quad format of IP addresses.** We learned what an octet is, how it gets its name, and its relationship to the decimal equivalent of an IP address.

- **Definition and explanation of the difference between a custom subnet and supernet.** We learned that a subnet takes bits away from available host IDs to make more networks. We also described the reverse process called supernetting that makes more available hosts by reducing available network IDs. We also learned a few of the requirements for each type of custom network implementation.

- **Calculation techniques for custom subnet masks based on host and network variables.** We learned how to custom subnet based on a particular situation using tables and information we extracted from each question. We then learned how to solve custom subnetting problems based on a particular situation.

- **Calculation techniques for IP address ranges associated with a specific subnet mask.** We learned how to calculate a range of IP addresses for a particular subnet as well as how to verify our work to assure that numbers in our tables map to the hosts we created.

● ● ● ● ● ● ● ● ● ● ● ● ●

Q & A

1. *Select all that apply.* Which of the following are valid TCP/IP addresses?

   a. 10.216.5.1:8080
   b. 204.5.4.255
   c. 151.204.224.255
   d. 204.193.192.254
   e. 0.5.45.224

2. *Select two.* Which of the following are valid Class B addresses?

   a. 121.100.131.4
   b. 193.204.5.1
   c. 129.131.140.7
   d. 206.151.224.45
   e. 191.193.204.22

3. *Select the best answer.* What is the maximum number of hosts that can exist with a network address 151.131.0.0 and subnet mask of 255.255.0.0?

   a. 254
   b. 16.7 million
   c. 65,536
   d. 65,534
   e. 16,384

4. *Select the best answer.* Which of the following best describes the definition of a custom subnet mask?

   a. A custom subnet mask allows a standard InterNIC assigned network to be logically divided to allow additional networks at the expense of hosts.
   b. A custom subnet mask allows a standard InterNIC assigned network to be logically divided to allow additional hosts at the expense of networks.
   c. A custom subnet mask allows a standard InterNIC assigned network to be logically divided to allow additional networks and hosts.
   d. A custom subnet mask allows a standard InterNIC assigned network to be logically divided to decrease available networks at the expense of hosts.
   e. None of the above describe the purpose of a custom subnet mask.

5. *Select two.* Which of the following best describes a supernet?

   a. Supernetting allows additonal networks to be added at the expense of host IDs.
   b. Supernetting allows additonal host IDs to be added at the expense of network IDs.
   c. Supernetting does not require any additional hardware to operate correctly.
   d. Supernetting requires special routers that support this network configuration option.

6. *Select the best answer.* Which of the following custom subnet masks illustrates a Class C network address with at least seven additional networks?

   a. 255.255.224.0
   b. 255.255.255.192
   c. 255.255.240.0
   d. 255.255.255.248
   e. 255.255.255.224

7. *Select the best answer.* Which of the following custom subnet masks would provide a Class B network with at least 1,500 hosts per network?

   a. 255.255.252.0
   b. 255.255.240.0
   c. 255.255.254.0
   d. 255.255.248.0
   e. None of the above.

8. *Select the best answer.* What is the correct subnet mask for a network ID of 210.100.192.0 to define 12 additional networks with 13 hosts per subnet?

   a. 255.255.240.0
   b. 255.255.255.240
   c. 255.255.248.0
   d. 255.255.255.248
   e. 255.255.255.224
   f. 255.255.224.0

9. *Select the best answer.* Mary was assigned an InterNIC address of 202.200.223.0. She wishes to subnet her network so that it has an additional four networks. What is the correct subnet mask Mary should apply?

   a. 255.255.255.224
   b. 255.255.255.192
   c. 255.255.255.240
   d. 255.255.255.248
   e. 255.255.255.128

10. *Select the best answer.* John has created a custom subnet mask of 255.255.255.192 for his class C network ID of 222.221.200.0. What is the appropriate IP range value for his newly created subnet 2?

   a. 222.221.200.(0–63)
   b. 222.221.200.(1–63)
   c. 222.221.200.(64–127)
   d. 222.221.200.(128–191)
   e. 222.221.200.(192–254)
   f. None of the above are suitable subnet 2 IP ranges.

11. *Select the best answer.* Harry has assigned the address 204.45.62.51 to one of his client computers. The custom subnet mask for his network is 255.255.255.240. What subnet does the client computer reside in?

    a. Subnet 2
    b. Subnet 3
    c. Subnet 4
    d. Subnet 5
    e. Subnet 6

12. Suppose the following situation exists:

Janice works in a small organization that uses TCP/IP for network transport and a Microsoft SQL server for database applications. InterNIC assigned Janice's company a network address of 221.200.192.0 and a subnet mask of 255.255.255.0. The organization is divided into four departments with roughly ten individuals in each. Each department needs to be secure and access the SQL Server. Lately, the company network utilization has increased to 87%. This has been causing delays in processing and productivity decreases. Management has asked Janice to come up with a viable solution that reduces network traffic by 50% and secures each department while still providing access to the SQL server.

Required Results:
    ■   Reduce network traffic by 50%.

    ■   Improve performance of the workstations and the SQL server.

    ■   Departmentalize the organization.

Optional Results:
    ■   Provide for growth in the organization.

    ■   Provide departmental security.

    ■   Minimizes cost.

Proposed Solution:
    ■   Configure three Windows NT servers as multi-homed computers.

    ■   Use a custom subnet mask of 255.255.255.224.

    ■   Assign each department to its own subnet.

    ■   Assign the SQL server to a separate subnet from the workstations.

    ■   Implement IP Forwarding and RIP for IP.

    a. The proposed solution meets both the required and optional results.
    b. The proposed solution meets the required results and two of the optional results.
    c. The proposed solution meets the required results and only one of the optional results.
    d. The proposed solution meets the required results and none of the optional results.
    e. The proposed solution does not meet requirements nor optional results.

13. *Select all that apply.* John is a network administrator for a large company. He has been assigned an network address of 191.132.0.0. John needs to subnet his network to reduce network traffic, yet allow at least 2,000 users to exist on each subnet. What custom subnet masks would allow John to accomplish his objective?

    a. 255.255.252.0
    b. 255.255.254.0
    c. 255.255.240.0
    d. 255.255.248.0
    e. 255.255.224.0
    f. 255.255.192.0

14. *Select the best answer.* Your company has been assigned a network ID of 222.222.100.0. One router divides the network. You need to assure that at least 32 host IDs will be available on each subnet. Which subnet mask will accomplish this objective?

    a. 255.255.255.252
    b. 255.255.255.248
    c. 255.255.255.240
    d. 255.255.255.224
    e. 255.255.255.192

15. *Select the best answer.* The decimal number 220 is expressed as what value in binary?

    a. 10011111
    b. 11011100
    c. 11101100
    d. 10111111
    e. 11111111

IP ROUTING

OBJECTIVES
By the end of this chapter, you should be able to:

- Describe the difference between a router, gateway, and multi-homed computer.

- Understand the difference between static and dynamic routing.

- Define the two most common routing protocols: RIP and OSPF.

- Use the ROUTE command to display and configure a static router.

- Successfully determine route paths between subnets.

- Integrate static and dynamic routers in a network.

Introduction

This chapter discusses the concept of routing TCP/IP networks. Now that you understand the principle of subnetting and why it is sometimes necessary to segment a TCP/IP network, it is also critical to be able to configure the devices that actually separate subnets: routers. We've been talking about routers, gateways, and multi-homed computers throughout the book up to this point. Now, we will see how to configure a router to route packets of information between different subnets.

We have already covered most of the terminology related to routing earlier in the book. This chapter will dig deeper into the nuts-and-bolts of routing and why it is important in TCP/IP.

Lesson 5.1 Routing Overview

Do I Need to Route My Network?

If you work in a small company, it may very well not be necessary for you to use a router or to subnet your network. As you will recall, the default gateway is not a required option for installation of TCP/IP. Many smaller networks that are localized in a LAN are not routed. However, if you plan to access the Internet or you implement a custom subnetting solution in your network, you will need to know the information in this chapter (and you will most definitely need to know this information if you plan to pass the TCP/IP test!).

What's the Difference between a Default Gateway, Router, and Multi-Homed Computer?

There really is not much difference at all! These three terms are used interchangeably when we talk about routing in TCP/IP. Let's take a quick review of these three terms since they are all so closely related:

Default Gateway. A default gateway is nothing more than the IP address of a router. It is the address TCP/IP uses to send packets to a remote network. A remote network is any network that is not on the same subnet as the host. Windows NT supports up to five default gateways that can be configured for any TCP/IP network interface.

Router. A router is a physical network device that manages packet forwarding between subnets. A multi-homed Windows NT computer is a type of router. Other routing devices include the dedicated physical devices from manufacturers like Cicso and Bay Networks. Additionally, back-office products like Microsoft Proxy Server also function as routers. The key to understanding a router is that they are always located between two network segments and they have at least two ports that connect the two segments together.

Multi-Homed Computer. A multi-homed computer is a fancy term for a Windows NT computer with at least two network cards installed in it. It serves the same purpose as a physical router and is an inexpensive routing alternative for smaller networks.

A simple routed network is illustrated in Figure 5-1.

So How Does a Router Work?

Routers are attached to at least two different segments of a network. Their job is to maintain a list of the possible routes to other routers and networks.

FIGURE 5-1
A Simple Routed Network.

A Simple Routed TCP/IP Network

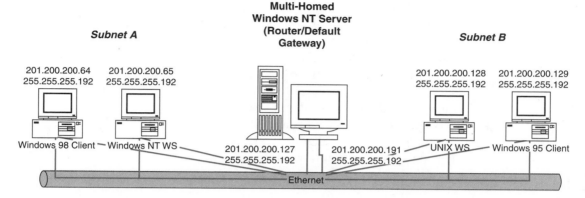

Routers *do not* contain the addresses of the clients they serve. They only contain lists of other routers. This list of routes is known as the **Route Table.** In a complex network, there are many different paths to a particular network. A properly configured router "knows" all the routes to a destination network and can forward the packets along any number of routes to get it there.

Another job of the router is to determine the best path to a remote network and to inform its fellow routers whether it is online and functioning. Of course, a router by itself cannot do this. It's a dumb piece of equipment. The act of building the route table, determining the shortest path to a destination network, and anything having to do with this process is controlled by one of two mechanisms:

1. **Static Routing.** We tell the router everything it needs to know to get its job done. When a network administrator follows this course of action, this is known as *static routing.* The network administrator manually enters the routes to all the other routers on their network. In a small network, this is a fine way to manage your routing. In a large organization with hundreds (or even tens) of routers, this can be a cumbersome, error-prone, and tedious chore! However, statically configured routers offer a higher degree of security on a network because paths to and from remote networks can be controlled completely by the network administrator.

2. **Dynamic Routing.** We use a router protocol like RIP or OSPF to allow the router to manage, build, and update its router table automatically. In

large organizations, this is the method of choice for managing routers. Let's take a quick look at the two most common protocols used in dynamic TCP/IP routing:

- **RIP.** RIP is an acronym for *Router Information Protocol.* RIP is a relatively simple routing protocol based on a "hop-count" metric. Hop-count signifies the number of "hops" across routers to a destination network. The maximum number of hops that RIP supports is 15. If it takes more routers to get there than that, the network is considered to be unreachable. RIP uses a distance-vector algorithm (formula) created by a very smart person named Mr. Nagle, hence, the algorithm is known as the Nagle Algorithm. RIP is a good dynamic routing protocol in smaller networks but can cause network congestion and update problems in larger environments.

  You should recall from chapter 3 that Windows NT includes a version of RIP for TCP/IP and IPX networks. These are protocols that can be loaded if you are using your server as a router in a multi-homed configuration.

- **OSPF.** OSPF is an acronym for *Open Shortest Path First.* OSPF uses a different type of algorithm to calculate paths through the network. It uses the Dijkstra algorithm, created by another very smart person named Mr. Dijkstra. OSPF is known as a link-state routing protocol. It calculates routes based on several variables including the number of hops, line speed, and cost. OSPF is more efficient than RIP. It is the dynamic routing protocol of choice in large inter-networked TCP/IP environments. OSPF is *not* supported within Windows NT, but is supported by most major router manufacturers.

This explanation of routers is provided to give you a basic understanding of a router's function in a network. While its overall purpose is simple in concept, they can be pretty tough to configure. Network engineers usually specialize in particular routers and manufacturers because of the complexity of the units. As a matter of fact, there are several professional certifications surrounding this area of networking offered by major manufacturers like Cisco and Cabletron. If this is an area you would like to explore in more detail, check out Cisco CCNA certification.

What Does a Route Table Look Like?

Route tables are ugly. Just kidding! Actually, they have some really important information in them. Figure 5-2 shows what a typical route table looks like in Windows NT using the ROUTE command.

This is a Windows NT routing table. Even though it looks complicated, it's really not all that bad. The following information is contained in the table:

FIGURE 5-2
Sample Routing Table.

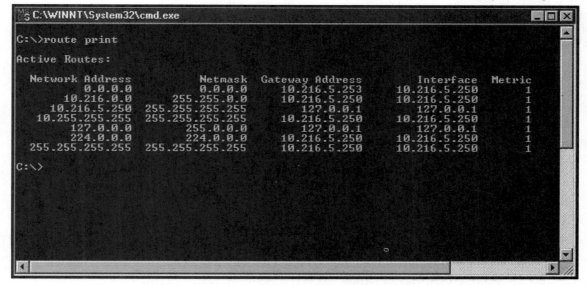

TABLE HEADINGS

Network Address. This is the Network ID we have been discussing throughout the book. Notice that we have the network ID of the computer itself—10.216.0.0, a Class A network of 127.0.0.0 (that's the loopback testing network), and a Class D network of 224.0.0.0 for multi-cast transmissions.

NetMask. This designates the particular subnet mask being used for each entry. Some of those masks look very different than what we have seen before. You will immediately notice masks of 255.255.255.255—these signify broadcasts. The 0.0.0.0 signifies the address of the default gateway. The other entries should look pretty familiar.

Gateway Address. This is the gateway to the network for each interface. You will see the default gateway address is listed in line one. It is 10.216.5.253. You may have also noticed that to TCP/IP, the gateway to the physical network is the IP address of the computer itself.

Interface. This is the IP address used for each entry. If we look at the interface entries, we can see that the computer's IP address is listed as well as the loopback address of 127.0.0.1. The rest of the entries specify such things as the method to get to a gateway and how to broadcast locally and remotely.

Each line in the table is used for a different purpose. These are briefly described below:

Default Gateway (0.0.0.0). This address signifies the default route for any destination network not specified in the table. This is my default gateway. If I opened my TCP/IP protocol options you would see that 10.216.5.253 is indeed the value entered for my default gateway.

Local Subnet Broadcast. This address is used by TCP/IP for broadcasting of the computer's address on a local subnet.

Network Broadcast. This address is used to broadcast across the entire internetwork.

Local Loopback. This is the 127.0.0.1 address we use to test our internal IP configuration.

Local Network. This address directs packets to hosts on the local network.

Local Host. This is the local computer's IP address.

EXERCISE 1 QUESTION AND ANSWER

Answer the following questions regarding information presented in Lesson 1. When you have completed the questions, review your answers with the instructor.

1. What is the difference between a gateway, router, and multi-homed computer?

2. What is a NetMask? What other term is it synonymous with?

3. What are the main differences between OSPF and RIP?

4. Why is RIP typically suited only for use in smaller TCP/IP networks?

5. Explain how a router works from a conceptual level.

6. What is the difference between static and dynamic routing? Which is better? Which is more secure? Why?

7. How do we display a computer's route table? What type of information is displayed in this table?

Lesson 5.2 The ROUTE Command

This lesson takes a look at the Windows NT command line utility ROUTE.EXE. ROUTE allows us to view, add, modify, and change the internal route table of a computer. ROUTE is automatically installed when the TCP/IP stack is added as a protocol.

ROUTE Command Overview

The Route command allows us to access the route table of a Windows NT Computer. Although we are usually working with NT Servers, this command is available on NT Workstation computers as well. ROUTE allows us to view, add, change, delete, and clear routing information for a TCP/IP computer.

In this lesson, we will be using the Route command predominantly to configure a multi-homed Windows NT computer so it can communicate across an internetwork. You may have already surmised that many of the parameters we entered when TCP/IP was first configured on our machines are found in the route table. Remember, TCP/IP needs to have routing information provided about every interface. This means that even our local computer interface (the NIC) and the loop-back testing address (127.0.0.1) need Route entries.

ROUTE is used to make a static entry in a route table for a particular network interface. Remember, static means manual to us. Route commands are stored in memory by default and are available as long as our machine is running. If we reboot a machine, the entry is lost and must be re-entered. We can enter a **persistent route** using a special switch. Persistent routes are permanently stored in the registry of the machine and are always available even if the computer is rebooted.

ROUTE Command Syntax

Using the ROUTE command to modify entries requires at least two, and sometimes three, pieces of information. We must tell the command the following information:

- **Destination Network Address.** This is the name of the destination network. For our purposes, this will always be a network ID like 151.131.0.0. This is a required field for all Route entries.

- **Subnet Mask.** In ROUTE, this is called the NetMask. It is the same thing as the venerable subnet mask we have been discussing throughout the book.

- **Gateway Port.** This is expressed as the IP address of the interface to a remote (or local) network. This is our gateway to the remote network. Think of the gateway ports as a tollbooth between states. We must pass through that port to gain entry to the other network (or state). This is also a required field for all entries.

NOTE: *You can also reference a network or host name in the ROUTE command provided there is an appropriate entry in either the LMHOSTS or HOSTS file. However, we will only be using IP addresses and network numbers. We will not be using this naming strategy in our exercises.*

We will be performing two main functions with the ROUTE command. The first is displaying the route table. The second is adding a route entry. The command syntax for these commands is provided below:

DISPLAYING ROUTE INFORMATION

To display ROUTE information on a local computer, use the following command at a Windows NT command prompt:

ROUTE PRINT

Display output looks exactly like Figure 5-2 presented earlier in this chapter.

ADDING A ROUTE ENTRY

To add a Route entry on a local computer, use the following command at a Windows NT command prompt:

ROUTE ADD <<Network Interface>> MASK <<Netmask>> <<Gateway Port>>

The Route Add command looks like that shown in Figure 5-3.

FIGURE 5-3
Entering the ROUTE ADD Command.

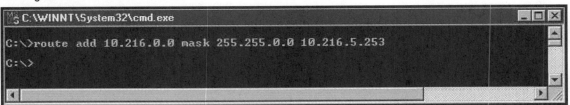

OTHER COMMANDS AND SWITCHES:

Help. To access ROUTE command help simply type **ROUTE** and press Enter. This will display all the command syntax and switches.

ROUTE help is displayed as shown in Figure 5-4 at the top of the next page.

Command Switches. Switches for ROUTE are added **BEFORE** you enter any other information. The switches available are as follows.

–p. This switch adds a persistent route entry to the table. Persistent entries are written directly to the Windows NT registry and are available even after a machine has been powered down. The command syntax is entered as shown in Figure 5-5 at right.

–f This switch clears all routes from the table. Figure 5-6 shows how the command syntax is entered.

FIGURE 5-4
ROUTE Command Help.

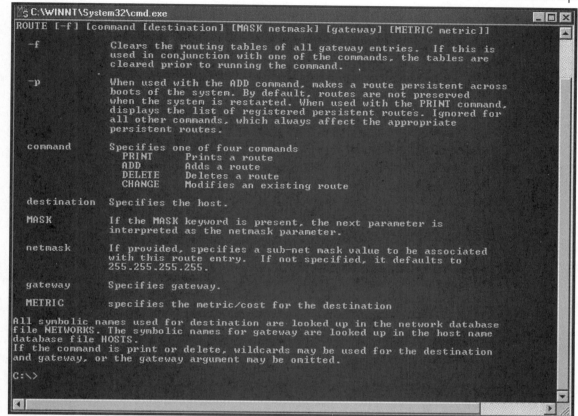

```
C:\WINNT\System32\cmd.exe                                              _ □ ×
ROUTE [-f] [command [destination] [MASK netmask] [gateway] [METRIC metric]]

    -f              Clears the routing tables of all gateway entries.  If this is
                    used in conjunction with one of the commands, the tables are
                    cleared prior to running the command.

    -p              When used with the ADD command, makes a route persistent across
                    boots of the system. By default, routes are not preserved
                    when the system is restarted. When used with the PRINT command,
                    displays the list of registered persistent routes. Ignored for
                    all other commands, which always affect the appropriate
                    persistent routes.

    command         Specifies one of four commands
                       PRINT       Prints a route
                       ADD         Adds a route
                       DELETE      Deletes a route
                       CHANGE      Modifies an existing route

    destination     Specifies the host.

    MASK            If the MASK keyword is present, the next parameter is
                    interpreted as the netmask parameter.

    netmask         If provided, specifies a sub-net mask value to be associated
                    with this route entry.  If not specified, it defaults to
                    255.255.255.255.

    gateway         Specifies gateway.

    METRIC          specifies the metric/cost for the destination

All symbolic names used for destination are looked up in the network database
file NETWORKS. The symbolic names for gateway are looked up in the host name
database file HOSTS.
If the command is print or delete, wildcards may be used for the destination
and gateway, or the gateway argument may be omitted.

C:\>
```

FIGURE 5-5
Entering a Persistent Route Entry.

```
C:\WINNT\System32\cmd.exe                                              _ □ ×
C:\>route -p add 10.216.0.0 mask 255.255.0.0 10.216.5.253
C:\>
```

FIGURE 5-6
Clearing All Route Entries.

```
C:\WINNT\System32\cmd.exe                                              _ □ ×
C:\>route -f
C:\>
```

Other ROUTE Commands.

ROUTE DELETE <<Network>> <<Gateway>>. You guessed it. This command deletes an entry from the table. Command syntax appears as shown in Figure 5-7.

FIGURE 5-7
Deleting Route Entries.

ROUTE CHANGE <<Network>> <<Gateway>>. Again, this is not rocket science. The command allows you to change an existing entry in the route table (Figure 5-8).

FIGURE 5-8
Changing Route Entries.

LAB
5.1 Using the ROUTE Command

• •

In this lab, you will explore the ROUTE command to edit and modify your computer's route table. It is important that you follow all the directions completely as you work through this lab. Otherwise, you may not be able to communicate without rebooting your computer! Your instructor will walk you through each component of this exercise. Follow along with his or her directions.

1. Open a Windows NT Command Prompt window.

2. Enter the ROUTE command and press Enter. What is displayed? Document all options in your notebook.

3. Print the current Route entries on your computer using the ROUTE PRINT command. Document your route table settings.

4. Add a route entry to the instructor's computer (your instructor's computer will be serving as our Gateway for this exercise) using the ROUTE ADD command.

5. Print the current route entries. What has changed?

6. Change the route entry you just made to your instructor's computer using the ROUTE CHANGE command.

7. Print the current route entries. What has changed?

8. Add a Persistent route to the instructor's computer using the ROUTE –p ADD command.

9. Print the current route entries. What has changed?

10. Clear all your routes using the ROUTE –f command.

11. Print the current route entries. What has changed?

12. Close the Windows NT Command Window.

13. Discuss the results with your instructor.

Lesson 5.3 Determining and Configuring Routes

Determining the route to a particular network can be confusing especially when one first looks at a routing table. As usual, there is a bunch of numbers that, at first glance, look like a real mess. But there is a complete method to the madness of the routing table. This section steps you through the process of determining a route between networks.

First Things First

Routing tables answer two really important questions: "Where do I want to go?" and "How do I get there?" If you remember these two questions as we work through our routing table problems, it will greatly ease the pain of building the route table.

Route tables are always expressed with two key pieces of information. The first is the *network number*—this is the Where do I want to go? question.

The second piece of information is the *Router IP address* that allows access to the remote network—this is the "How do I get there?" question.

The Typical Route Table Problem

This section shows you how to approach routing table problems. If you follow the prescribed approach, this type of problem will be easy to solve. The thing that makes route tables confusing is the fact that many of the numbers seem very similar. In fact, they are. It is for this reason that you must take a *very* methodical approach to building a route table. When working on router tables, it is best to take one table at a time. Additionally, you must make sure all routes are covered by all routers. It is easy to get confused about routes unless you apply a system to working the information out. When you are working these problems, use the following process.

1. Read the question and figure out what it is asking! It is very important to carefully read the problem and extract all the pertinent information at your disposal. A missed word or phrase can cause a completely incorrect answer.

2. Build route tables containing the following information:

Network	Network Number	Router Port
Home Network A	Network ID number	IP address of home router port on 'A' segment
Home Network B	Network ID number	IP address of home router port on 'B' segment
Remote Subnet C	Network ID number	Gateway of other router port on 'B' segment

3. Determine your answer before you look at the choices! Look for *your* answer in the list provided. If you have been methodical, your answer will always be correct.

Let's try this methodology with the scenario provided in Figure 5-9.

The Scenario

Henrietta, a network administrator, needs to configure the router tables of two Windows NT server multi-homed computers. Her network appears in

FIGURE 5-9
A Sample Routing Scenario.

Route Table Configuration

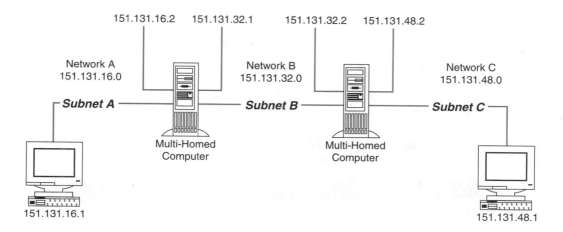

FIGURE 5-9
A Sample Routing Scenario.

Figure 5-9. She needs to configure the route tables to enable a computer on Subnet A to communicate with Subnet C. What are the correct route entries she must enter?

a. On Router 1,
   ROUTE ADD 151.131.48.0 MASK 255.255.224.0 151.131.32.2

b. On Router 2,
   ROUTE ADD 151.131.16.0 MASK 255.255.224.0 151.131.32.1

c. On Router 1,
   ROUTE ADD 151.131.32.0 MASK 255.255.224.0 151.131.32.2

d. On Router 2,
   ROUTE ADD 151.131.32.0 MASK 255.255.224.0 151.131.16.2

e. None of the configurations will work.

STEP 1—GATHER INFORMATION

We have a great deal of information provided to us in Figure 5-9. Let's sort it out:

■ We have 3 subnets connected by two routers.

■ The routers are multi-homed computers.

- There are workstations on Subnets A and C.

- Subnet A is on network 151.131.16.0

- Subnet B is on network 151.131.32.0

- Subnet C is on network 151.131.48.0

- Our subnet mask is 255.255.224.0

- We need to have computers communicating between Subnets A and C.

With this information, we can determine everything needed to construct and configure route tables on the two multi-homed computers.

STEP 2—BUILD A ROUTE TABLE FOR EACH ROUTER

MASTER ROUTE TABLES

ROUTER A

Network	Network Number	Router Port
Home Network A	151.131.16.0	151.131.16.2
Home Network B	151.131.32.0	151.131.32.1
Remote Subnet C	151.131.48.0	151.131.32.2

ROUTER B

Network	Network Number	Router Port
Home Network A	151.131.48.0	151.131.48.2
Home Network B	151.131.32.0	151.131.32.2
Remote Subnet C	151.131.16.0	151.131.32.1

Ok, now you're really confused! Hang in there! Let's look at this a little more carefully.

Router A Explanation. Router A is physically connected to two segments of the network—Subnets A and B. These are our home networks. Our remote network is Subnet C. All the network numbers are provided for these subnets. Home Network A has a network number of 151.131.16.0 and Home Network B has a network number of 151.131.32.0. Remote network C has a network number of 151.131.48.0. This provides the answers to our "Where do we want to go?" question.

To gain access to the networks, we have to enter the port that allows us access to the subnet we wish to traverse (the gateway). For Router A, if we want to gain access to the 151.131.16.0 network we would go through the 151.131.16.2 port. This answers our "How do we get there?" question. Likewise, if we want to gain access to the 151.131.32.0 network, we would go through port 151.131.32.1. Finally, if we want to gain access to the 151.131.48.0 network, we would go through 151.131.32.2.

Router B Explanation. Router B is physically connected to two segments of the network—Subnets B and C. These are our home networks. Our remote network is Subnet A. All the network numbers are provided for these subnets. Home Network C has a network number of 151.131.48.0 and Home Network B has a network number of 151.131.32.0. Remote network A has a network number of 151.131.16.0. This provides the answers to our "Where do we want to go?" question.

To gain access to the networks, we have to enter the port that allows us on the subnet we wish to traverse. For Router B, if we want to gain access to the 151.131.48.0 network we would go through the 151.131.48.2 port. This answers our "How do we get there?" question. Likewise, if we want to gain access to the 151.131.32.0 network, we would go through port 151.131.32.2. Finally, if we want to gain access to the 151.131.16.0 network, we would go through 151.131.32.1.

It is easy to see how quickly you could get turned around and confused when configuring a route table. This is why you should *always* always draw a picture *and* create a table. Do this one step at a time!

STEP 3—NOW THAT YOU HAVE COMPLETED YOUR ROUTE TABLES, LOOK FOR THE CORRECT ANSWERS IN THE ROUTE ADD COMMANDS FOR THE DIFFERENT ROUTERS

Determine the answer before you look at the choices! Look for *your* answer in the list provided. If you have been methodical, your answer will always be correct. As you will see in the problem, we are only concerned with the route to the remote network. From our tables, we know the following:

To access Remote Network C (151.131.48.0) from Router A , we must use the 151.131.32.2 port on Subnet B. As you recall from the previous lesson, the ROUTE command to add the entry is:

ROUTE ADD <<Network ID>> MASK <<Subnet Mask>> <<Destination IP Address Port>>

So our answer for Router A will be

ROUTE ADD 151.131.48.0 MASK 255.255.224.0 151.131.32.2

To access Remote Network A (151.131.16.0) from Router B, we must use the 151.131.32.1 port on Subnet B. Our answer for Router B will be

ROUTE ADD 151.131.16.0 MASK 255.255.224.0 151.131.32.1

This means answers *A* and *B* are the correct answers to this question. Once you have built these tables, it will not matter what routes are displayed. You will have all the answers at your fingertips. In this problem, only the routes to remote subnets were required.

This will take a little practice to perfect the process but it is not really all that hard if you take it one step at a time.

5.2

Configuring Static Route Tables

● ●

Compute the route tables for each scenario presented in this lab. Be sure to share your results with the instructor once you have completed this lab. If you are having problems, be sure to ask for help!

Problem Scenario 1

Select the best answer. Brian, a network administrator needs to configure the router tables of two Windows NT Server multi-homed computers. The netmask is 255.255.255.0. His network appears in Figure 5-10. Brian needs to configure the route tables to enable a computer on Subnet A to communicate with Subnet C. What are the correct route entries he must enter?

A. On Router 1, ROUTE ADD 131.161.16.0 MASK 255.255.255.0 131.161.16.1

On Router 2, ROUTE ADD 131.161.8.0 MASK 255.255.255.0 131.161.16.2

B. On Router 1, ROUTE ADD 131.161.24.0 MASK 255.255.255.0 131.161.16.1

On Router 2, ROUTE ADD 131.161.8.0 MASK 255.255.255.0 131.161.16.2

C. On Router 1, ROUTE ADD 131.161.24.0 MASK 255.255.255.0 131.161.16.2

On Router 2, ROUTE ADD 131.161.8.0 MASK 255.255.255.0 131.161.16.1

D. None of the configurations will work

FIGURE 5-10
Problem Scenario 1.

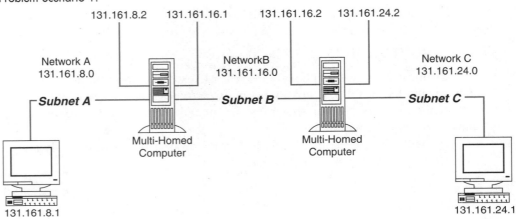

Problem Scenario 2

Dawn, a network administrator, needs to configure the router tables of one Windows NT server multi-homed computer. The netmask is 255.255.255.252. Her network appears in Figure 5-11. Dawn needs to configure the route table to enable a computer on Subnet A to communicate with Subnet B. What are the correct route entries she must enter?

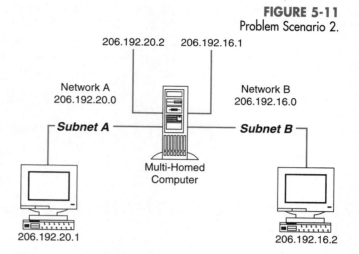

FIGURE 5-11
Problem Scenario 2.

A. ROUTE ADD 206.192.20.0 MASK 255.255.255.252 206.192.16.2

B. ROUTE ADD 206.192.20.0 MASK 255.255.255.252 206.192.16.1

C. ROUTE ADD 206.192.16.0 MASK 255.255.255.252 206.192.20.1

D. ROUTE ADD 206.192.16.0 MASK 255.255.255.252 206.192.20.2

E. None of the configurations will work.

Problem Scenario 3

Susan, a network administrator, needs to configure the router tables of three Windows NT server multi-homed computers. Her subnet mask is 255.255.224.0. Her network appears in Figure 5-12. Susan needs to configure the route tables to enable a computer on Subnet A to communicate with Subnet D. What are the correct route entries she must enter?

A. On Router 1, ROUTE ADD 129.100.96.0 MASK 255.255.224.0 129.100.64.2

On Router 1, ROUTE ADD 129.100.128.0 MASK 255.255.224.0 131.100.64.2

On Router 2, ROUTE ADD 129.100.32.0 MASK 255.255.224.0 131.100.64.1

On Router 2, ROUTE ADD 129.100.128.0 MASK 255.255.224.0 131.100.96.1

On Router 3, ROUTE ADD 129.100.64.0 MASK 255.255.224.0 131.100.96.2

On Router 3, ROUTE ADD 129.100.32.0 MASK 255.255.224.0 131.100.96.2

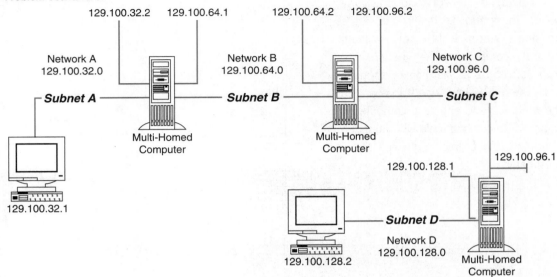

FIGURE 5-12
Problem Scenario 3.

129.100.32.2   129.100.64.1   129.100.64.2   129.100.96.2

Network A   Network B   Network C
129.100.32.0   129.100.64.0   129.100.96.0

— **Subnet A** —   — **Subnet B** —   — **Subnet C** —

Multi-Homed   Multi-Homed
Computer   Computer

129.100.128.1   129.100.96.1

129.100.32.1   — **Subnet D** —

Network D
129.100.128.2   129.100.128.0   Multi-Homed
Computer

B. On Router 1, ROUTE ADD 129.100.96.0 MASK 255.255.224.0 129.100.64.1

On Router 1, ROUTE ADD 129.100.128.0 MASK 255.255.224.0 131.100.64.1

On Router 2, ROUTE ADD 129.100.32.0 MASK 255.255.224.0 131.100.64.2

On Router 2, ROUTE ADD 129.100.128.0 MASK 255.255.224.0 131.100.96.2

On Router 3, ROUTE ADD 129.100.64.0 MASK 255.255.224.0 131.100.96.1

On Router 3, ROUTE ADD 129.100.32.0 MASK 255.255.224.0 131.100.96.1

C. On Router 1, ROUTE ADD 129.100.128.0 MASK 255.255.224.0 129.100.96.2

On Router 1, ROUTE ADD 129.100.96.0 MASK 255.255.224.0 131.100.96.2

On Router 2, ROUTE ADD 129.100.128.0 MASK 255.255.224.0 131.100.64.1

On Router 2, ROUTE ADD 129.100.32.0 MASK 255.255.224.0 131.100.64.2

On Router 3, ROUTE ADD 129.100.32.0 MASK 255.255.224.0 131.100.128.2

On Router 3, ROUTE ADD 129.100.64.0 MASK 255.255.224.0 131.100.128.2

D. None of the configurations will work.

Lesson 5.4 Configuring Dynamic Routing in Windows NT

This lesson discusses the process for enabling dynamic routing in a Windows NT environment. In the previous lesson, we learned how to configure a static route table. In this lesson, we will learn how to configure a Windows NT multi-homed computer to use the RIP for IP protocol included with the operating system. Additionally, we will take a look at how to integrate static and dynamic routers on the same network.

Dynamic Routing and Windows NT

When Windows NT is configured as a multi-homed TCP/IP computer, it is possible to implement a dynamic routing algorithm to ease the administrative burden of statically configuring each route table in the network. Windows NT comes with the RIP for IP protocol as part of the operating system. If you are also running IPX (a NetWare network), NT has the IPX version of this protocol: RIP for IPX. To enable RIP for IP, you add the protocol using the Network Control Panel.

The process is quick and easy with no configuration required on your part except for the selection and adding of the protocol. Once installed, RIP for IP will handle router table updates of your multi-homed computer without your intervention. However, you must remember that *all* the routers on your network must have RIP enabled for this to work. Remember that RIP is a protocol like any other! For two routers to communicate using RIP, they must *both* have the protocol installed.

How Does RIP for IP Work?

Transport. RIP for IP uses the UDP protocol for transport. You should remember that UDP is a broadcast-based transport mechanism offering nonguaranteed transmission. It is not surprising that RIP uses this protocol to communicate. In essence, the protocol is asking all the other routers on the network for changes. If one doesn't respond, it could care less! This is a perfect use for a broadcast. RIP uses the well-known UDP port 520 for all its communications.

Router Updates. By default, RIP sends a broadcast every thirty seconds. This means that all routers on a network are broadcasting their information to other routers *all the time*. In a large network with many routers, this can generate a great deal of network traffic. This is why in large inter-networking environments, routing protocols like OSPF are chosen. In a smaller network, RIP is a good, inexpensive choice for dynamic routing.

Types of RIP Routers. By default, all RIP routers send and receive broadcasts of their route tables. It is possible to configure a RIP router to only receive other router broadcasts and not transmit any of its own. A router configured in this fashion is known as a *Silent RIP Router.*

Hop Metrics. RIP determines destinations and distances to remote networks using a hop count. A hop is defined as one jump across a router. Remote networks that are more than 15 hops away are considered unreachable. You might think this would be a real problem, but remember that all the other routers are connected together. Other routers will have different hop counts to the destination than the source and it would be rare that transmissions would fail because of an unreachable destination.

Installation of RIP for IP

Installing RIP for IP is a snap. To install the protocol, follow the outlined procedure below.

1. Open the Network Control Panel. Your screen should look like Figure 5-13.

2. Assure that TCP/IP is already installed on the computer. You can do this by checking the protocol tab and making sure there is an entry for TCP/IP as shown in Figure 5-14.

3. Click on the Services Tab and click the Add button. Select the RIP for IP protocol in the window provided. Your screen will look something like Figure 5-15.

4. You will be prompted to supply the Windows NT Server CD if you do not already have it in your machine.

5. The protocol will be loaded, and you will be prompted to restart your computer for the changes to take effect. That's all there is to adding RIP for IP!

NOTE: *If you have previously applied* any *service packs to your Windows NT installation, you must reapply the service pack once the computer has rebooted. Odd things happen when versions of software are out of synchronization!*

FIGURE 5-13
The Windows NT Network Control Panel.

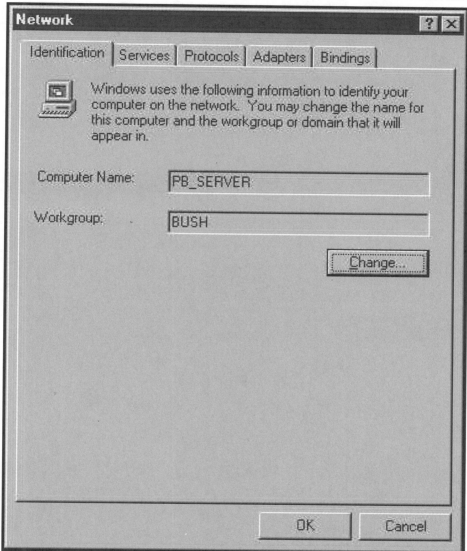

FIGURE 5-14
The Network Control Panel/Protocol Tab.

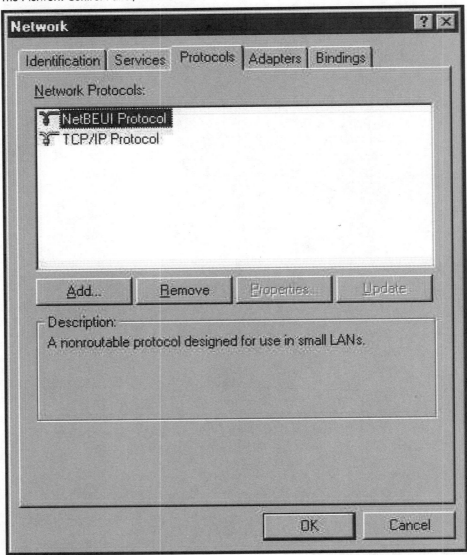

FIGURE 5-15
Adding RIP for IP.

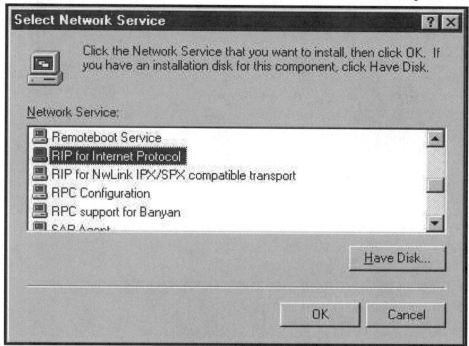

Using Static and Dynamic Routers on the Same Network

If your network uses both static and dynamic routers, you will need to make some manual entries in the router tables of all computers (static and dynamic). It should come as no surprise that a static router will not update a RIP-enabled router (or vice versa). The principle of building the route tables is exactly the same as we discussed earlier. Let's take a look at an example, using the information in Figure 5-16.

FIGURE 5-16
Static/Dynamic Routing Example.

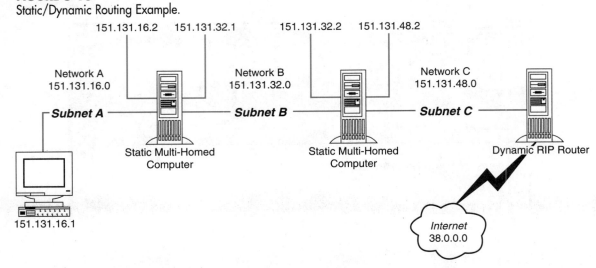

Routing entries you would be required to make are highlighted in bold text. Your tables should look like this:

STATIC ROUTER A TABLE		
NETWORK	**NETWORK ID**	**GATEWAY ROUTE**
Home Network A	151.131.16.0	151.131.16.2
Home Network B	151.131.32.0	151.131.32.1
Remote Network C	**151.131.48.0**	**151.131.32.2**
Internet	**38.0.0.0**	**151.131.32.2**

STATIC ROUTER B TABLE		
NETWORK	**NETWORK ID**	**GATEWAY ROUTE**
Home Network C	151.131.48.0	151.131.48.2
Home Network B	151.131.32.0	151.131.32.2
Remote Network A	**151.131.16.0**	**151.131.32.1**
Internet	**38.0.0.0**	**151.131.48.2**

RIP ENABLED DYNAMIC ROUTER C TABLE

NETWORK	NETWORK ID	GATEWAY ROUTE
Home Network C (RIP Enabled)	N/A	N/A
Internet (RIP Enabled)	N/A	N/A
Remote Network B	**151.131.32.0**	**151.131.48.2**
Remote Network A	**151.131.16.0**	**151.131.48.2**

Notice that we have added all possible routes between the networks. This situation gets really ugly when working with large numbers of routers. This is why most network administrators use dynamic routing to build their route tables.

Summary

This chapter explored both static and dynamic IP routing within Windows NT. Within this chapter we covered the following material:

■ **The difference between routers, gateways, and multi-homed computers.** We learned that these terms are very closely related. Routers and multi-homed computers serve essentially the same purpose—to forward packets to remote networks. These devices serve as gateways to remote and local networks. The routes between different networks are controlled by routing tables that reside on these devices.

■ **The difference between static and dynamic routing.** We defined and examined the two methods of routing in an internetwork. We also discussed the two most popular dynamic routing protocols: RIP and OSPF.

■ **Use of the ROUTE command.** We learned how to access and use the Windows NT ROUTE command to display and configure a static or dynamic router.

■ **How to configure routes between subnets.** We learned a process for building static route tables between different networks and practiced this method several times throughout the lesson.

■ **Installation of RIP for IP.** We learned how to install the RIP for IP protocol within Windows NT.

■ **How to integrate static and dynamic routers in an internetwork.** We learned that when working with static and dynamic routers, we must make static entries to inform the routers of all possible paths to remote networks.

● ● ● ● ● ● ● ● ● ● ● ● ● ●

Q & A

1. *Select all that apply.* The main purpose of a router is to

   a. Forward client packets to other routers.
   b. Maintain all the client IP addresses in its route table.
   c. Maintain all other router's addresses in its route table.
   d. Determine the best path to a destination network.
   e. Maintain both client and router addresses in its route table.

2. *Select the best answer.* Lea needs to install routers on her Windows NT network to divide it into three segments. What would be Lea's most cost-effective installation option while reducing her administrative support?

   a. Install 2 Windows NT servers as multi-homed computers and enable IP forwarding on both machines. Nothing else is required.
   b. Install 2 Windows NT servers as multi-homed computers, enable IP forwarding, and enable RIP for IP on both machines.
   c. Install 3 Windows NT servers as multi-homed computers, enable IP forwarding, and enable RIP for IP on all machines.
   d. Install 2 Windows NT servers as multi-homed computers, disable IP forwarding, and enable RIP for IP on both machines.
   e. None of the above.

3. *Select the best answer.* John works in a large organization. He is in the process of selecting a method for configuring his routers on his network. What would be John's best choice?

   a. Static routing.
   b. Dynamic routing using RIP.
   c. Dynamic routing using OSPF.
   d. Dynamic routing using INFR.
   e. None of the above.

4. *Select the best answer.* What ROUTE switch/command option enables a user to create persistent route table entry?

   a. ROUTE –p CHANGE
   b. ROUTE –f ADD
   c. ROUTE –f CHANGE
   d. ROUTE –p ADD
   e. ROUTE ADD

5. *Select the best answer.* When integrating static and dynamic routers, one must

   a. Do nothing. The routers will automatically update each other.
   b. Enter route entries *only* on the static routers.
   c. Enter route entries *only* on the dynamic routers.
   d. Enter route entries on both the static and dynamic routers.

6. *Select the best answer.* Which of the following custom subnet masks illustrates a Class C network address with at least 12 additional networks?

   a. 255.255.224.0
   b. 255.255.255.192
   c. 255.255.255.240
   d. 255.255.255.248
   e. 255.255.255.224

7. *Select the best answer.* Which of the following custom subnet masks would provide a Class B network with at least 3,500 hosts per network?

   a. 255.255.252.0
   b. 255.255.240.0
   c. 255.255.254.0
   d. 255.255.248.0
   e. None of the above.

8. *Select the best answer.* What is the correct subnet mask for a network ID of 210.100.192.0 to define six additional networks with 16 hosts per subnet?

   a. 255.255.240.0
   b. 255.255.255.240
   c. 255.255.248.0
   d. 255.255.255.248
   e. 255.255.255.224
   f. 255.255.224.0

9. *Select the best answer.* RIP considers a network unreachable after how many hops?

   a. 10
   b. 12
   c. 15
   d. 22
   e. 16

10. *Select the best answer.* Windows NT accepts a maximum of how many default gateways?

    a. 1
    b. 3
    c. 4
    d. 5
    e. 10

11. *Select the best answer.* John is a network administrator attempting to install a routed network. He has three subnets. Hosts on Subnet A can communicate with Subnet B and Hosts from Subnet B can communicate with Subnet C but hosts on Subnet C cannot communicate with Subnet A. What is the most likely cause of the problem?

    a. IP forwarding is not enabled on the routers.
    b. The static route entries have not been added for Router A.

    c. RIP for IP has not been installed on Router B.

    d. The static route entries have not been added for Router B.

    e. RIP for IP has not been installed on Router A.

    f. The static route entries have not been added for both routers.

12. Suppose the following situation exists:

Michael needs to segment his Class C network into 3 subnets. He must implement a cost-effective and low-maintenance solution that does not require any additional hardware or software. Michael has two Windows NT Fileservers on his network.

Required Results

- Reduce network traffic by 50%.

- Improve performance of the workstations.

- Departmentalize the organization.

Optional Results

- Provide for growth in the organization.

- Provide departmental security.

- Minimizes cost.

Proposed Solution

- Configure two Windows NT servers as multi-homed computers.

- Use a custom subnet mask of 255.255.255.224.

- Assign each department to its own subnet.

- Enable RIP for IP on both NT servers.

- Implement IP forwarding on both multi-homed computers.

    a. The proposed solution meets both the required and optional results.

    b. The proposed solution meets the required results and two of the optional results.

    c. The proposed solution meets the required results and only one of the optional results.

    d. The proposed solution meets the required results and none of the optional results.

    e. The proposed solution does not meet requirements nor any optional results.

13. *Select all that apply.* What criteria should you apply when selecting a route management mechanism?

    a. Security

    b. Size

    c. Network traffic

    d. Number of routers

    e. All of the above.

    f. None of the above.

FIGURE 5-17

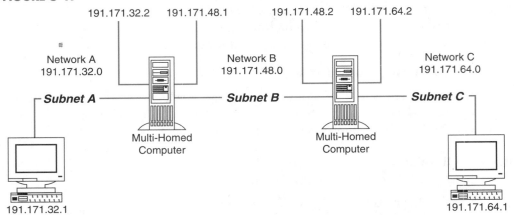

191.171.32.2   191.171.48.1   191.171.48.2   191.171.64.2

Network A   Network B   Network C
191.171.32.0   191.171.48.0   191.171.64.0

Subnet A   Subnet B   Subnet C

Multi-Homed   Multi-Homed
Computer   Computer

191.171.32.1   191.171.64.1

14. *Select the best answer.* Wanda has two multi-homed computers connecting three subnets as illustrated in Figure 5-17. Wanda's subnet mask is 255.255.255.0. What route entries must Wanda use to allow all computers on all subnets to communicate?

   a. On Router 1, ROUTE ADD 191.171.64.0 MASK 255.255.255.0 191.171.48.2
   On Router 2, ROUTE ADD 191.171.32.0 MASK 255.255.255.0 191.171.48.1

   b. On Router 1, ROUTE ADD 191.171.32.0 MASK 255.255.255.0 191.171.32.2
   On Router 2, ROUTE ADD 191.171.64.0 MASK 255.255.255.0 191.171.64.2

   c. On Router 1, ROUTE ADD 191.171.48.0 MASK 255.255.255.0 191.171.48.1
   On Router 2, ROUTE ADD 191.171.48.0 MASK 255.255.255.0 191.171.48.2

   d. On Router 1, ROUTE ADD 191.171.64.0 MASK 255.255.255.0 191.171.64.2
   On Router 2, ROUTE ADD 191.171.32.0 MASK 255.255.255.0 191.171.32.2

   e. None of the configurations will work.

15. *Select all that apply?* What components are required to use the ROUTE ADD command?

   a. Network address
   b. Gateway address
   c. Router address
   d. Subnet mask
   e. FQDN

NETBIOS, BROWSING, AND WINS

OBJECTIVES

By the end of this chapter, you should be able to:

- Describe the purpose of a NetBIOS name and resolution in a Microsoft network.

- Understand the basic relationship between NetBIOS names, the computer browsing process, and TCP/IP–NetBIOS name resolution.

- Configure and implement LMHOSTS files in a Microsoft network.

- Explain common problems and resolutions using NetBIOS naming schemes in a routed network.

- Define the relationship between the LMHOSTS file and WINS

- Install and configure the Microsoft WINS service.

- Perform administration of WINS servers including management of replication and review of the WINS dynamic database.

- Explain the process a Microsoft client uses to resolve NetBIOS names.

- Explain how WINS can be integrated with a DNS server for expanded name resolution functionality.

- Describe the purpose and function of the NBTSTAT utility in troubleshooting and gathering NetBIOS information.

Introduction

This chapter explores NetBIOS name resolution, the Windows NT browsing process and the Windows Internet Name Service. We have talked at a high level about NetBIOS and WINS previously. In this chapter, we dig deeply into these extremely important name resolution mechanisms in a Microsoft network.

As you will recall, WINS is used to resolve NetBIOS names into IP addresses. NetBIOS names are most often used to provide a friendly name for a computer and it is the primary mechanism for naming a Microsoft client. Several important concepts are tied to NetBIOS name resolution in a TCP/IP network, including network browsing, the LMHOSTS file and NetBIOS Name Servers (NBNS) like WINS.

Lesson 6.1 NetBIOS Naming Overview

This lesson provides an overview of the NetBIOS naming scheme, its importance to a Microsoft client, and how NetBIOS works with TCP/IP in a Microsoft network to provide one method of name resolution.

What Is NetBIOS?

NetBIOS is actually a session-layer protocol used to submit and process networking requests from a client. NetBIOS names are user-friendly. By this I mean they are easy for a human being to understand. The most common illustration of a NetBIOS name is a Microsoft computer name. The computer name is in fact a NetBIOS name and NetBIOS is integrated tightly into Microsoft networks. It is also the primary mechanism for identifying a Microsoft Client on the network. As we will see later, the entire computer browsing process is NetBIOS-based. However, this presents somewhat of a problem in a TCP/IP network since all IP understands is an IP address! This whole chapter is dedicated to dealing with this problem.

NetBIOS is the primary communications mechanism used by the NetBEUI protocol. NetBEUI, as you will recall, is a broadcast-based protocol (as are all NetBIOS transmissions) that is fast and efficient in small LAN environments. Microsoft operating systems use NetBIOS for all sorts of things and it is integrated deeply into all their operating systems.

Just like TCP/IP, there are rules for using NetBIOS names. We will further explain these and additional mechanisms as we work through the chapter. However, here are some of the more important rules that apply to NetBIOS names:

- **Every NetBIOS name must be unique.** Just like every TCP/IP address must be unique, so must every NetBIOS name. You cannot have a duplicate NetBIOS name on a Microsoft network. It will generate an error just like if you have a duplicate IP address.

- **There are naming rules and conventions for using NetBIOS names.** As is the case with any protocol, there are certain rules and regulations that govern the creation of NetBIOS names. You must follow these rules for the protocol to operate correctly.

- **Like must equal like.** Computers that do not use NetBIOS naming schemes cannot natively communicate with each other. For instance, if we were running strictly TCP/IP on a client and had we no method for resolving NetBIOS names into IP addresses, Microsoft computers would have a nasty time trying to communicate. NetBIOS for TCP/IP (NBT) helps to address this issue in Microsoft networks. It is for this reason that we spend time making basic equations that map different naming schemes to other naming schemes.

NetBIOS Requirements and Registered Names

NetBIOS names consist of alphanumeric characters, unlike IP addresses, which are comprised only of numbers. A NetBIOS name consists of sixteen bytes of information. Fifteen of these bytes are used to create the user-friendly name. The sixteenth byte is used to identify the computer's role in the network.

In terms of rules of NetBIOS naming, the same rules we used for naming of computers in Windows apply here (since they are the same). There can be no spaces in the names, almost all characters (alpha and numeric) are allowed except for the "special" ones (@,!,*, etc. . .) and the name is limited to fifteen characters. Based on the role of the computer, the sixteenth byte is automatically assigned. This applies to all facets of the service.

COMMON NETBIOS IDENTIFIERS

When you use a tool like NBTSTAT or WINS, entries in NetBIOS show all 16 bytes of information. The sixteenth byte is presented in a hexadecimal format that doesn't really mean too much unless you know what the code means. The most common types of NetBIOS names are presented in Table 6-1.

As you will see later in the chapter, on first glance it looks like WINS has multiple entries for certain clients in its table. However, if you look at the hex-code in the last placeholder, it will define exactly what was registered by the service. If you are unsure of the meaning or purpose of the different services, refer to your Windows NT documentation.

TABLE 6-1 COMMON REGISTERED NETBIOS COMPUTER NAME TYPES

REGISTERED NAME	HEX CODE	MEANING
Computer Name	00h	The Workstation Service Registered Name
Computer Name	03h	The Messenger Service Registered Name
Computer Name	20h	The Server Service Registered Name
Username	03h	Name of the user logged on to the computer
Domain Name	1Bh	The Domain Name registered by the server

NETBIOS RESOURCE ACCESS

NetBIOS names apply to computers, domains, and network resources on the network. Every time you share a resource (printer or folder) the resource is using a NetBIOS name. Although we will be focusing predominantly on the use of NetBIOS names in computer and domain naming, it is helpful to understand that resources use NetBIOS names. As you are well aware, all computer resources in a Microsoft network are accessed using the Universal Naming Convention (UNC). A UNC consists of two pieces of information: the computer name and the share name. They should look very familiar as in the following example:

NET USE G: \\PB-SERVER\I386

This command maps drive G: to the PB-SERVER computer, I386 Share.

A Word on Naming Conventions

When you work in a large organization, it is important to develop a flexible and expandable NetBIOS naming scheme. Unlike TCP/IP where everyone *has* to use an IP address in a specified format, NetBIOS naming will accept almost anything for a client computer, share, domain, and/or printer. This can make for a messy situation if you are attempting to name computers and shared resources especially if you have not planned the implementation out completely. Keep the following in mind if you are developing a NetBIOS naming scheme:

Make the Name Understandable and Flexible. Nobody likes esoteric and obtuse resource names that mean nothing to anyone except the person who developed the naming scheme! The rule of thumb is "Keep it Simple and Understandable," so even the president of the company can find a resource on the network!

Plan for Duplicate Naming Situations. This is where good planning comes in. Just like when you develop a UserID strategy for your domain, you should follow the same principles in creating a NetBIOS naming scheme. Keeping the names unique is of the utmost importance. With 15 available characters and a little planning, this can be accomplished pretty easily.

Create "Easy" Resource Names. Nobody likes names that are difficult to type and remember. If you work in a network that requires you to actually type the NetBIOS name for connections, this is very important. Even if you are using a browser to connect, a list of 50 computers in a browse list is useless if you can't remember the server you need to connect with! If you type an incorrect name or select the wrong computer, you will never be able to connect. So, try to keep the names easy to remember and typable.

Be Consistent. Use the same naming strategy across the enterprise so no matter where a user is located, they will be able to use the same naming strategy to connect to their hosts. Document and distribute this information to the organization. It will greatly ease your support load as an administrator if everyone is on the same page when it comes to connecting to a computer resource.

Implement the Policy Company Wide. If you are working in a decentralized environment, this can be a real challenge (especially if your users are able to share resources on the network). However, try to get everybody to use the same naming strategy or better yet, do it for them and lock down the workstations using polices and profiles!

As usual, doing your planning work on the frontend before you implement the solution will save you a huge amount of work on the backend.

Broadcast Resolution Basics

NetBIOS is a broadcast-based transmission mechanism. This means it sends a message out on the network to *every* computer on a segment. All computers must process the request. If the request is meant for them, they process it and respond. If it is not, the packet is discarded. When working in a small LAN environment, this is fine. But once you start adding multiple computers, you can cause a lot of traffic using this type of resolution mechanism. Moreover, if a network card starts to malfunction, a pesky condition called a "broadcast storm" may result bringing your network to its knees.

This whole broadcast thing presents some problems when we have to use this type of mechanism in a routed network. As you are well aware, broadcast transmissions do not traverse routers (that's one of the main reasons they exist). It is possible to turn broadcasting "on" for a router, but that sort of eliminates its purpose of limiting traffic between subnets. In a Microsoft network with nothing but NetBIOS broadcasting enabled, hosts cannot see any remote computers because the whole process of browsing and broadcasting is limited to the local segment the computer "lives" on. Later we will see how to use LMHOSTS and WINS to work our way around this nasty limitation when operating in a routed TCP/IP environment.

A Quick Fix—NetBIOS Scopes

In an effort to limit broadcast traffic in a NetBIOS environment, a special type of network divider can be used called a **NetBIOS scope.** The scope is not a physical device, but a division or local grouping of computers on a local subnet. If you implement a NetBIOS name scope, you are grouping computers who need to communicate together. The scope limits the hosts to only communicating with each other and not any other computers outside of the scope, or group, they belong to. This reduces broadcast traffic but limits access between computers. So, there is a trade-off here.

NetBIOS scopes are identified using the NetBIOS name, a period, and the group name (scope ID) where they belong. It looks something like this:

PB-SERVER.HOME

The computer name comes first, then the scope ID. They are separated by a period.

TCP/IP and NetBIOS Names?

What we have learned up to this point is that Microsoft clients use NetBIOS as their primary mechanism for establishing network communications and identifying themselves to each other. Yet, we are also attempting to use TCP/IP as our main mechanism for network connectivity. This is not a "like equals like" situation by any stretch of the imagination! To address this, Microsoft includes a special type of "middle-man manager," called NBT. NBT stands for *NetBIOS for TCP/IP*. This is how Microsoft clients are able to use TCP/IP while still using a NetBIOS naming standard. This does not solve all our problems though.

Now we have *both* a NetBIOS name and IP address to deal with. The only thing the Microsoft client cares about is its NetBIOS name. The only thing TCP/IP cares about is its IP Address. Enter NetBIOS name resolution! To effectively manage this conversion/equation process, some type of mapping needs to be made between the IP address and NetBIOS name. This is done in a Windows NT environment using one of the following methods.

- **Internal Name Cache.** Cache is frequently used information that is stored in memory. Once a host is known to a computer, its location is stored in memory and can be used by NetBIOS without rebroadcasting. NetBIOS checks its internal cache first to see if an entry exists for a computer. If it does, it will use this and not send a message out on the network. Name Cache can be displayed using the NBTSTAT utility included in a standard Microsoft TCP/IP installation.

- **A NBNS Server.** This is a NetBIOS Name Server. WINS is a type of NBNS. These type of servers allow a centralized store for NetBIOS naming information and resolution. If a NBNS is in use on a network and the client is configured to use it, the client will check the NBNS for an entry before it broadcasts. This has the effect of enhancing performance in the network because most of the workstations will have entries on the NBNS and the connection made will not have to be processed by every computer on the network—only the NBNS server. Microsoft uses the WINS server to resolve IP addresses to NetBIOS names.

- **LMHOSTS or HOSTS Files.** In some instances, special files called the LMHOSTS and HOSTS can be used to resolve a NetBIOS and FQDN name to an IP Address. LMHOSTS and HOSTS files must reside locally on each client computer. One of the things a Microsoft client will do (if the file is installed on a machine) when attempting to resolve a NetBIOS name is "parse" (read through) the file looking for a mapping that matches the computer request.

- **A DNS Server working with a WINS Server.** Microsoft clients can also use DNS servers and HOSTS files to assist in the resolution process. You will learn more about how this works in the next chapter on DNS.

- **Broadcast.** If all else fails, a broadcast on the network is made for Net-BIOS resolution.

NBT Name Management

A methodical and formal process is used to register a name in Net-BIOS. In brief, three things occur during the process. Two are initiated by the clients who need to register themselves. The third is for clients wishing to communicate on the network. As you will see in later chapters, the process and steps may have a different name, but the services are all basically doing the same thing.

Name Registration. NetBIOS *registers* and *releases* names. One of the first things a client does when it boots is register itself with a WINS server using a "directed" (it knows exactly where to send the request) or broadcast message identifying both its NetBIOS name and TCP/IP address.

Name Discovery. When a Microsoft client wishes to communicate with another host on the network, it must "discover" or find that host. If WINS is enabled, it can do this by querying the server for the IP address mapping based on the computer name. If this is not in place, a broadcast will be sent to find the host.

Name Release. When a computer ceremoniously exits the network (shuts down normally) it will send another message to the WINS server saying "I'm leaving now, you can release my address mapping." Once a release has been issued, the NetBIOS name and IP address are available for another client to use. This keeps both computer names and IP addresses unique on the network.

EXERCISE 6.1 TERMINOLOGY AND CONCEPTS REVIEW

Answer the following questions based on this lesson's content. When you have completed this exercise share your responses with the instructor for validation and additional discussion.

1. What types of uses does NetBIOS have in a Microsoft network?

2. Why is NBT important to NetBIOS–TCP/IP communications?

3. What are the main methods NetBIOS uses to resolve names?

4. Why does NetBIOS present a problem in routed networks?

5. What is the purpose of a NetBIOS scope? What are its benefits? Its limitations?

6. Describe the concept of broadcast transmissions.

7. What steps constitute the process of registering a name in a NBT environment?

8. Why is it important to develop a standardized NetBIOS naming scheme?

9. What is the sixteenth byte of a NetBIOS name used for? Name two ways we display this information.

10. List several mechanisms used by Microsoft clients to resolve NetBIOS names to IP addresses.

Lesson 6.2 Browsing and NetBIOS

This lesson takes a look at how the browsing process works in Windows networking and its interaction with NetBIOS. In this lesson, we will briefly describe browsing, components used in the process, and issues that arise in enterprise-routed networks related to the construction of browse lists. This lesson is not designed to detail the entire browsing process—only to provide an overview in the Microsoft TCP/IP environment. If you would like to learn more about the browsing process, consult with any Microsoft Windows operating system resource kit.

Microsoft Browsing Overview

When you open Network Neighborhood you are viewing a *browse list* of the computers who are available on the network. Browsing is a NetBIOS function. This is why all computers in a browse list have a NetBIOS name. Individual computers in a browse list are grouped by their association with either a workgroup or domain. That's where that sixteenth byte of the NetBIOS name we discussed in the last lesson comes into play. Any workstation can view and connect to a resource if the Workstation service on their computer is started. However, for a computer to be listed in a browse list, it must have its Server Service enabled. This means the host has something to share. Remember that any computer can be both a workstation and server. This is why all computers in a browse list appear the same.

The Browsing Process in a Nutshell

This browse list is constructed through an organized process called *elections*. It is important to note that the election process is not really democratic! Certain machines will always win elections based on their type, release version, and function in the network. The following rules apply to the browsing process.

- **Domain Controllers will always win a domain master browser election and they will always be the master browser for the domain they service.** A higher version of an operating system (e.g., Windows NT 4.0 vs. 3.51) will win an election over a lesser machine operating system version.

- **A Windows NT server will always win a master or backup browser over a client workstation.** Here again, a higher version of an operating system (e.g., Windows NT 4.0 vs. 3.51) will win an election over a lesser machine operating system version. Additionally, a Windows NT Workstation will always win an election over a Windows 95 or 98 client.

Elections and building browse lists can generate a great deal of traffic. Because of this, a hierarchy of machines was developed to address this issue and minimize traffic. As described above there are three main types of browsers. These are

- **Domain Master Browser.** In a Windows NT environment, the computer who is the Domain Master browser holds the master copy of the browse list for the computers it services. A PDC serves two roles: It is the domain master browser as well as the master browser.

- **Master Browser.** A master browser maintains the browse list for the network it services. Any computer can be a master browser—it all depends on how the election goes (see the rules above). A master browser's job is to update backup browser's with browse list information.

- **Backup Browser.** In the event a master browser goes offline, a backup browser can be elected to a master browser. However, the backup browser's main job is to distribute the browse list to clients. Here again, any computer can be a backup browser for a network—it just depends on how the elections proceed.

Figure 6-1 shows how this works.

Lists are updated periodically. Browser traffic can be managed, optimized, and manipulated through various registry settings. In a default configuration it is possible that a browse list might not be updated for more than 45 minutes. Depending on your situation, you may want to work with these settings. Refer to your Windows NT support materials to gather more information on the actual registry keys and settings you can modify.

Problems Browsing across Routers?

Browsers constantly trade information to keep their individual lists (and their clients) up to date. On a local subnet, the process works quite well.

FIGURE 6-1
The Browser Function.

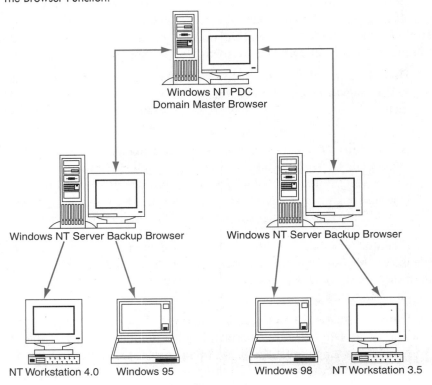

Windows NT PDC
Domain Master Browser

Windows NT Server Backup Browser

Windows NT Server Backup Browser

NT Workstation 4.0   Windows 95

Windows 98   NT Workstation 3.5

Browser Clients

However, because this process uses broadcasts, lists are not typically available across routers. We have to do some special configuration on our NT servers to make browse lists available across an internetwork. The two methods we use deal with the use of the LMHOSTS file and WINS. We will talk in just a bit about how this works and what we have to do.

Lesson 6.3 Before There Was WINS, There Was LMHOSTS

Before we dig deeply into WINS, it will be helpful to understand the LMHOSTS file in a little more depth. As you are already aware, the primary purpose of the LMHOSTS file is to resolve NetBIOS name to IP addresses. However, there is much more we can do with this file. We will be discussing the LMHOSTS file in detail within this lesson.

The LMHOSTS File and Its Purpose

The LMHOSTS file contains mappings of IP addresses to Microsoft networking computer names (which are NetBIOS names). Microsoft LMHOSTS files are compatible with Microsoft TCP/IP. Before WINS came into existence, the LMHOSTS file was the primary mechanism for resolving NetBIOS names to IP addresses. LMHOSTS, like the HOSTS file, is a flat text file and can be edited with any standard text editor like NotePad. However, the LMHOSTS file has some additional information and parameters that make it more useful for resolving names.

The LMHOSTS file provides a basic mapping between a NetBIOS name and IP address. A typical entry might appear as follows:

10.216.5.250   PB-SERVER   #Windows NT Member Server

The first entry specifies the IP address, the second the NetBIOS name. The "#" sign designates a comment. Comments should be added *after* the name mapping entry or on their own line.

When the Microsoft client needs to resolve PB-Server to an IP address, it parses (reads through) the LMHOSTS file looking for an entry like the one we created. If it finds the entry, the computer resolves it. For a long time this was the only way to resolve hostnames in a Microsoft network. It works wonderfully but . . .

The file must be located locally! Like the HOSTS file, LMHOSTS files are typically located on each local computer. This means that any changes to the file must be replicated across an entire organization. This can be a very time consuming job in a large network with many clients. That is why WINS was created. WINS lets you manage your NetBIOS name resolution centrally.

However, certain specific applications require LMHOSTS files and if you are not running WINS on a network, you will have to use this file unless you like a great deal of broadcast traffic! In this case, the LMHOSTS file is typically managed centrally by an administrator and then automatically updated on a regular basis through some type of replication mechanism like Windows NT directory replication or login script processing.

How Microsoft TCP/IP Uses the LMHOSTS File

Microsoft TCP/IP loads the LMHOSTS file into memory when the computer is started. In addition, there are a couple of additional entries that allow certain regularly used addresses to be loaded into the local NetBIOS cache or to access name resolution through a particular domain.

One common use for a LMHOSTS file is to enable browsing and file/printer services across an enterprise-routed network. By specifying the

FIGURE 6-2
Sample Multiple Subnet LMHOSTS Implementation.

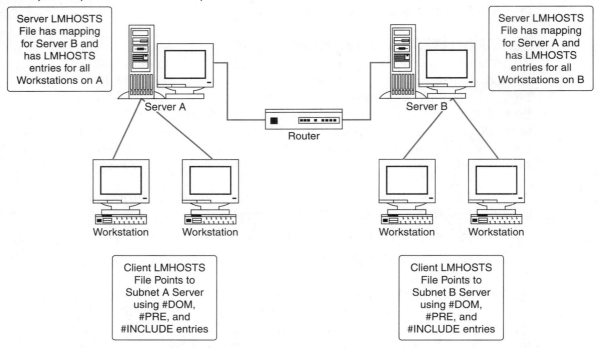

Server LMHOSTS
File has mapping
for Server B and
has LMHOSTS
entries for all
Workstations on A

Server A

Router

Server B

Server LMHOSTS
File has mapping
for Server A and
has LMHOSTS
entries for all
Workstations on B

Workstation   Workstation

Workstation   Workstation

Client LMHOSTS
File Points to
Subnet A Server
using #DOM,
#PRE, and
#INCLUDE entries

Client LMHOSTS
File Points to
Subnet B Server
using #DOM,
#PRE, and
#INCLUDE entries

name and IP address in the file, the computer is able to use IP to traverse the router, eliminating the need for NetBIOS broadcast name resolution. Usually, this type of arrangement is configured between servers located on remote subnets. The clients point to the server using a special entry in their LMHOSTS file. In this arrangement, the server acts like a static database for hosts on the other subnet. Figure 6-2 is a simple illustration of what we're talking about.

If you are looking at those # commands and scratching your head, fear not! The next section describes what each of these special entries is for.

Additional LMHOSTS Commands

There is more we can do with the LMHOSTS file than just map IP addresses to NetBIOS names. LMHOSTS has some additional functionality that allows you to point and use other LMHOSTS files as well as load some entries into NetBIOS cache. The options listed in Table 6-2 can be used in LMHOSTS using Microsoft TCP/IP:

TABLE 6-2 LMHOSTS COMMAND SET SUMMARY

COMMAND	USED TO
#PRE	Causes an entry to be preloaded into the name cache. By default, entries are not preloaded into the name cache. #PRE must be added for entries that appear in #INCLUDE statements (*see below*) otherwise #INCLUDE will be ignored.
#DOM:*domain*	Added after an entry to associate that entry with the domain specified by the *domain* entry. This keyword affects how the browser and Logon services behave in routed TCP/IP environments. To enter a #DOM entry you must also add the #PRE keyword to the line as shown in the examples below.
#INCLUDE *filename*	This command forces the system to seek the specified *filename* and parse it as if it were locally located on the client. Specifying a Universal Naming Convention (UNC) *filename* allows you to use a centralized LMHOSTS file on a server.
	To use this command, add a mapping for the server before its entry in the #INCLUDE section and also append #PRE to ensure that it is preloaded otherwise the #INCLUDE will be ignored.
#BEGIN_ALTERNATE	This command is used to group multiple #INCLUDE statements. It's sort of like a paragraph marker for a group of #INCLUDE statements. Any single successful #INCLUDE statement causes the entire group to succeed.
#END_ALTERNATE	This command signifies the end of a #INCLUDE grouping starting with a #BEGIN_ALTERNATE. These two commands must be used in combination to work correctly.
#	Signifies a general comment for the file.

Let's look at how a file might appear for one of the clients in our example:

```
200.216.94.98   SERVERA #PRE  #Load ServerA into NetBIOS Cache
200.216.94.98   SERVERA #PRE  #DOM:DOMAIN1 #SUBNET GROUP
#BEGIN_ALTERNATE
#INCLUDE \\SERVERA\LMHOSTS #Forces use of Server LMHOSTS file
#END_ALTERNATE
```

The server side entry might look something like this:

200.216.94.91   Workstation 1
200.216.94.92   Workstation 2
200.216.128.98   SERVERB #PRE #Load ServerB into NetBIOS Cache
200.216.128.98   SERVERB #PRE #DOM:DOMAIN2 #SUBNET GROUP

#BEGIN_ALTERNATE

#INCLUDE \\SERVERB\LMHOSTS #Forces use of Server B LMHOSTS file

#END_ALTERNATE

In this manner, all the computers will be able to see the hosts on the remote network. The same process would be completed on Subnet B.

NOTE: *Notice that the #PRE entries are all placed at the end of the file. This is done to speed the parsing process since LMHOSTS files are all processed from top to bottom. The #PRE entries have already been entered into Cache when the machine booted, so there's no point in having LMHOSTS look at them again. Placing them at the bottom helps to assure this will not happen.*

LAB

Creating a LMHOSTS File

Follow all instructions and test your configuration when complete.

TO CREATE A LMHOSTS FILE

1. Locate the sample LMHOSTS file on your NT Workstation or Server computer. The file is stored in the \WINNT\SYSTEM32\DRIVERS\ETC directory and is called LMHOSTS.SAM.

2. Open this file using a text editor like NotePad and make the following entries:

\<Instructor IP Address\>   MASTER
\<Your partner's IP Address\>   JOEBOB

3. Save the file as LMHOSTS with no extension. If you are using NotePad, you will have to use NT Explorer to remove the .TXT extension that will be placed on the file by default.

TO TEST YOUR NEW LMHOSTS FILE

1. Open a Windows NT Command Window.

2. PING MASTER and JOEBOB. What responses do you receive? Were they successful?

3. What conclusions can you draw from this procedure?

Tips on Creating and Managing LMHOSTS Files

When creating the LMHOSTS file keep the following in mind:

- Entries in the LMHOSTS file are not case-sensitive.

- Each entry should be placed on a separate line. When the file is parsed, each record entry is demarcated by a carriage return.

- The IP address should begin in the first column, followed by the corresponding computer name.

- The address and the computer name should be separated by at least one space or tab. Use the # character sparingly. Comment lines add to the parsing time, because each line is processed individually. It is best used to comment the special sections of the file.

GUIDELINES FOR USING LMHOSTS FILES

When you use a LMHOSTS file, make sure you keep it up to date and organized. Follow these guidelines:

- Consider using a LMHOSTS file in small TCP/IP networks. It's far more efficient than broadcasting! If you are working in a larger routed environment, consider using WINS. It's much easier to deal with and maintain (more on this in the next lesson).

- Update the LMHOSTS file whenever a computer is changed or removed from the network. Set up directory replication or some other mechanism to assure everything is replicated to your clients on a regular basis.

- Use #PRE statements to load popular entries into the local computer's name cache and remember this statement MUST be used if you are planning on implementing the #INCLUDE and the ALTERNATE statements.

- Don't get #INCLUDE happy! Try to keep things simple and pull the files from one central server. As usual, keep it as simple as possible!

- Place the most frequently accessed servers at the top of the file. Since the file is parsed from top-to-bottom, this will improve performance.

Lesson 6.4 The Windows Internet Naming Service (WINS)

This lesson covers the Windows Internet Naming Service (WINS) and its importance in a Microsoft TCP/IP network. In this lesson, we will learn the function of a WINS server, several mechanisms that can be used to direct WINS in handling client requests, and the purpose/function of a WINS proxy. Make sure you read this lesson before you begin the lesson on installation and configuration of WINS.

WINS Defined

WINS is a dynamic database included with Windows NT server that allows clients to register and release NetBIOS name/IP address mappings. When you implement WINS, you will significantly reduce network traffic and have all the tools necessary to manage some of the browsing and name resolution issues we discussed in an enterprise wide Microsoft TCP/IP Internetwork scenario.

WINS was developed to make the process of resolving NetBIOS names to IP addresses easier, centralized, and automatic (well, mostly automatic). WINS is a dynamic database, which means it functions with no administrative intervention in terms of entering and managing records assuming all the clients are WINS based. If you have non-WINS enabled clients, you can still use the service by configuring a "Static Mapping" (more on this later).

WINS manages the name resolution process automatically unlike a statically maintained database like DNS. Once the clients are configured to use a WINS server, all NetBIOS name registrations, requests, and releases are managed by the service. This makes WINS gobs easier to maintain than LMHOSTS files!

Unfortunately, WINS uses broadcast mechanisms to operate and so, it too is limited in traversing a router. However, Microsoft has several mechanisms that allow us to circumvent this issue and most others related to NetBIOS name resolution. We will look at the primary mechanism to manage inter-network implementations of WINS called "Push/Pull Replication" in just a little bit.

NetBIOS for TCP/IP (NBT)

We briefly discussed NBT in the last few lessons. Now, we will take a little closer look at some key information that our clients use to connect to a WINS server (or not) and how they will process name resolution. This section discusses name resolution modes that WINS clients use. This is a very important option that *must* be configured in DHCP if you plan to use WINS scope options in your DHCP lease. See chapter 8 for more information on this.

Name Resolution Modes

As we have seen previously, there are several mechanisms a client can use to resolve a NetBIOS name. WINS can handle all combinations of these nodes. *These configuration options are for the client to tell it how to connect to a resource.* By specifying a name recognition method, you assure the correct mechanism will be used by the service to resolve the name. There are five different modes a WINS client can operate in. They are referred to as *nodes,* which is really another name for a client on the network. These node types are described in Table 6-3.

Client configuration of node types can be manually completed by making a registry change. However, in most cases, the client will pick the correct mechanism based on how you've configured TCP/IP.

TABLE 6-3 WINS CLIENT RESOLUTION MODES

NODE TYPE	WHAT IT IS AND WHEN TO USE IT
B-Node	This is a broadcast node. If your clients only work on a local subnet, you can use this type of resolution node for your clients. Be forewarned though, this node type does not travel across a router!
P-Node	This is a directed name resolution request to a NBNS server like WINS. If all clients use WINS exclusively, you could use this node type to configure the WINS clients.
M-Node	This node type uses both B and P nodes depending on the situation. It was a precursor to the H-Node that is used far most frequently. With M-Node, the client will try a P-Node registration first. If that doesn't work, it will use a B-Node transmission to resolve the address.
H-Node	This node type is the "hybrid" type. It too uses both P and B nodes to resolve names. *It is the recommended (and only) option you should use when configuring a WINS server and is required when you setup WINS in DHCP.*
Microsoft Enhanced B-Node	This is the LMHOSTS file implementation we discussed in the last chapter. All Microsoft clients use this method of checking the LMHOSTS file as part of their resolution process. You do not configure this—it just works if you're using a LMHOSTS file.

The NetBIOS Name Resolution Process

Microsoft clients go through a very structured approach to resolving NetBIOS names to IP addresses. Be sure you understand what is taking place since it will make your troubleshooting much easier! The resolution process is outlined below:

1. **Check Name Cache.** The first thing that happens when a client requests a resource on the network is the local name cache is checked for a NetBIOS to IP address mapping. If it is found, the address is resolved and communications begin. If not, the client will try step 2.

2. **Check Name Server.** If a WINS server has been installed, the client will make three attempts to query the WINS database for resolution. If successful, the WINS server returns the mapping and the computer begins to communicate. If not, the client will try step 3.

3. **Broadcast on the local network.** If the client has been unable to resolve the address thus far, it will broadcast on the local network. If it receives a reply, it will resolve the address. If not, the client will try step 4.

4. **Parse the LMHOSTS file.** If the broadcast doesn't work, the LMHOSTS file is then parsed to see if an entry exists there. If so, it will be resolved. If not, things really get serious.

5. **Check anything else available to the client.** The client will attempt to use a HOSTS file or DNS to resolve the address. If everything fails, the user will receive an error message.

What about Non-WINS Clients Who Need to Access NetBIOS Computers?

It would be nice if our world worked with all the same operating systems! But, this is not the case. Many times, UNIX or other hosts need to communicate with NetBIOS servers. When this happens, we still need a way to get to the host and a method for name resolution. To do this, we use something called a WINS Proxy.

WHAT'S A WINS PROXY?

A proxy is defined as a *go-between* or *helper*. A WINS proxy sits between a non-WINS enabled client and NetBIOS hosts helping to resolve the name for the non-WINS client. A WINS Proxy Agent listens for broadcasts by non-WINS clients and forwards (proxies) the request to a WINS server on behalf of the client.

This is a useful feature to enable in a heterogeneous network. To enable a WINS Proxy, you must make a registry change on the computer who will be the proxy. There is no tab or applet that allows you to do this. A Windows NT workstation or server can be a WINS Proxy Agent. If you wish to configure a Proxy Agent, modify the following key:

HKEY_LOCAL_MACHINE\SYSTEM\CurrentControlSet\Services\NetBT\Parameters
Set the "EnableProxy" key to a value of "1".

EXERCISE 6.2 TERMINOLOGY AND CONCEPTS REVIEW

Answer the following questions based on this lesson's content. When you have completed this exercise share your responses with the instructor for validation and additional discussion.

1. Describe the Microsoft browsing process, explaining what browsing is used for and why it is important in a Microsoft network.

2. What is the difference between a domain master browser, master browser, and backup browser?

3. What is the order of precedence for machines to win a browser election?

4. What is a WINS proxy? What is it used for? How can it be enabled?

5. Describe the process a client goes through to resolve a remote host's IP address based on a NetBIOS name.

6. What are the major node types a client uses to register its names with a WINS server? What node type must be configured on a DHCP server?

7. What is the purpose of a #PRE entry in the LMHOSTS file? A #DOMAIN?

8. Describe how you might configure LMHOSTS files to allow remote access across a router.

9. Why should you place #PRE entries at the bottom of your LMHOSTS file?

10. What are the benefits and drawbacks of using an LMHOSTS file versus WINS?

Lesson 6.5 Installing and Configuring WINS

This lesson walks you through the process of installing and configuring the WINS service on a Windows NT server computer. The lab at the end of this lesson will allow you to practice what you have learned in this lesson by installing and configuring your own server.

In this lesson we will be focusing on WINS basic installation requirements, configuration, and some of the more advanced topics associated with WINS like push/pull replication and creation of a static WINS entry.

Installing the Service

Before we actually begin the installation process, the first thing we must do is verify that our computer meets minimum requirements for the installation. To install WINS on your machine the following criteria must be met:

■ You must be using a Windows NT server computer. The computer can be either a member or domain controller. For high traffic networks, it is recommended that you install WINS on a member server to minimize load on the server. Multiple services may be installed on the computer as long as performance remains acceptable.

- The NT server should have a statically configured IP address, subnet mask, and, if required, a default gateway. WINS can be installed on a server acting as a DHCP client but it is not recommended.

- If you are planning on implementing any type of fault tolerant WINS configuration, you will need a minimum of two WINS servers on the network. These servers will be known to the clients as a Primary and Secondary WINS server, respectively.

- If you are working in a routed network, placement of your WINS servers will be key. In most instances, WINS servers will need to be placed on each subnet and configured for push/pull replication (more on this later).

Installing the WINS service begins in the Network Control Panel. To install the service follow the outlined process.

1. Open Control Panel and then the Network Control Panel applet. Select the Services Tab. Your screen should appear as in Figure 6-3.

2. Click **Add,** and highlight the "Windows Internet Name Service" in the list box. Your screen should look like Figure 6-4.

3. Click **OK.** The files will be copied from your Windows NT distribution CD or share. When complete, you will be prompted to restart your computer. If space allows, it is nice to copy the \I386 directory onto your NT box so you don't need to keep referring to the CD.

4. Restart your computer. Log in as "Administrator." When you log back in, reapply any Service Packs installed on your machine. Restart the computer when prompted. It is also recommended to update your emergency repair disk after any software installs or updates.

That's it on the server! You have successfully added the WINS service.

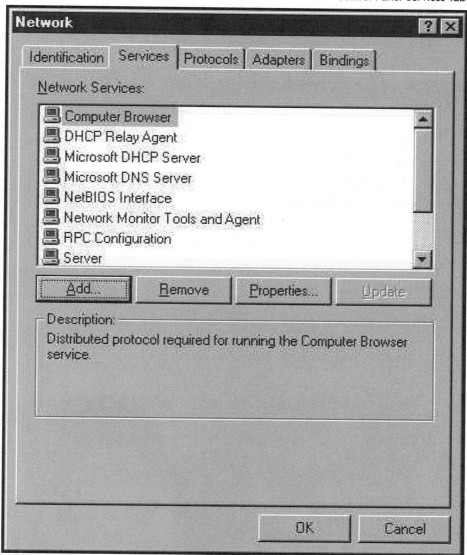

FIGURE 6-4
WINS Service Add Service Dialog.

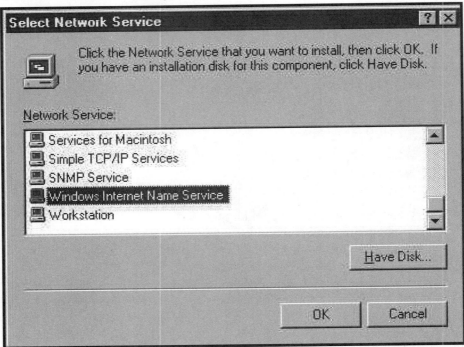

Starting and Stopping the WINS Service

Starting and stopping the WINS Service can be accomplished using two methods. The first involves use of the Control Panel Services applet. The second method is completed at the command prompt. If you need to stop, pause, or start the WINS service, follow the outlined procedures below:

USING THE SERVICES APPLET TO STOP, START, AND PAUSE WINS

1. Open the Control Panel, Services applet and scroll down the list of services until you arrive at the Windows Internet Name Service entry. Your screen should look like Figure 6-5.

2. To Pause or Stop the service, click the appropriate button. Once paused or stopped, the Start button becomes available for you to start the service. That's it!

FIGURE 6-5
Services Applet.

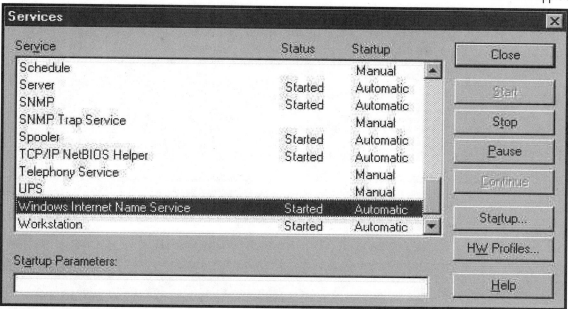

FIGURE 6-5
Services Applet.

FIGURE 6-6
NET STOP WINS Command.

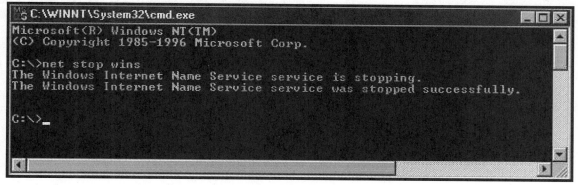

USING THE NET COMMAND TO START AND STOP THE WINS SERVICE

1. Open a Windows NT Command Prompt. Type the following command.

NET STOP WINS

Your screen should look like Figure 6-6.

FIGURE 6-7
NET START WINS Command.

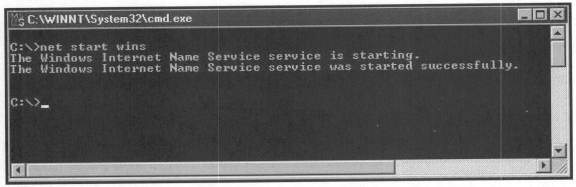

FIGURE 6-8
NET PAUSE WINS Command.

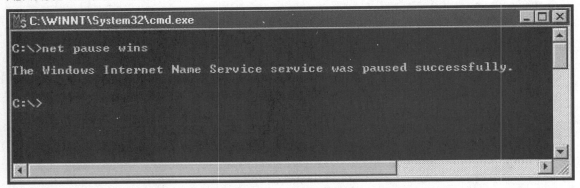

2. To restart the WINS Service type the following command:

   NET START WINS

   Your screen should look like that in Figure 6-7.

3. To pause the WINS Service type the following command:

   NET PAUSE WINS

   Your screen should look like Figure 6-8.

Configuring a WINS Client

Configuring a WINS Client is simple. To enable WINS resolution on a statically configured Windows NT computer, follow this outlined procedure.

1. Open Control Panel, Network. Click on the Protocols Tab. Your screen should look like Figure 6-9.

Network Control Panel Protocols Tab.

FIGURE 6-9
Network Control Panel Protocols Tab.

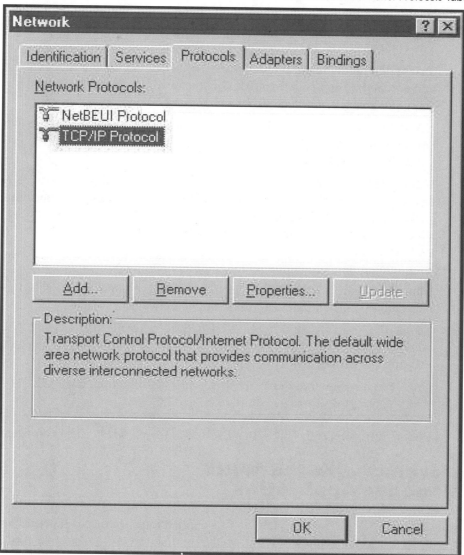

2. Click on TCP/IP Protocol, then click on the Properties button. Then click on the WINS Address Tab. Your screen should look like Figure 6-10.

At this dialog, you can configure the WINS client. Let's look at the entries you can make

Primary WINS Server. Specify the IP address of the primary WINS server using this entry. All NetBIOS name resolution requests will be initially processed using this NBNS address.

Secondary WINS Server. Specify the IP address of the secondary WINS server using this entry area. The secondary server will be used if the Primary server's resolution fails.

Enable DNS for Windows Resolution. If you have a special entry made in the DNS Server (see chapter 7) for WINS resolution, you can check this box. This tells TCP/IP to attempt resolution using the Microsoft DNS Service if other modes of NetBIOS name resolution fail.

Enable LMHOSTS Lookup. This box is checked by default and tells TCP/IP to perform a LMHOSTS lookup as part of the resolution process. You can import a LMHOSTS file from another computer if this box is checked as well. The file can reside on the network or on disk.

Scope ID. You can configure a NetBIOS scope using this field. If you were using this field, you would enter the name of the scope you wish the computer to belong to.

3. Once you have entered the appropriate client information, click **OK.** You will be prompted to restart your computer.

4. Restart your computer. That's it! WINS is configured on the client computer.

Working with the WINS Manager Application

Once WINS has been successfully installed, we manage the application using the WINS Manager application. This application controls all functions of WINS. To access the application click on the Start button, Administrative Tools, WINS Manager selection. WINS Manager will start. Your screen should look like Figure 6-11.

To display the WINS database, click on the "Mappings" Menu option and select "Show Database." This will display the WINS database. Your screen should look like Figure 6-12.

The Show Database view has several options that are all related to sorting and displaying the data contained in the WINS database. You can view data in WINS by sorting on any number of criteria including IP address, computer name, and all the radio buttons listed in the panel, or by setting a filter (this is a sort based on criteria you set). The database can be refreshed (or updated) by clicking on the Refresh button.

FIGURE 6-10
WINS Address Tab.

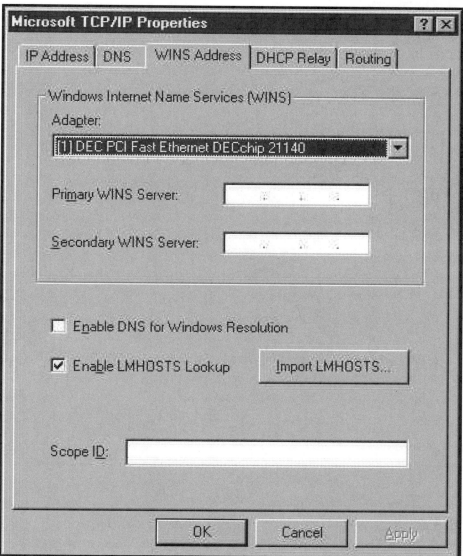

FIGURE 6-11
WINS Manager Main Display.

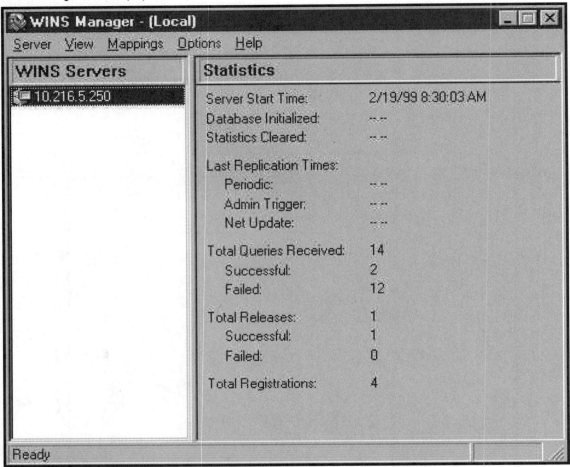

Notice in the mappings section the sixteenth byte of the NetBIOS name is displayed designating the type of information being reported by WINS. Also of interest is the Version ID column. WINS manages entries in its database by Version numbers. Later versions of the same entry take precedence in the database. The Expiration Date column designates when the name registration will expire. This and several other parameters governing the name resolution process can be managed based on your individual requirements. This is the area we will look at next.

Managing Registration Parameters

To manage the WINS registration parameters, follow this outlined process.

FIGURE 6-12
Viewing the WINS Database.

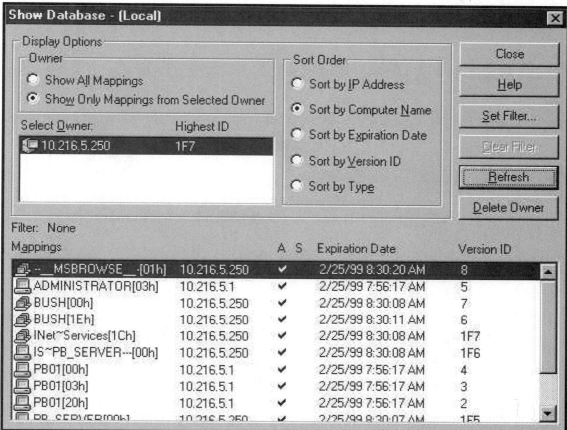

1. Click the Server menu and select the Configure option. It is here that you can change the way WINS manages registrations, renewals, and extinction parameters. Your screen should look like Figure 6-13.

   Figure 6-13 displays all the default settings for WINS parameters. Clicking on the Advanced button will provide several other options as well. Changing the registration parameters is simple—just type in the settings you want in a HH/MM/SS format for any entry. The other parameters surrounding pull and push are used for WINS replication. We will discuss these in just a bit.

2. If we click on the Advanced button, we will have several additional options available. Figure 6-14 shows what your screen would look with this button selected.

FIGURE 6-13
WINS Configuration Dialog.

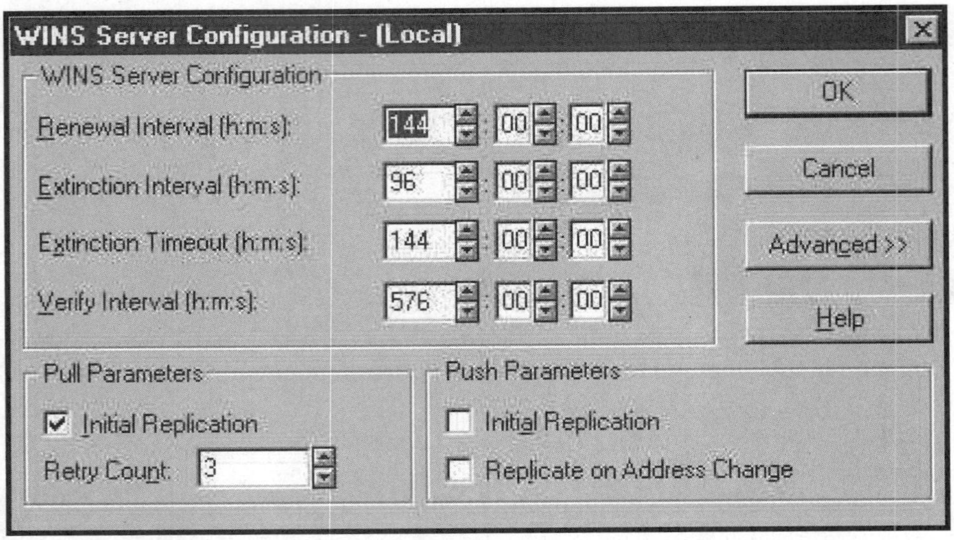

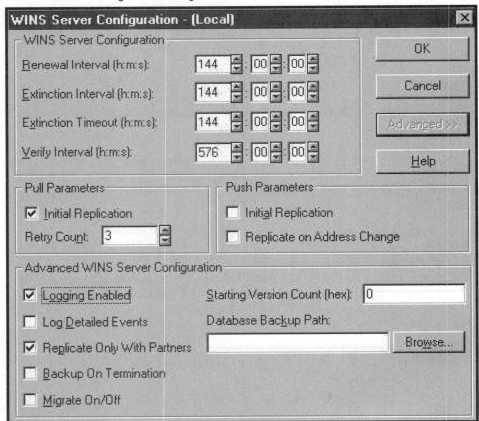

FIGURE 6-14
WINS Advanced Configuration Dialog.

In the Advanced configuration dialog, you configure parameters that effect how WINS logs registrations, backs up data, migrates data, and version counting parameters. Normally, you will not need to work in this area for a basic WINS install except to possibly specify a Database Backup path.

Configuring Static versus Dynamic Mappings

As you can see, once a WINS client is enabled, the name registration process is completely automatic. As an administrator, you are basically watching for problems—you do not have to configure anything beyond what we have done to this point. However, if you have a non-WINS client and you wish to establish a NetBIOS name mapping you must manually configure this entry. This is called a *Static WINS Mapping*. In this section we will see how to complete this task.

To configure a static WINS client in the database, follow the outlined procedure below:

1. To display the Static configuration dialog, click on the Mappings menu option and select Static Mappings. Your screen should look like Figure 6-15.

   Adding a Static Mapping is a simple procedure of clicking the Add Mappings button. When you do this you will be presented with the dialog as shown in Figure 6-16.

FIGURE 6-15
Static Mapping Dialog.

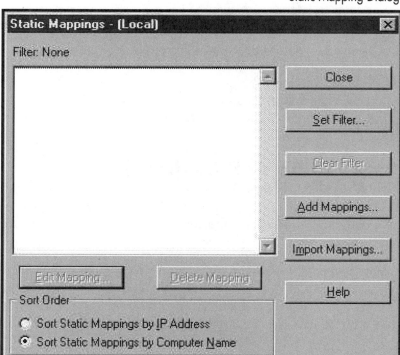

2. Enter the name of the computer and its IP address and then select the type of name registration record to create. When you are done, press the Add button and your entry will be added the WINS database. Click Close to close the dialog.

The Type radio buttons define the type of entry to make in the database. Many times, you will use the *Unique* entry which makes a unique mapping to a NetBIOS name. The other options define whether the entry is a workgroup (Group), domain name, Internet group (groups resources for easy browsing and access), and multi-homed computers (computers with more than one IP address).

Understanding and Configuring WINS Replication

This section of the lesson discusses WINS replication. Along with procedures for configuring this important feature, there is some additional theory we must understand as well.

WHY REPLICATE?

If you are working in a routed network and you want browse lists and computers to be able to access resources across the enterprise, you will have to use WINS replication. Replication is a database term for *copy*. In essence, when we replicate, we are synchronizing all our WINS servers with the same entries. This allows all computers on all subnets to communicate with each other. WINS provides a more eloquent solution for remote subnet access to resources than the LMHOSTS solution we discussed in the previous lesson.

PUSH VERSUS PULL REPLICATION

WINS uses two types of replication. This section briefly describes each and when you should use them.

Push Replication. In this situation, you are pushing the WINS database to another server. Push partners are usually used on fast WAN links. In a push situation, replication occurs based on a preselected number of changes in the WINS database. When the threshold is reached, the WINS server initiates the push to the configured servers. You can push changes to multiple servers. Push servers cannot be configured to replicate at a specific time so as an administrator, you must determine an appropriate threshold value that allows for updates to be made without impacting performance on the WAN link. On an initial push, the entire database is transferred to the push partner. After this is completed, only records that have changed are transferred.

Pull Replication. In this replication scenario, you are pulling information from another WINS server. Pull replication is typically used across slow WAN links since the administrator can configure replication to occur at predesignated times when traffic on the link is not heavy (e.g., late in the evening). Pull replication occurs automatically whenever a WINS server is stopped and then restarted.

When WINS servers replicate between themselves they are known as **Replication Partners** since they are sharing information. In most instances, the servers are both Push and Pull partners of each other. Replication can occur automatically, or you can force it to occur by issuing a *trigger* to the database. A trigger is nothing more than a switch that executes a command. It's sort of like pulling the trigger of a gun—pull the trigger, and the gun fires.

Armed with this information we are now ready to configure replication.

NOTE: *To implement WINS replication you need at least two WINS servers!*

CONFIGURING PUSH/PULL REPLICATION

To configure WINS replication, follow this outlined process.

1. Select the Server menu and click on the Replication Partners option. This will bring up the WINS replication configuration dialog. Your screen should appear like that in Figure 6-17.

FIGURE 6-17
Replication Partner Configuration Dialog.

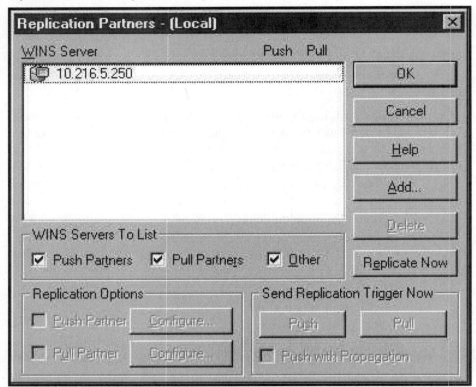

2. To add a new replication partner click on the Add button. Enter the IP address or NetBIOS name of the WINS server you wish to replicate with. When complete, your screen should look something like Figure 6-18.

Let's look at some of the options we have available to us:

WINS Servers to List. These checkboxes allow us to filter what is displayed in the view panel in Figure 6-18. Right now, my computer is showing all servers. When working within a large volume of WINS servers, it is useful to only view the particular ones you are attempting to modify.

Replication Options. For the highlighted server, this is where we select the type of replication we want to occur. We can also configure the individual replication parameters for each server using the Configure buttons.

Send Replication Trigger Now. This forces push and/or pull replication immediately. If you send a trigger, replication will be queued and completed as soon as possible. The Replicate Now button will force replication based on the configuration of the selected WINS server.

FIGURE 6-18
Push/Pull Partner Configured.

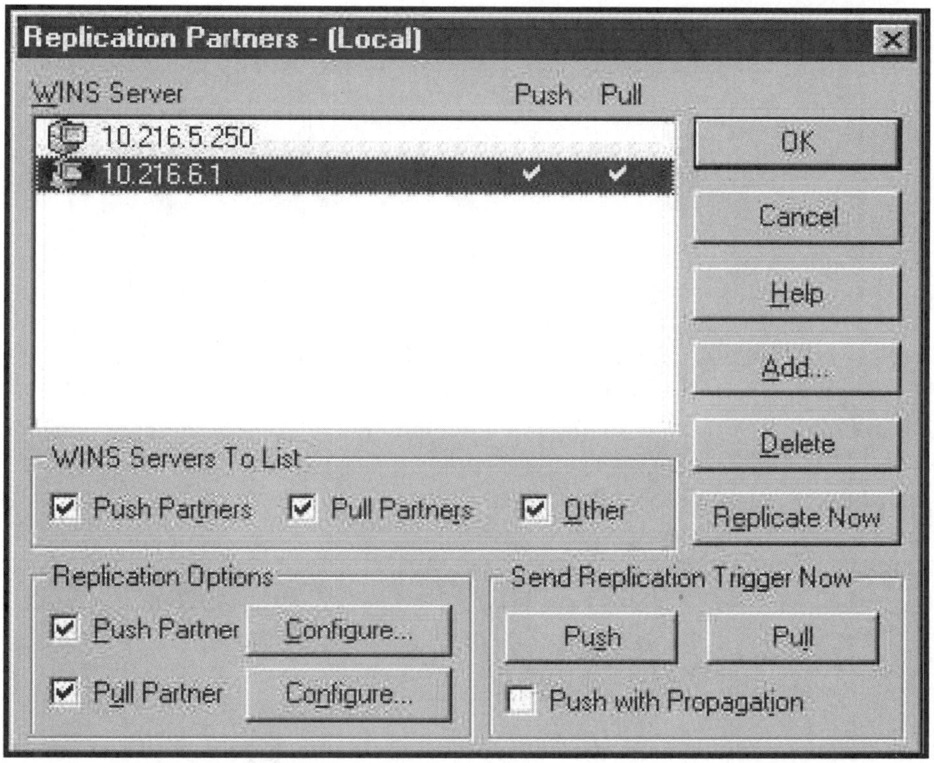

Push with Propagation. This will push information to all push partner WINS servers configured for WINS push replication, propagating the changes down the chain of WINS servers. If the check box is not selected, only the selected server will receive a push from the WINS server.

Let's take a look at the Configure buttons for replication.

PUSH REPLICATION CONFIGURATION

The push configuration does not have very much we can configure (see Figure 6-19). The Update Count field is all we can modify. This tells the WINS server when to replicate based on a predetermined number of changes. A small number here will force replication frequently assuring databases are synchronized. A larger value will reduce network traffic but other WINS servers will not receive updates as quickly. As usual, there is a trade-off between the accuracy of information and network performance.

FIGURE 6-19
Configure Push Replication Dialog.

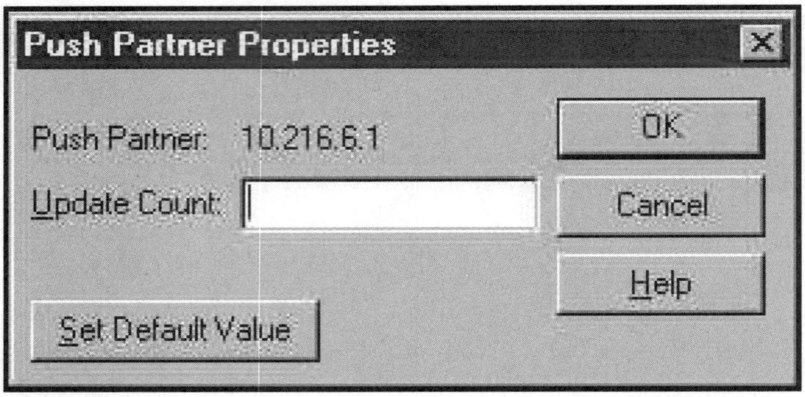

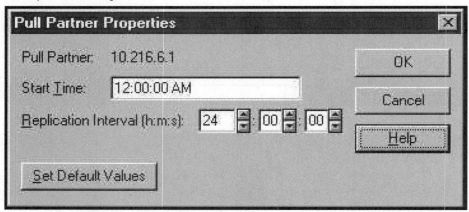

FIGURE 6-20
Pull Replication Configuration.

Type a number in the Update Count field. If you want this to be the default update count for the WINS server, click on the Select Default Value. When you have completed the entry, click OK for the changes to be saved.

PULL REPLICATION CONFIGURATION

The pull configuration allows us to specify two pieces of information (Figure 6-20). The first is an hour, minute, second entry specifying the time we want to replicate. This first value is not required but is necessary if you need to specify a particular time for replication to occur due to a slow WAN link or other considerations. The second value is required and designates how often pull replication should occur. In Figure 6-20, I have configured push replication to occur once a day (every 24 hours) at 12:00 A.M. in the morning.

If you wish to use these parameters as defaults, click on the Set Default Values button.

When you have completed the configuration, click on the OK button and your replication setting will be saved.

Integrating WINS and LMHOSTS

In some instances you may have to use both WINS and LMHOSTS files to enable browsing and remote subnet access. You might need to do this if you had a network with only one or two WINS servers and several other subnets that needed access. Remember that WINS can enable browsing across the subnets using replication. If a WINS server does not exist on a subnet, the only way to enable remote resource access is to use LMHOSTS files as specified in the previous lesson.

Wherever possible, you should try to use one method for name resolution. We always want to keep our management as simple as possible. If you need to use both mechanisms, keep the configuration as simple as possible to allow function, yet minimize your support time.

LAB

6.2 Installing and Configuring WINS

This lab allows you to practice and reinforce the concepts and configurations demonstrated in this lesson. To complete the lab, you must meet the minimum requirements outlined in the beginning lesson. Also, if you plan on completing the replication component of the lab, you will need two Windows NT WINS servers to configure. I have purposely not provided detailed instructions so you can practice the installation and configuration demonstrated earlier. Try to complete the lab from memory based on what you have learned. Answer all questions and share your results with the instructor when you have completed the lab.

On the Windows NT Servers:

1. Install the WINS service on two Windows NT servers.

2. Practice starting, pausing, and stopping the service using both mechanisms discussed in the chapter. What is different about the command line version versus the Services applet? Is there an order you must follow? If so, document it.

3. Configure both Windows NT servers as WINS clients providing primary and secondary WINS addresses of each WINS server you have configured.

4. Practice adding a static WINS entry for a unique computer. Ask your instructor for a valid computer and IP address to add. Review the entries in the database. Can you find the static entry you just made? What is its sixteenth byte identifier?

5. Configure Push/Pull replication between the two servers. Set the push interval to 100 records. Set the pull replication to occur automatically every 30 minutes.

6. Force replication using a trigger.

7. Open the WINS database and review the entries in your WINS database. Document the types of information stored for a computer, a domain, and a user.

8. If your installation is routed, try setting up Push/Pull replication between two WINS servers located on remote subnets. Push your changes to the remote server immediately. Did the replication work?

9. Discuss the results of this lab with your instructor.

Lesson 6.6 WINS Troubleshooting and Maintenance

This lesson takes a look at some common troubleshooting techniques and general maintenance you may be required to implement when you are working with a WINS server. In this lesson, we will discuss a useful command line utility called NBTSTAT as well as the mechanisms used in backing up and restoring your WINS server database.

General WINS and NetBIOS Troubleshooting

Because NetBIOS resolution uses several different methods to resolve names, it can be difficult to troubleshoot complicated installations. Some general recommendations for troubleshooting NetBIOS name resolution problems in Microsoft TCP/IP are found in the following list:

Check "dumb" things first. Always check the cables and connections before you proceed to rip a machine apart. Many problems can be resolved just by plugging a cable back into a wall jack!

PING the IP address. If a client reports they are unable to connect using a NetBIOS name, try pinging a host using its IP address. If this works, then it is indeed a name resolution problem. If it does not, it is most likely something to do with the general TCP/IP configuration.

Check the WINS addresses. Check to see if the WINS addresses are configured properly in TCP/IP properties for the client. Also, check to make sure the Hybrid node type is being used for name resolution on client. You can use the IPCONFIG /ALL utility to display this information.

Check the LMHOSTS file. If the client is using a LMHOSTS file, make sure the entries are correct and all the dependencies for the various # switches have been met. If you are running LMHOSTS on the servers, check those files as well.

Try browsing the local subnet. Can you see other computers? If not, there may be a general network problem or the master browser may have been taken offline. You can still try to connect using the Find Computer applet off the Start menu. If you can type a NetBIOS name and find the computer, everything is fine. Remember, it can take a while for a browse list to be rebuilt on a computer due to the way browsing works.

Check the WINS server. Is the service running? If it failed because of a corrupt database, restore it using the procedures in this lesson. Try the client again. Generally, if the WINS server goes down, clients will still be able to communicate on their local subnets using broadcasts. However, they will not be able to access folks on remote subnets using NetBIOS names. When you have many users reporting a problem like this, check the WINS server immediately for problems with replication configuration or the database.

Is a NetBIOS scope in place? If so, understand the limitations the scope places on communications. If clients need more access either expand or disable the scope.

This is by far not the exhaustive list of tests you can perform. But, in general, most problems can be resolved if you look at these areas.

The NBTSTAT Utility

NBTSTAT is a command line utility used to assist in troubleshooting NetBIOS name resolution problems or just to provide some basic information on the NBT interface. NBTSTAT is installed when TCP/IP is first configured. There are many options for NBTSTAT and they are case-sensitive. Some of the most useful are described here.

NBTSTAT –n. The –n switch presents a listing of the current NetBIOS names registered by the client. NBTSTAT –n produces output as follows as illustrated in Figure 6-21.

FIGURE 6-21
NBTSTAT –n Command Output.

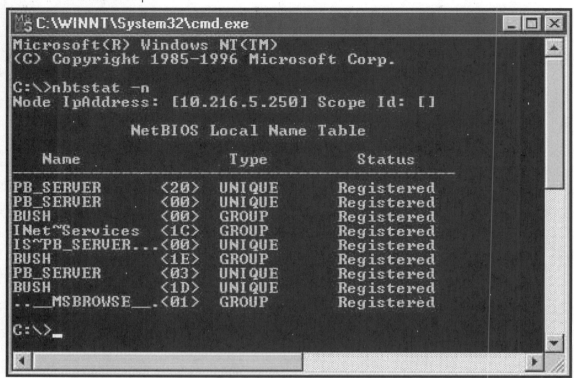

```
     C:\WINNT\System32\cmd.exe                        _ □ ×

Microsoft(R) Windows NT(TM)
(C) Copyright 1985-1996 Microsoft Corp.

C:\>nbtstat -n
Node IpAddress: [10.216.5.250] Scope Id: []

                NetBIOS Local Name Table

      Name              Type           Status
    ─────────────────────────────────────────────
    PB_SERVER    <20>   UNIQUE         Registered
    PB_SERVER    <00>   UNIQUE         Registered
    BUSH         <00>   GROUP          Registered
    INet~Services<1C>   GROUP          Registered
    IS~PB_SERVER...<00> UNIQUE         Registered
    BUSH         <1E>   GROUP          Registered
    PB_SERVER    <03>   UNIQUE         Registered
    BUSH         <1D>   UNIQUE         Registered
    ..__MSBROWSE__.<01> GROUP          Registered

C:\>_
```

NBTSTAT –c. The –c switch provides a listing of NetBIOS names loaded in NetBIOS cache. This is useful if you are preloading NetBIOS entries using a LMHOSTS file and you want to see if the load worked correctly. The output of the command is shown in Figure 6-22.

My computer is not using any static entries and therefore I do not have anything in cache. If I had preloaded some entries using an LMHOSTS file, they would be displayed here.

NBTSTAT –R. The –R switch allows you to manually reload cache entries specified in a LMHOSTS file. This is useful if you make changes in the LMHOSTS file and wish to refresh the cache without restarting the computer. The commands output is shown in Figure 6-23.

To access help on NBTSTAT, simply type **NBTSTAT** and press Return. A list of commands and switches available for use will be displayed.

FIGURE 6-22
NBTSTAT –c Command Output.

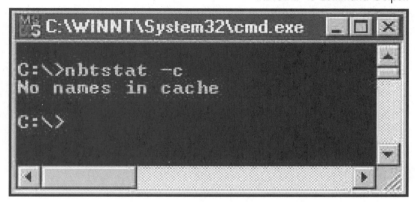

FIGURE 6-23
NBTSTAT –R Command Output.

WINS Database Maintenance

Typically, little or no maintenance is required on a WINS database. However, it is always a good policy to backup the WINS database periodically. This section reviews the procedures required to backup, restore, and compact the WINS database should the need arise.

BACKING UP THE DATABASE

A WINS backup is not completed automatically. You must configure it. To do this, you go to the Server menu and select the Configuration option as described earlier in the chapter. Once there, select the Advanced button and then configure a backup directory. Once configured, the WINS database will be automatically backed-up once a day on a twenty-four hour interval.

RESTORING THE WINS DATABASE

If WINS reports a corrupt database, it can be restored using one of the following methods.

Stop and restart the WINS service. WINS will automatically detect the corrupt file and restore the backup copy from the directory you specified earlier. You may use either Start/Stop method discussed in this chapter.

Use the Restore Local Database Menu Option. From the WINS Manager application, select the Mappings menu and then click on Restore Local Database. The database will be restored based on the backup directory you specify.

NOTE: *You must configure the backup database options for the Restore function to operate!*

Compressing the WINS Database

WINS automatically compacts the database on a regular basis so you should never have to do any manual compaction. If for some reason you must do this, there is a special utility included with WINS called the JETPACK utility. This utility compresses the WINS database. To complete the process, you must specify a temporary "working" file for compaction in the command. The command is as follows:

JETPACK wins.mdb temp.mdb

Temp.mdb can be any name you want to specify. When you execute the command, the database is compacted. When complete the temporary file is deleted.

NOTE: **Always** *stop WINS before attempting any database maintenance and make sure you have a backup copy of the file!*

Summary

This chapter covered NetBIOS name resolution and its importance in the Microsoft TCP/IP protocol. We learned the following concepts and skills in this chapter.

NetBIOS Naming. We learned what a NetBIOS name is, some of the important characteristics of NetBIOS names, and how NetBIOS naming is integrated within Microsoft Networking.

NBT. We learned about NBT and its relationship to both NetBIOS transport and TCP/IP. We also learned the process of how a Microsoft client goes about resolving names.

LMHOSTS. We learned about the purpose, function, and how to configure a LMHOSTS file on a client. We also looked at methods for allowing NetBIOS browsing and resource access across routed networks.

The Microsoft Browsing Process. We learned how the Network Neighborhood Browse List is built, how different computers function on a network, and what limitations browse lists have when being run in a routed network.

WINS. We learned why WINS is an important and useful tool in managing NetBIOS name resolution. We also learned how to install and configure WINS to provide name resolution, static mappings, and push/pull replication between computers.

Troubleshooting. We learned some useful techniques and tools for troubleshooting a WINS installation including NBTSTAT. We also learned how to backup, restore, and compress the WINS database.

● ● ● ● ● ● ● ● ● ● ● ● ●

Q & A

1. *Select the best answer.* John is a network administrator of a small TCP/IP installation. He wishes to limit NetBIOS broadcast traffic on the network. What is the best mechanism for allowing John to complete his objectives?

   a. Implement IP routing.
   b. Configure several NetBIOS scopes.
   c. Configure RIP for IP.
   d. Install a router.
   e. None of the above.

2. *Select the best answer.* Mark wants to enable browsing across two subnets. He has installed two WINS servers; one on each remote subnet. What must Mark enable to allow users to access computers and resources on the remote subnet?

   a. DNS replication.
   b. NetBIOS scopes.
   c. LMHOSTS files.
   d. WINS replication.
   e. RIP for IP.

3. *Select the best answer.* Bruce wants to allow a measure of fault tolerance in his WINS server network, enabling a client to use multiple WINS servers should one fail. How can Bruce implement this objective?

   a. Install primary and secondary WINS servers on the client.
   b. Configure the client to access primary and secondary WINS servers.
   c. Implement multiple LMHOSTS files pointing to the WINS servers using the #INCLUDE command.
   d. Configure the client to access a NetBIOS WINS scope and use DNS parameters.
   e. None of these solutions will work.

4. *Select the best answer.* Sandy needs to restore her WINS database because of a corrupted file. However, she never configured a backup directory for the file. How can Sandy restore her WINS database?

   a. Do nothing. The database will be automatically restored when WINS detects it is corrupt.
   b. Use the Restore Local Database option, then restart the WINS service.
   c. Manually copy the database to the WINS subdirectory.
   d. Replicate as a pull partner to refresh the entire database.
   e. This cannot be accomplished.

5. *Select the best answer.* When configuring DHCP to lease WINS entries, what NBT node resolution type should be selected?

   a. B-Type.
   b. P-Type.
   c. M-Type.
   d. H-Type.
   e. Microsoft Enhanced B-Node Type.

6. *Select all that apply.* What additional name resolution mechanisms can be used to resolve NetBIOS names to IP addresses if the standard tools and methods fail?

   a. Secondary WINS servers
   b. LMHOSTS files
   c. DNS
   d. HOSTS files
   e. WINS replication

7. *Select the best answer.* Dawn needs to implement WINS replication across a slow WAN link. She wants to be sure that she does not impact network performance. What type of replication should Dawn implement?

   a. Push replication at night.
   b. Pull replication during the day.
   c. Push replication during the day.
   d. Pull replication at night.
   e. You cannot configure replication to occur at a specified time period.

8. *Select the best answer.* Harry manages a small TCP/IP network that is not WINS enabled. He needs to provide NetBIOS name resolution for his clients while limiting broadcast traffic. What should Harry do?

   a. Install HOSTS files on both the server and clients.
   b. Install HOSTS files on all the clients.
   c. Install LMHOSTS files on both the server and all the clients.
   d. Install a LMHOSTS file on the clients only.
   e. Install a HOSTS file on the server only.

9. *Select the best answer.* Samantha needs to provide name resolution services to non-WINS UNIX clients on a heterogeneous-routed TCP/IP network. What can Samantha do to provide this service?

   a. Install the WINS Manager on a UNIX server.
   b. Implement a WINS proxy on a NT workstation.
   c. Implement broadcast resolution on all the UNIX computers.
   d. Configure a LMHOSTS file on the UNIX computers.
   e. NetBIOS name resolution cannot occur for a non-WINS enabled client.

10. *Select the best answer.* Jack needs to troubleshoot a client's NT workstation WINS resolution problem. What utilities could Jack use to display the NetBIOS node type in use on the DHCP configured client?

    a. NBTSTAT
    b. NETSTAT
    c. PING
    d. IPCONFIG
    e. WINIPCFG

11. *Select the best answer.* Martha needs to refresh the NetBIOS name cache on a Windows NT workstation. What command should Martha use?

    a. NBTSTAT –C
    b. NBTSTAT –c
    c. NBTSTAT –r
    d. NBSTAT –R
    e. NBTSTAT –p
    f. None of these commands will work.

12. *Select the best answer.* Tom is having problems with browse lists being retained on his network. He has several controllers installed. Some are Windows NT 3.51, some are version 4.0, and his test lab is using a Windows NT 5.0 Beta 2 controller. Why is Tom's browse list being reset constantly?

    a. The NT 5.0 Server is conflicting with the browse masters on the network.
    b. The NT 5.0 server is constantly being restarted.
    c. The election process does not operate properly with multiple versions of Windows NT.
    d. The Domain Master Browser is malfunctioning.
    e. None of the above are the problem.

13. *Select all that apply.* Of the following computers, which can serve as master browsers for a network?

    a. Windows NT servers
    b. Windows 3.11 clients
    c. Windows NT workstations
    d. UNIX workstations
    e. Windows 95 clients

14. *Select all that apply.* The LMHOSTS file contains several additional keywords that assist in managing a routed network implementation of Windows NT using NetBIOS name resolution. What commands would allow a host to be preloaded in name cache and specify a domain controller?

    a. 10.10.10.10   PDC1   #PRE
    b. 10.10.10.10   PDC1   #DOM:DOMAIN1 #PRE
    c. 10.10.10.10   PDC1   #INCLUDE #DOM:DOMAIN1 #PRE
    d. 10.10.10.10   PDC1   #PRE #DOM:DOMAIN1
    e. 10.10.10.10   PDC1   #INCLUDE #DOM:DOMAIN1

15. *Select the best answer.* Nancy is troubleshooting a TCP/IP configuration for one of her users. The user reports that she is unable to connect to any resources using an IP address but can see herself in Network Neighborhood. What is the most likely problem?

   a. The primary WINS server is incorrect.
   b. The LMHOSTS file has incorrect entries.
   c. WINS is not enabled.
   d. The Use DNS for WINS Resolution is not enabled.
   e. There is a local TCP/IP configuration problem.

THE DOMAIN NAME SYSTEM AND MICROSOFT DNS SERVER

OBJECTIVES

By the end of this chapter, you should be able to:

■ Describe basic terminology surrounding DNS implementations.

■ Describe DNS generically and the various methods available to resolve FQDN names to IP addresses using the service.

■ Explain the relationship between HOSTS files and DNS and how Windows NT uses both to assist in the name resolution process.

■ Define commonly used DNS configurations and servers given requirements.

■ Explain the function of common DNS database files including cache, and reverse lookup files.

■ Install and configure the Microsoft DNS service.

■ Perform basic administration of DNS domains and zones.

■ Explain how DNS can be integrated with a WINS server for expanded name resolution functionality.

■ Describe the purpose and function of the NSLOOKUP utility in troubleshooting and gathering DNS server information.

Introduction

This chapter explores DNS and the Microsoft DNS Server service. We have talked at a high-level about DNS previously. Now it is time for us to delve deeper into this extremely important name resolution mechanism in a TCP/IP network.

As you will recall, DNS is used to resolved Fully Qualified Domain Names (FQDN) into IP addresses. The material in this chapter is not designed to be the be all to end all of DNS—entire books are written on administration of DNS servers! However, this chapter will provide you with an excellent foundation for both the Microsoft exam and your continuing studies in TCP/IP name resolution technologies.

Lesson 7.1 DNS Overview

This lesson provides an overview of the history and terminology required for you to fully grasp the DNS service and its relationship to the HOSTS file. Information in this lesson will be used throughout the balance of the chapter—so be sure you understand the definitions, terms, and concepts presented in this lesson before you begin working with DNS.

What Is DNS?

DNS is a hierarchical, static database that stores IP addresses and FQDN information for TCP/IP hosts. It also stores various information about the types of hosts on the TCP/IP network. The server allows a computer application and users to use user-friendly FQDN names for hosts on a network. In terms of structure, it closely resembles a directory tree used for file management. Each "directory" is associated with a level of DNS server. The servers all work together to piece together and resolve a FQDN to an IP address.

DNS is often described as a telephone directory of sorts. Multiple books (servers) cover different geographic regions and states (domains) and the combination of all the books together forms a master telephone directory (the overall DNS name space). When you use a telephone book, you are in essence performing a phone number lookup to a person's name and address. DNS does exactly the same thing except it looks up an IP address, based on a FQDN entry (which, as we will see later, is comprised of all the information necessary to resolve and route the address to the appropriate host). DNS also allows us to lookup a FQDN based on a known IP address. This is called a **Reverse Lookup.**

This whole process of looking up things is called a **query.** A query is nothing more than a search for information. Query is a common term used across all databases to define a search for something. We can use the term "lookup" and "query" synonymously.

A Little DNS History

Way back in the stone age of TCP/IP (the 1970s), DNS did not exist. When TCP/IP was first developed, a simple text file was used for all FQDN name resolution. As you recall, this file is known as the HOSTS file. This file was maintained by one institution and all requests for name resolution went through this institution. Some poor soul spent a great deal of time adding and deleting entries in this file, which was fine in the beginning when there were not all that many host to IP mappings. As TCP/IP increased in popularity, this file became cumbersome to maintain, was error prone, and required clients to periodically download updates. This caused heavy network traffic against the master maintenance site as more and more clients came onboard. As you should also recall, the HOSTS file needs to be located locally on a machine for name resolution to occur.

As is the case with all things computer, we came up with a better idea! An extremely bright scholar named Dr. Paul Mockapetris thought that this whole name resolution process could be better administered if it were distributed and managed between sites. The sites would need to be connected in some fashion to allow all the different sites to resolve each other's names and presto! DNS was born.

The original objective of DNS was to replace the HOSTS file with a small and efficient database system allowing for individual and modularized name space management and administration, unlimited combined database size and reasonable performance across the then new TCP/IP inter-network ARPANET. Today, DNS has indeed lived up to its expectations! With literally millions of Internet hosts, DNS is still the primary method of name resolution and it continues to grow in scope and use. It has lived up to all its initial objectives (and probably exceeded everybody's expectations of what it could do!).

Databases and DNS

Databases are nothing more than large storage banks of information that can be queried and results reported to users. *DNS is a hierarchical, client/server-based, distributed database management system.* Yikes—That's a mouthful! However, if we take a look at this statement we will find that it is a lot of complicated words that net into some very simple concepts:

Hierarchical. A directory-like structure from generic to specific needed to be created. This defines a hierarchical database. In database-ease, there are two types of databases: hierarchical (like IBM's IMS database) and Relational (like Microsoft's SQL Server). When DNS was developed, relational technology was in its infancy and almost all databases were hierarchical. If this whole thing were developed today, it would probably would have been done using a relational database.

Client-Server Based. We are using a client to request information and a server to resolve it. In DNS, clients can be both the initiating host and a lower level DNS server. Servers return DNS responses to the clients. In this manner we can move up and down (called *traversing*) the DNS tree to find the correct resolution to a client DNS query.

Distributed Database. DNS is not located in any one spot. The system is based on the basic principle of distributed management, meaning that lots of little databases all work together to comprise the master directory tree. This makes DNS extremely *extensible* (a fancy term for expandable) and modular.

Now that we understand where and why this whole system was created, lets look at some of the terminology required for us to understand how this whole system is "put together."

Lesson 7.2 The Nuts-and-Bolts of DNS

Resolvers and Name Servers

At the most generic and fundamental level, DNS consists of two types of hosts: the Resolver and the Name Server. A brief definition of each is provided here.

Resolver. This is a fancy name for the client who is making the request for name resolution! A resolver is usually a type of program that acts on behalf of the host to request the name resolution from the other type of DNS computer—the Name server.

Name Server. A name server is exactly what it appears to be. It is the "telephone book" of FQDN to IP mappings for a particular area. Resolvers pass their name resolution requests to the name server to find the answer to their name lookup or query. The name server will either return the mapping from its database or begin the process of querying other name servers to resolve the FQDN. There are several methods of query which we will discuss in just a bit.

Armed with this basic knowledge of terms, we can now take a look at how DNS generically deals with name resolution in its directory management structure.

The Name Resolution Process

DNS uses three methods to resolve addresses. Depending on the particular situation, more than one of the methods outlined in this section may be (and often times is) used. What is important to remember as you work through this section is that all these mechanisms work together for name resolution. You should understand the basic process of resolution once you have worked your way through the following paragraphs.

There are three types of name resolution queries that a client (or resolver) can make of a DNS server. Don't forget that a DNS name server as well as a requesting client host can be a resolver to another DNS name server. The three types of resolution are explained here.

RECURSIVE QUERIES

Recursive queries are usually executed from a local client to a DNS server. The basic premise behind a recursive query is that the DNS server cannot refer the client's request to another server. The name server, in effect, will manage the rest of the resolution process if it cannot itself resolve the address. Recursive queries will either return a name mapping or an error.

Name servers responsible for processing these type of requests may end up forwarding the client request onto other DNS servers for resolution. As the owning DNS server receives information on the name resolution, it caches (or stores in memory) the responses it receives from all the other servers. Assuming all goes well, the name will be resolved to the requested FQDN and this information is then returned to the initial resolver (the client). If it doesn't go well, an error message will be returned.

ITERATIVE QUERIES

Iterative queries are usually performed between servers. In this type of query, a DNS server will return its best-known information to the requesting server. This can consist either of the resolved name to IP address mapping or the address of another name server who might be able to resolve the request. To resolve one FQDN for a client, several iterative queries may be issued to other name servers. Each one should get the owning server a little closer to resolving (or not) the FQDN for the client.

INVERSE QUERIES

The last type of query that can be issued is known as an *inverse query*. This is also referred to as a reverse lookup. In this situation, the resolver knows the IP address but needs to resolve that IP address into a FQDN. We are doing the exact opposite mapping that we have been discussing up to this point. Inverse queries are processed using a special domain that must be configured on each DNS server. This domain is called **in-addr.arpa.**

This whole in-addr.arpa thing will be explained in greater depth in just a bit. Suffice to say, it looks very weird upon first glance. For now, it is fine to just understand what an inverse query is.

CACHING OF RESULTS

You have seen the effect of caching before using ARP. It is a method of storing frequently used information for a time period in memory. Lots of things use caching besides TCP/IP protocols and utilities—hard disks, CPUs, programs, and many others. The principle of use is exactly the same for all these components regardless of their function: To speed things up!

DNS servers completing recursive queries cache results they have received from the iterative queries they issued. In the event another requestor asks for the same FQDN, the DNS server can immediately answer the request without marching through another several iterative queries to find the same information. Cached query results are stored in physical memory—so resolution is blazingly fast while the entry exists.

Cached information is stored for a period of time before being flushed from memory. This amount of time is referred to as the TTL, or *Time To Live.*

The DNS administrator decides on the TTL for the data. Once the name has been resolved and it is cached, the server begins decrementing (lowering) the value of the TTL. When the value reaches 0 (zero), the information is flushed from memory. If another "hit" occurs while the TTL is live, it will be reset to the value specified by the administrator and then begin decrementing again.

There is a trade-off here: smaller cache values will mean that the FQDN is updated more regularly but this puts more load on the server. Longer TTLs will reduce load on the server but you run the risk of a FQDN resolution entry being out-of-date. In most instances, the default values for TTL will work just fine. The rule is "If it isn't broken, don't fix it!"

OK, now we understand how the resolution process occurs. Now let's look at some DNS specific terminology that will help us to configure the Microsoft DNS server later in the chapter.

Lesson 7.3 Putting More Pieces in Place

DNS, not unlike many computer systems, is laden with terminology that is specific to its implementation. It will be difficult for you to manage any DNS server without some basic understanding of these terms and their placement in DNS. This section will help to define all the terms you will need to configure Microsoft's DNS Server later in this chapter.

The "Big Directory in the Sky." As we said previously, DNS is nothing more than a bunch of directory trees all hooked together with little databases. The composite of all these databases and the entire DNS tree structure is globally known as the **DNS Name Space.** DNS Name Space is also used to refer to an individual domain's area of responsibility. Each component of the tree can have a name up to 63 characters in length. The components are all separated by periods resulting in our notation of www.anywhere.com.

The top of this tree is called the **Root Domain.** The root domain uses a null (nothing) label, but when referring to the root domain it can be symbolized by a lone period (.). In the United States, there are seven root domain name servers, and they are administered by InterNIC.

The next level in the hierarchy is divided into a series of directories called **top-level domains.** The top-level domains are assigned organizationally using identifiers like "com", "gov", "org", "edu", and by country. All top-level domains have name servers administered by InterNIC. Top-level domains contain individual domains, subdomains, and hosts.

Domain. Each discrete node in the DNS Name Space is called a *Domain*. This type of domain is very different than a Windows NT domain! A DNS domain is a branch in the DNS tree that can occur anywhere in the DNS Name Space overall tree structure. It is much like adding a subdirectory in DOS. There is no limit to the number of domains in DNS—it is important however to understand that all the domains are organized in a very specific structure.

Domains can be further segmented on DNS servers into *Subdomains*. A subdomain is a member of its parent. It is like creating a subdirectory within another directory. Individual domains and subdomains are usually managed by individual organizations or ISPs. Root level domains are managed by InterNIC.

Zone. A zone is a portion of a DNS domain that contains database records (also known as a resource record) for individual computers. Zones are associated with a particular domain. There can be many zones within a domain. A single DNS server can manage one or multiple zones depending on the situation. If the DNS server has resource records associated with it, it is said to have *authority* over that zone. All the subdomains and their associated zones are hooked together in an association with the organization's domain name. This domain name is known as the zone's **Root Domain.**

Resource Records. Zones are comprised of database records for individual computers called resource records. Resource records are used to configure a DNS server and categorize workstations based on the particular function of different computers in the domain. Resource records include such entries as the SOA, A, CNAME, and MX record types. We will learn more about these in a bit.

Host Names. This is the name you refer to a host by in DNS. It does not have to be the NetBIOS name of the computer. Computers in DNS can have multiple names called **"aliases."** For instance, one server can serve as both a ftp and www server. In this case, the machine would have two entries in the DNS database, one specifying it as an ftp server and the other specifying it as a www server. To a client, it appears as two separate machines when in reality it is really only one. The hostname is limited to 256 characters, but they are usually much shorter to facilitate easy use.

Got all that terminology? It's OK if it doesn't sink in right away. Think about it a bit and then review this section. It's all very organized once you get used to it! We're almost done with the terminology we need to manage DNS. The only thing left for us to explore are the types of DNS servers. These are discussed in the next lesson.

Lesson 7.4 DNS Name Server Types

DNS name servers store information about portions of the individual domains, resources, and zones. There are three main types of DNS servers that we will need to know. These are discussed below:

PRIMARY NAME SERVERS

A primary name server is a DNS server that "owns" resource record data. In other words, it has locally (the records "live" on its hard disk) entered information for a particular zone. If one needs to change the DNS entries on a server, these changes are *always* performed on a primary name server.

SECONDARY NAME SERVERS

A secondary name server gets its data from another DNS server (usually but not always a primary name server). A secondary server actually receives a copy of the zone database it services. However, this copy cannot be modified on the secondary server. It is in effect, "read-only." All entries to the zone must be made on the primary name server. The copy process used to transfer the database is referred to as a *Zone Transfer.*

The source of the zone information for a secondary name server is referred to as a *Master Name Server* (another name for the Primary Name Server). When a secondary name server initializes, it contacts the master name server and begins a zone transfer. Zone transfers also can occur periodically (provided that data on the master name server has changed). This is set as an option in a special resource record called the Start of Authority (SOA).

Why Use a Secondary Name Server? There are three main reasons to place secondary name servers in the DNS server mix. These rationales are not all that different than any of the other reasons you are already familiar with regarding PDCs and BDCs! Secondary name servers are put in place for one or all of the following reasons:

Fault Tolerance. If you want to implement any type of fault tolerance in the DNS hierarchy, at least two DNS servers are required for any particular zone. One of these must be a primary and the other would be a secondary. In the event the primary went down, the secondary could still service requests although you would be unable to make any changes to the database. This is essentially the same setup Windows NT uses in the PDC/BDC fault tolerance management strategy.

Network and Client Optimization. Secondary name servers serve a very important role in network optimization in large-scale WAN-based DNS implementations. A significant reduction in response time can be initiated by using secondary name servers on the other side of a slow WAN link. This reduces query traffic across the link since only an occasional zone transfer is necessary and speeds resolution for the clients. The same principle applies to placement of Windows NT BDCs on the other side of a slow WAN link for better network performance and speed in validating logons.

Load Balancing. Use of multiple secondary servers has the effect of reducing the overall load on a primary DNS server. Several DNS servers can be configured for a client to use and it really doesn't care which one it gets—as long as its request is answered. Adding secondary name servers tends to increase performance for clients as well as reducing the load on the primary server. Here again, Windows NT PDC/BDC configurations use this type of setup for load balancing.

ONE FINAL WORD ON SECONDARY NAME SERVERS:

I bet you thought you had everything you needed to know about secondary servers. . . . Not quite. Secondary servers can also serve as primary servers! Good grief! It's not all that hard to understand though. Remember that there can be multiple zones associated with one DNS server. It is totally possible for one DNS server to be a secondary name server for one zone and the primary for another.

CACHE SERVERS

The last type of DNS server you can configure is called a *Cache Server.* These specialized servers are not authoritative for any zone, they have no database, and their sole purpose in life is to resolve DNS queries using cached information.

We've talked about this caching thing before. All DNS servers do this to store results from FQDN queries to other servers. It's fast! The big difference with a dedicated DNS cache server is that that's all they have—cached results. As you might expect, a cached server can only exist in an environment where there is a primary and/or secondary server running in the mix. Caching servers forward almost all of their initial queries until their internal cache can be built. However, once that cache is built, look out! Resolution occurs at a lightning pace because data is being read directly from memory. It should come as no surprise that caching servers are used to enhance performance in a DNS environment without using a bunch of computer resources. However, a caching server cannot be used for any type of fault tolerance. If the server is brought down for any reason, the cache must be rebuilt from ground zero.

Obviously, the more memory dedicated to the cache, the more data that can be held. So, if you are planning on using a cache server, it should be equipped with plenty of memory dedicated to its primary purpose.

Variations on a Basic Theme

Primary, secondary, and caching servers are also classified by how they access local and wide area networks. DNS servers are classified as either forwarders or slaves. Now, you don't have to be a computer genius to figure out the purpose of these subclasses of the servers we have just discussed. A forwarding server is allowed to access the WAN to process its iterative queries. A slave server must send its requests through a forwarding server for processing if the record cannot be resolved in the local zone. Within this arrangement there are two types of DNS servers: *exclusive* and *non-exclusive.*

Nonexclusive DNS servers attempt to use a designated forwarding server first. The forwarding server does all the hard work, while the nonexclusive DNS server waits for the results. If the request is not resolved, then the nonexclusive server will attempt to resolve the address on its own.

Exclusive DNS servers rely completely on forwarding servers for resolution. The DNS server using an exclusive mode for resolution is known as a slave server. If the name cannot be resolved using a forwarder, the name resolution process fails. This is where their name comes from—the DNS server is a slave to the forwarder to whom they send their requests. They are completely dependent on resolution from the forwarder. A caching server should almost always be configured as an exclusive server because it is completely dependent on other servers for the construction of its local cache.

DNS Server Planning

DNS server planning is similar to planning any implementation of servers. There are several items you will need to be concerned with that are specific to DNS but generally, all the things we worried about with WINS and NT servers in terms of WAN links, redundancy, and load-balancing must be taken into account and planned for. In general, you will need to do the following if you are planning an Internet presence using DNS:

Pick and Register a Domain Name. At a bare minimum, you will need to pick a domain name and get that name registered with InterNIC if you are planning on implementing a Internet-attached DNS Server. This is not required if you are using a DNS server for Intranet access.

Plan, Plan and then Plan more! The importance of designing your overall network and defining placement of servers on the front-end cannot be stressed enough. Understanding your environment and planning accordingly will save you a huge amount of rework (and aggravation) in the long term. Ask yourself the following questions.

Do I really need to manage my own DNS Servers? In many cases, it may not be required. Your Internet Service Provider is typically very capable of hosting your DNS management. Unless you are working for a very large organization that requires constant maintenance and entry of hosts and resource records, an ISP may be a very good choice. Many ISPs provide primary and secondary DNS hosting as part of your monthly connection charges.

Do I require a fault tolerant configuration? If you do and you are implementing your own DNS System you will require at least one primary server and a secondary server.

Will my sites be connected via a slow WAN link? If so, you will want to consider using either a secondary or caching server on the termination end of the link. For really slow links (less than 56K) consider using a caching server since this type of server does not have to do a zone transfer and will minimize traffic on the line. However, make sure you understand the trade-offs between secondary and caching servers.

How many zones will I really need? Can I get by with just one primary domain or will I need to further break out the DNS tree to include subdomains? This question will be defined by organizational requirements. Be sure to plan for this as you design your DNS structure.

How many users will be accessing the DNS Server? Understanding this parameter will help you to determine whether additional servers will be required to load-balance your DNS traffic. Nothing is more frustrating to a user than slow connect and resolution times! You can add secondary and/or caching servers as required to help manage load balancing in your network environment.

Lesson 7.5 Common DNS Files and Resource Records

This lesson looks at some common resource records and files used with DNS generally, and Microsoft DNS Server specifically. As was the case with DHCP, there are many different types of resource records and files associated with DNS. The information in this section is not intended to provide the complete authority on DNS record and file types. It is designed to introduce you to the most common types of records and files you will encounter.

DNS Database Files

The following files are not used by default by Microsoft DNS Server. These files are flat text files that contain information allowing a DNS server to initialize. Since all the work we do in Microsoft DNS manager is done via the GUI interface provided by the application, editing these files is not required. However, they are used in other types of DNS implementations. If you needed to import data from another DNS server you could do so by using these files. Samples of the flat files are located in the \WINNT\System32\DNS\Samples subdirectory.

DNS BOOT FILES

The Boot File. This file controls the initialization of a DNS Server. It contains information on the location of all the files listed here as well all domains for which the DNS server will have authority. Normally, Microsoft DNS server does not require this file but you can make modifications in the registry to use it if required.

The Database File. This is the "master" DNS database for a zone. It contains all the resource entries for the zone. This file is typically named based on the domain name the DNS Server services. For instance, if we were working at Compaq, the name of this file might be "compaq.com.dns". A sample of this file and the type/syntax of entries is located in the samples subdirectory and is called "Place.dns".

The Cache File. This file contains all the addresses for the root Internet DNS servers at InterNIC. This file is configured by default and is used by Microsoft DNS Server to begin its iterative queries for any zone outside its authority. The file's name is Cache.dns. If a DNS server is only serving an internal Intranet, this file should be modified with appropriate entries for the authoritative domains within its namespace.

The Reverse Lookup File. This file contains the information necessary for a resolver to complete a reverse lookup using the special in.addr.arpa domain. The file contains various resource records similar to those found in the database. Additionally, pointer records are found in this file.

It is not necessary for you to be able to edit or maintain these files for use of Microsoft DNS Server, so we won't complicate matters. What is important is that you understand what these files are, what they do, and when you might be required to use them.

Common DNS Resource Records

As you recall, DNS resource records allow computers in a DNS database to be defined for a particular purpose. This includes defining a DNS server. There are many types of records that are usable by DNS to identify host computers. The table on the following page outlines the most common types of resource records we will encounter when looking at a DNS server.

Lesson 7.6 FQDN Name Resolution Revisited

Throughout this book we have been discussing name resolution using a FQDN. By this point in our education we are pretty familiar with the two mechanisms we use to resolve FQDN's to IP addresses: DNS and the Hosts

COMMON DNS RECORD TYPES

RECORD TYPE	BRIEF DESCRIPTION
SOA	Identifies the start of a zone of authority
A	A host address
NS	The authoritative name server for the domain
PTR	A pointer to another part of the domain name space
CNAME	The canonical name of an alias
MX	Identifies a mail exchange server for the domain
WINS	Allows DNS server to use a WINS server to lookup the host portion of a DNS name
WINS-R	WINS reverse lookup. This resource record instructs the name server to use a reverse lookup request for IP addresses that are not given in PTR records contained in a reverse lookup domain. This record is used with, and configured exclusively with, the in-addr.arpa domain.
HINFO	Host information—this is often used to identify the CPU and OS used by the host computer

file. This lesson looks a little deeper into the actual internal process a Microsoft client uses to resolve a hostname.

DNS, WINS, and HOSTS Files

It is not uncommon for several types of name resolution to be in effect in any particular network situation. Different circumstances like application and operating system requirements may require the use of DNS, HOSTS, LMHOSTS, WINS or a combination of any of these methods. Microsoft clients use a very structured and organized approach to resolving NetBIOS and FQDN names. This section takes a quick look at that process and what you can expect when running flat file and database name resolution mechanisms.

The Microsoft Host Name Resolution Process

Microsoft clients use all the tools available to try and resolve hostnames. There is a definite method to its madness, and it follows the same process each time a client requests a resource on a hostname. This process is somewhat similar to how NetBIOS name resolution occurs in the previous chapter with a couple of extra steps that integrate DNS and WINS into the mix:

1. The first thing a Microsoft client checks when a hostname access request is made is if the local hostname is the same as the one being requested. If this is the case, the name is resolved internally with no additional network activity.

2. Assuming the host is remote (anywhere but local), the client will then parse (read through) the HOSTS file if one has been configured on the workstation. Remember that HOSTS and LMHOSTS files must reside locally on a client to be used! If an entry exists for the hostname in the HOSTS file, it is resolved and transmissions begin.

3. If no HOSTS file is present or there is no entry in the HOSTS file for the remote host, the client will then send off a request to its configured DNS servers attempting to resolve the name. If an entry is found using DNS, host resolution occurs and communications begin.

4. If DNS is unsuccessful in resolving the address, the client resorts to checking its local NetBIOS name cache and the LMHOSTS file. If it doesn't find the host there, it queries a WINS server to see if it can be resolved. If an entry is found using either mechanism, host resolution occurs and communications begin.

5. If nothing else works, the client makes a broadcast on the local subnet attempting to find the host.

6. If that doesn't work, an error message is generated.

As you can see, the client attempts to minimize network traffic by trying local methods first before issuing requests across the network. If at any step the name is resolved, the process stops. This resolution mechanism provides an efficient and complete way of resolving names no matter what system is being used.

Lesson 7.7 Installing and Configuring Microsoft DNS Server

This lesson steps you through the process of installing and configuring the Microsoft DNS Server. As was the case with WINS, many of the steps in installing the software will be similar. However, the similarities stop there! Whereas WINS is dynamic and updates itself automatically, DNS has no such mechanism. Much of what we will do in this lesson focuses on the process for adding and configuring a DNS server with a zone and several key resource records. The lab at the end of this section will allow you to install and test your own DNS server using the steps outlined in this section.

General Installation Requirements

DNS should use a static IP address configuration for installation. While DNS can be installed on a server that is a DHEP client, this is not recommended.

Also, it is important the DNS properties of the NT server you install DNS on is configured with a domain and host name. The DNS Service pulls information from your internal TCP/IP configuration. For the exercise, we will be working in the classroom.com domain. Your computer name will be the host name used when you complete the lab. To check this information, you will need to look at the DNS tab of the TCP/IP protocol properties in Network Control Panel. This tab appears in Figure 7-1.

Assuming this information is in place, when DNS is installed and you create a zone, the service will automatically add a SOA record for the zone and A and NS records corresponding to the server. If the host and domain names are not configured, then only a SOA record for the zone will be created! You will have to manually add the other records.

FIGURE 7-1
The DNS Tab.

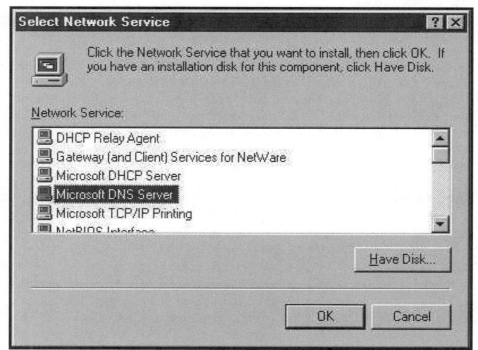

Installing the Microsoft DNS Server Service

1. Installing the Microsoft DNS Server Service is like installing any other network service. We begin the process by opening the Network Control Panel and selecting the Services Tab. Click on the Add button and highlight the Microsoft DNS server. Your screen should look like Figure 7-2.

2. Select **Microsoft DNS Server** and click **OK.** Files will be copied from your distribution directory and you will be prompted to restart.

3. When the computer restarts, be sure to reapply any service packs you installed under Windows NT. Restart your computer when prompted.

4. When the computer reboots, the Microsoft DNS Server Service will start automatically

That's it for the installation of the software! Now, on to configuring Microsoft DNS Server!

Basic Configuration of Microsoft DNS Server

Microsoft DNS Server requires quite a bit of configuration to function correctly. Because DNS uses a static database, entries must be manually configured by the user. All DNS servers require this manual configuration—it is just the nature of the beast. This section of the lesson will lead you through the process of initially configuring the Microsoft DNS Server for operation and adding a few key resource record entries. As is the case with many different computer systems, there is a certain order things must be completed in. This section takes a methodical step-by-step approach to configuring the server. In general, you should always follow this order when working with DNS otherwise unpredictable results may occur. Keeping that in mind, let's get started:

THE BLANK SLATE

When you first open Microsoft DNS Server, it is configured as a caching server with entries pointing to the root domain servers at InterNIC. This is the default configuration for DNS since we have not told the service anything else about zones or resources that might be part of the DNS domain structure. In most cases, we will need to do more configuration to identify the server as either a primary or secondary DNS machine. Keeping this in mind, let's start by opening the DNS Manager application and configuring a zone for our server.

To open the DNS Manager application, click on Start, Administrative Tools, and select the DNS Manager application. When DNS Manager opens, your screen should look something like Figure 7-3.

FIGURE 7-2
DNS Server Entry on Services Tab.

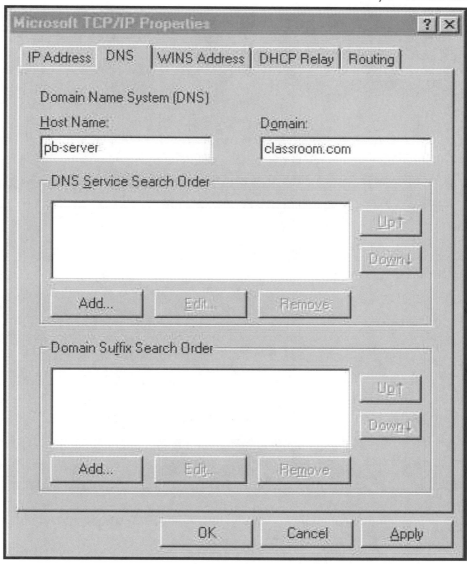

FIGURE 7-3
DNS Manager Screen.

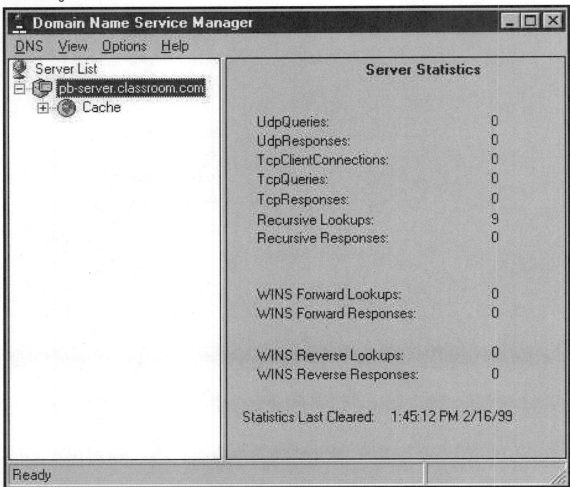

STEP 1—ADDING A ZONE

As we have learned all DNS information is grouped and controlled by zones. Before we can do anything meaningful with the server we must first create a zone

To do this, right-click the server name to initiate a shortcut menu for the server. Then, click **New Zone.** Your screen should appear as that in Figure 7-4.

Click on the New Zone option.

STEP 2—DETERMINE PRIMARY OR SECONDARY ZONE

After selecting New Zone from the menu, a dialog box appears that asks if the zone being created is a primary zone (information stored locally) or a secondary zone (information obtained from a master server by means of a zone

FIGURE 7-4
Creating a New Zone.

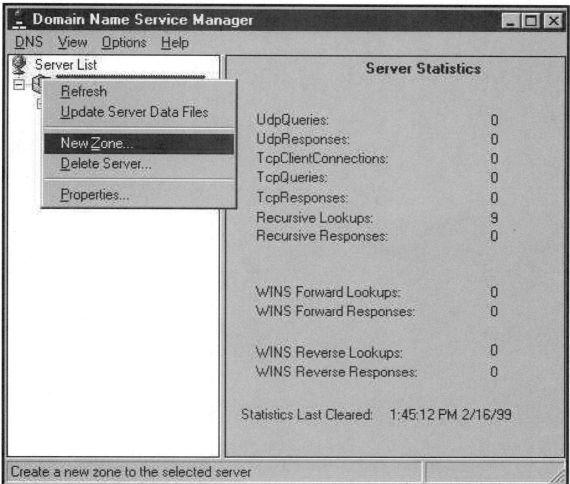

transfer). At this stage of the process, you can select one or the other but not both. Your screen should look like Figure 7-5.

Primary zones require no additional setup at this stage of the configuration. However, if we need to add a secondary zone, we must specify the zone and master (primary) DNS server name in this dialog. If we were configuring a secondary name server, we would configure the zone name to match the primary DNS server's name. We would then be prompted to enter the IP address of the master (primary) name servers (the name servers with which the secondary name server will do zone transfers for this zone). Once the zone is added, DNS Manager would immediately initiate a zone transfer to get the information from the primary.

FIGURE 7-5
Selecting a Zone Type.

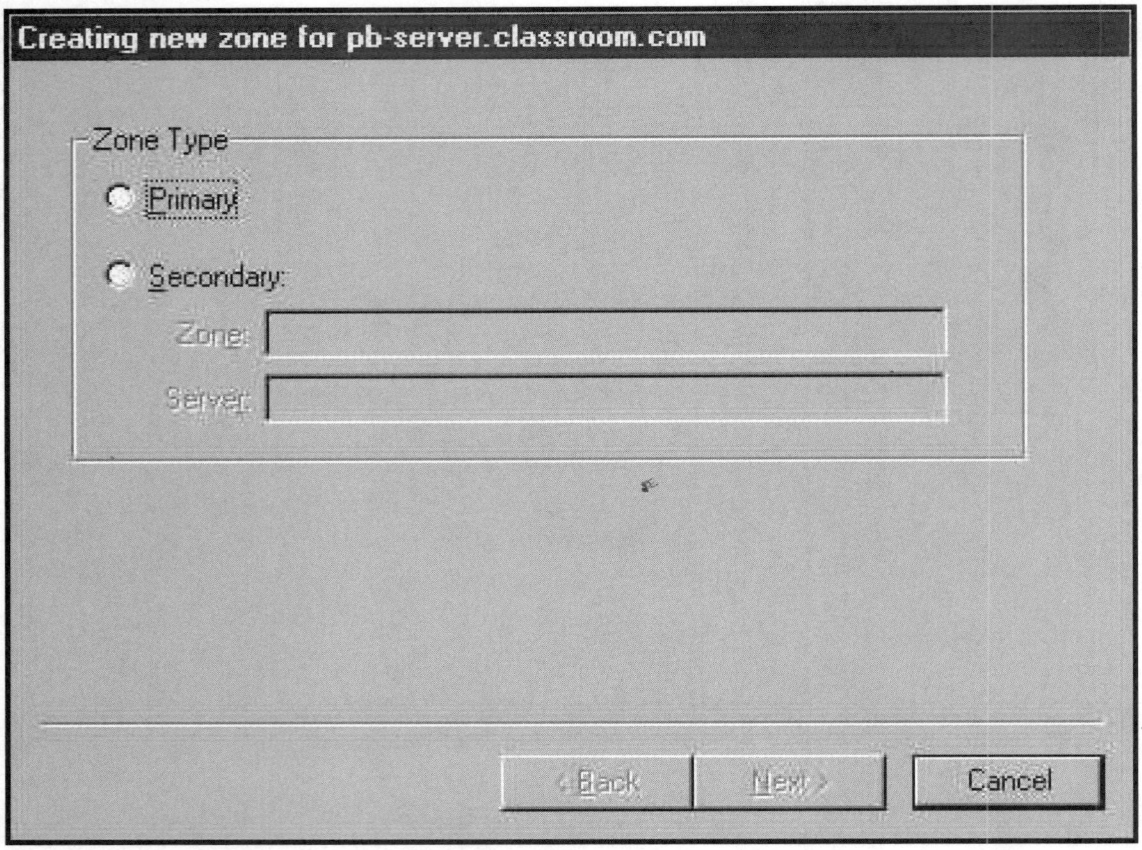

Creating new zone for pb-server.classroom.com

Zone Type
- ○ Primary
- ○ Secondary:
  - Zone:
  - Server:

[< Back] [Next >] [Cancel]

But, let's keep things simple at this point and just configure a primary zone. To do this, select the Primary Zone radio button and click Next.

To configure the zone and server name, drag the hand icon to point to the secondary zone on the destination server in the DNS Manager main window. Now we can name the new primary zone.

STEP 3—NAMING THE ZONE

Regardless of the type of server we are configuring, the next step in configuring DNS is to enter a Zone Name and Zone File for the server. This will determine how our new zone appears in the DNS Manager and what file name it is stored under on disk. Once you have entered the information, press the Tab key. DNS Manager will automatically create a file with the name of your zone appended with the .DNS suffix. When complete, your screen should look something like Figure 7-6.

Click the Next button when you have made the entry.

FIGURE 7-6
Zone File Name.

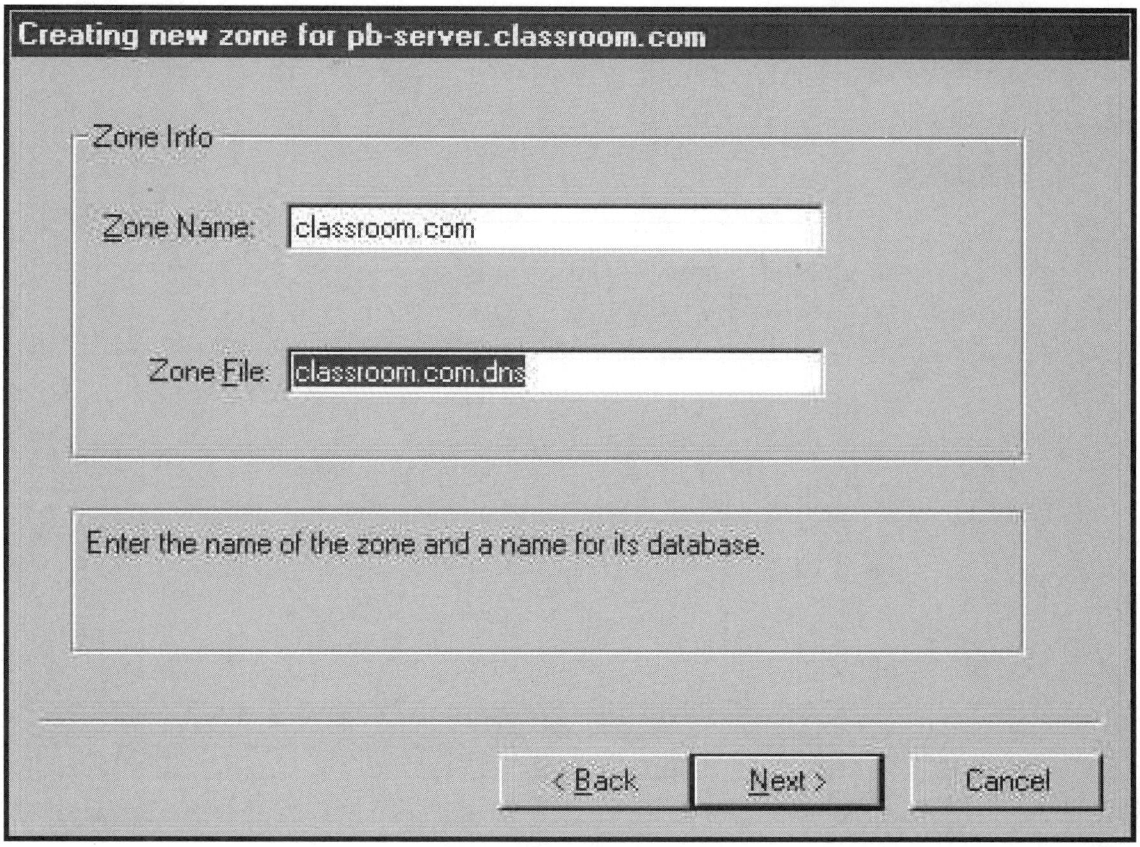

Creating new zone for pb-server.classroom.com

Zone Info

Zone Name: classroom.com

Zone File: classroom.com.dns

Enter the name of the zone and a name for its database.

< Back   Next >   Cancel

Now that we have created a DNS database file, we are ready to view our newly created zone. Click Next one more time and you will be returned to the main view of DNS Manager. Your screen should look like Figure 7-7.

Let's take a look at what has happened. We now see that a new zone (domain) has been added to the server called classroom.com. Within that zone, Microsoft DNS Server has entered some resource records to identify our DNS server. Every DNS server will have both the NS and SOA entries if they are a primary server. As you will recall, the NS entry specifies the "Name Server" computer. The SOA record is the "Statement of Authority" for this zone. The other two records that were added are "A" type records identifying this computer's IP address and hostname. My DNS server has two addresses because two network cards are installed in this NT Server. Your machine will likely only have one "A" entry specifying the computer name and IP address.

FIGURE 7-7
Viewing a Zone.

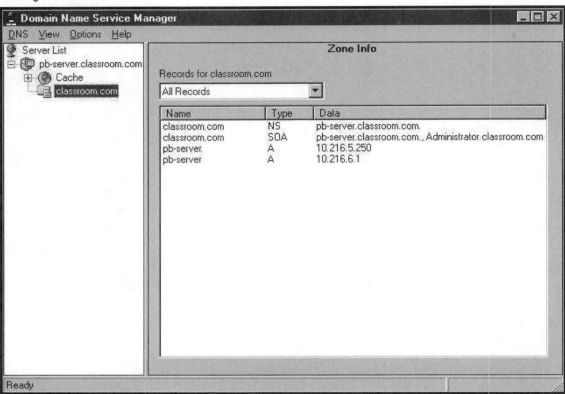

The A entry is very important and is one reason why DNS should have a static IP address. The entry identifies this computer as a primary zone to DNS—it wouldn't be very good if we were getting all sorts of different IP addresses from a DHCP server—because this entry would not change to reflect the new DNS Server leased address!

All these entries can of course be modified. To do this, you would highlight the resource record by clicking once on it. Then right-click and select the Properties option. The properties for the selected resource record will be displayed. Please note that depending on the type of record, options will vary. I have opened the NS record for the DNS server. Your screen would look something like Figure 7-8.

STEP 4—DEFINING FORWARDER OR SLAVE SERVER (OPTIONAL)

If you need to configure your DNS server to be a forwarder or slave server, right-click on the Server icon and select Properties for your DNS servers. Then select the Forwarders tab. Your screen would look something like Figure 7-9.

FIGURE 7-8
Properties of Selected Resource Record.

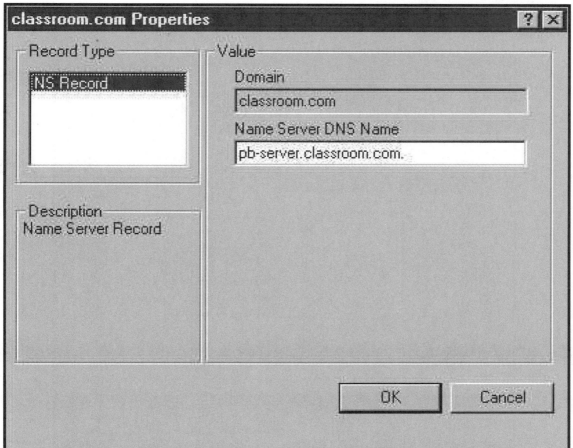

To enable the forwarding gesture check the Use Forwarder(s) box. This will enable the rest of the buttons. At this point, you add the IP addresses of the DNS servers that you would forward your DNS queries to. If you do not check the Operate as Slave Server checkbox, your DNS server will act as a nonexclusive forwarder. Checking the Operate as Slave Server checkbox means your server will be an exclusive forwarder. To complete the process, click the OK button and your settings will be saved.

NOTE: *If you have a need to add additional zones to your DNS server follow the same procedure for each of them. Once all zones have been added to the server, subdomains under the zones can be added. To add a subdomain, click New Domain from the shortcut menu of the desired zone. The Add process is very similar to what we have done in this section.*

FIGURE 7-9
Defining Forwarder.

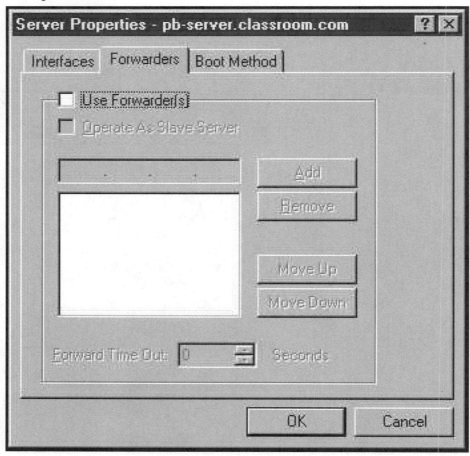

Congratulations! You have successfully configured a basic DNS server installation. In the next section, we will add some resource records and look at some of the more advanced features of Microsoft DNS Server.

Adding Resource Records

Now that your DNS server is configured with a primary zone, we can begin the process of entering some information that DNS can use to identify hosts that "live" in your domain. This process requires us to add resource records.

Adding resource records is fairly similar to what we did in creating a new zone. To add a resource record in DNS, follow the outlined procedure in this section.

FIGURE 7-10
Adding a Resource Record.

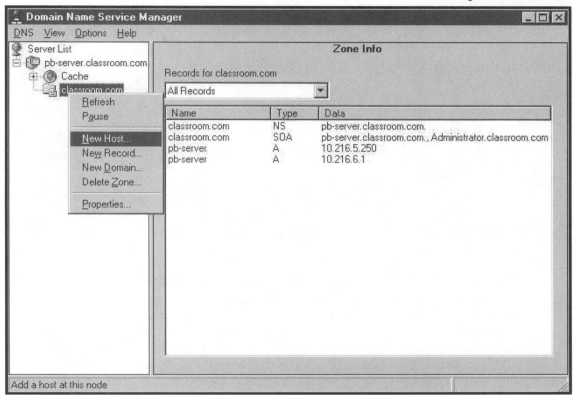

STEP 1—ADD AND CONFIGURE THE RESOURCE RECORD

Adding a resource record is really a snap. Right-click a zone or subdomain and then click New Host or New Record on the shortcut menu. Your screen should look like Figure 7-10.

If you are entering a machine for the very first time, you should add a new host first and then associate the host with other records.

STEP 2—ADDING A NEW HOST RECORD

To add a new host, enter a host name and its IP address This dialog box is for the creation of A (Address) records only. The Add Hosts dialog appears in Figure 7-11.

Click on the Done button when you have completed entering the information. Your entry will be added to the DNS zone. Now is an excellent time to explain this whole reverse lookup procedure since that Create Associated PTR record is staring at us in this picture and it should be checked as part of the addition of a new record!

FIGURE 7-11
Adding a New Host Record.

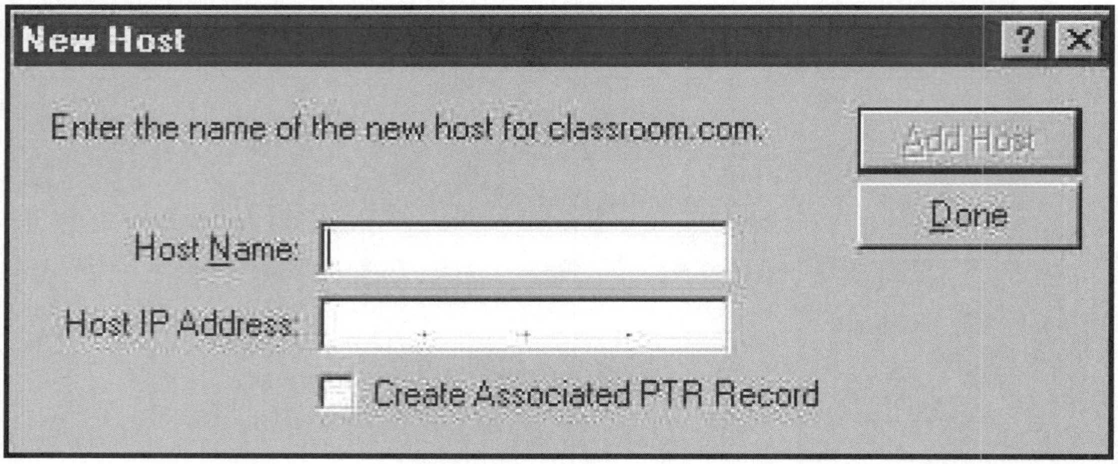

New Host ☐ ? ☐ X

Enter the name of the new host for classroom.com.

[Add Host]

[Done]

Host Name: [   ]

Host IP Address: [.   .   .   ]

☐ Create Associated PTR Record

IN-ADDR.ARPA and Reverse Lookup

As you recall from earlier in this chapter, inverse queries occur when a resolver has the IP address of a host but needs the host name for a particular machine. Because there is no direct correlation in DNS between the domain names and the associated IP addresses they contain, only a thorough search of all domains can guarantee a correct answer. To deal with this rather annoying limitation, a special domain called *in-addr.arpa.* was created.

Nodes in the in-addr.arpa domain are named after numbers in the dotted decimal representation of IP addresses. The fact of the matter is IP addresses get more specific from left to right and domain names get less specific from left to right. To resolve a domain name from this mess, the order of IP address octets must be reversed when building the in-addr.arpa domain. This looks very weird when you first view it in an in-addr.arpa entry. The IP address I use for my machine is **10.216.5.250.** In in-addr.arpa notation for it would appear as **250.5.216.10.**

The in-addr.arpa domain is not built automatically for your zone. You must add a new zone for the DNS server based on your network class ID. However the "Add" process for the zone is exactly the same as for the zone we just created. To set up a reverse lookup zone create a new primary zone using the following notation to delineate your network class:

For a Class A address of 15.100.210.5, the entry would be: 15.in-addr.arpa

For a Class B address of 151.131.220.5, the entry would be: 131.151.in-addr.arpa

For a Class C address of 208.196.220.9, the entry would be: 220.196.208.in-addr.arpa

Once the domain is built, special resource records called PTR (pointer) records can be added for each new host name that is added to the DNS zone. Hence that checkbox illustrated in the screen-capture in Figure 7-11. You do not need to add the PTR record. It will be added automatically once the in-addr.arpa domain is configured and the checkbox is selected.

To make this a little clearer, let's look at an example:

IP address is 10.216.5.250
Host name is pb-server

To find pb-server based on the IP address **10.216.5.250,** a resolver queries the DNS server for a PTR (pointer) record of **250.5.250.10.in-addr.arpa.** The PTR record that would be found contains the host name corresponding to the IP address 10.216.5.250. This is the information that is returned to the resolver. If the PTR record does not exist, reverse lookup name resolution will not occur! This is why configuring the domain and adding PTR resource records is important.

NOTE: *Part of the administration of a DNS name server is ensuring that pointer records are created for hosts so these inverse queries can be satisfied. To do this, make sure you select Add Associated PTR Record whenever you add a new host.*

Now that the new "A" host record has been added, we can associate the computer with any number of aliases. The type of record we use to create an alias is called a CNAME record. Creating this type of record will allow us to provide other names to a host that are more meaningful.

STEP 3—ADDING ADDITIONAL RECORDS (OPTIONAL)

At this point in the process, it is not required that you enter any additional information for a host for name resolution to occur in most cases. This step is optional. However, the record we will add (called a CNAME) allows us to alias a computer by a different name. A good use for this record is in configuring a web or ftp site. In this example we will add a CNAME record to add a website on my server. We will call this alias "ftp". The ftp value will allow us to refer to the host as ftp.classroom.com. The process for adding this record is very similar to what we did when we added the "A" record in the previous step. To add the CNAME record, do the following. Right-click a zone or subdomain and then click New Record on the shortcut menu. Your screen should look like Figure 7-12.

STEP 4—ADDING A NEW RESOURCE RECORD

To add a new CNAME resource record, scroll down the left-hand list and highlight the CNAME entry. Enter the alias "ftp" (aliases cannot have

FIGURE 7-12
Adding Additional Records.

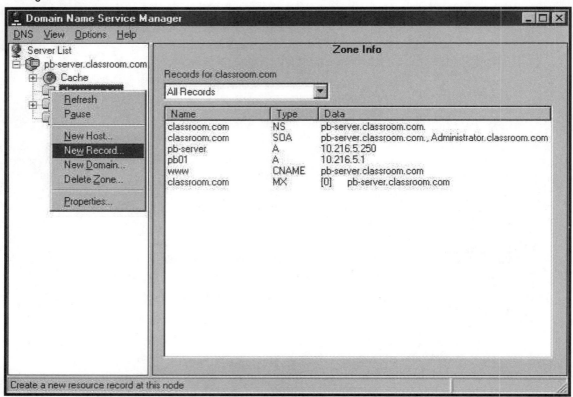

any periods), and the host name of the aliased computer "pb-server.class-room.com". When complete, your screen should look like Figure 7-13.

Click on the OK button when you have completed entering the information. Your entry will be added to the DNS zone. Congratulations! You have just added an alias name of ftp.classroom.com to the classroom.com zone. You can now access my IIS website using the FQDN ftp.classroom.com.

Advanced Configuration of Microsoft DNS Server

This section of the installation and configuration lesson looks at how to add and integrate WINS resolution into your DNS server as well as how to set zone update parameters for your DNS server.

THE DNS-WINS CONNECTION

Microsoft DNS Server has the ability to use a WINS server to assist it in resolving host names to IP addresses. The whole process is completely isolated from the client computer. To enable this feature in DNS, a special record used

FIGURE 7-13
Adding a New Resource Record.

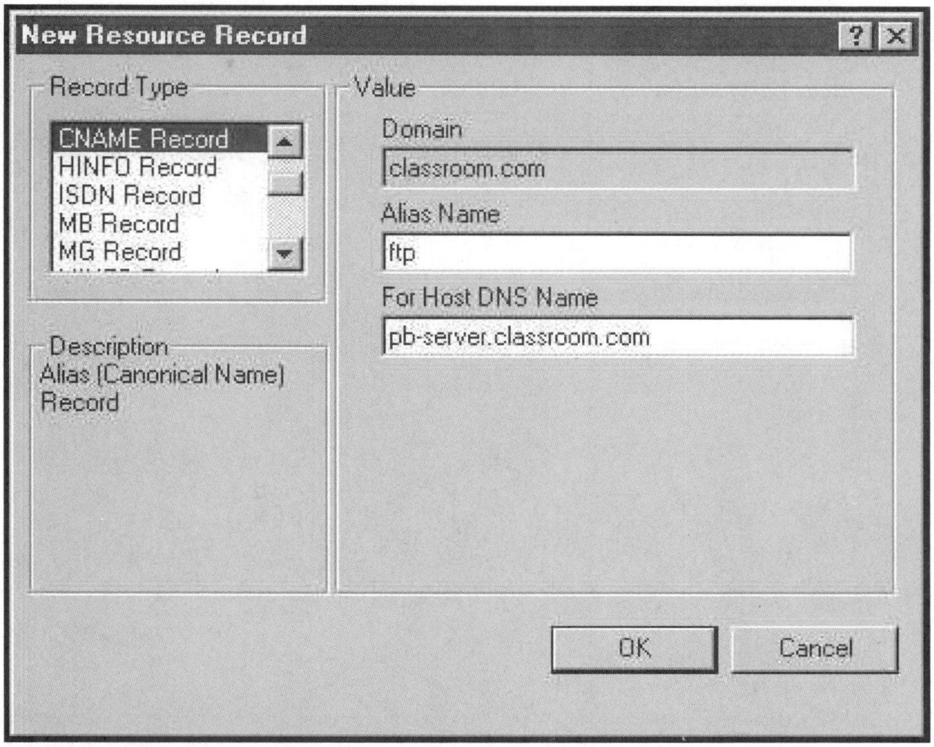

only with the Microsoft DNS server is added called the WINS record. We will see how to configure this record in just a bit.

This WINS record allows a DNS server to query a WINS server to assist in resolving a computer name to IP address. The DNS server handles all the zone information processing and uses WINS to finish the task of associating the computer name with the FQDN. For instance, a host might ask for a resource named atlntdev located in the padev.com domain. This resource does not have an "A" record or "CNAME" record entered for it, so DNS does not know what to do. If the WINS resolution record is in place, the DNS server will query the WINS server asking "Who is atlntdev?" WINS will return the IP address to the DNS server and this information will be passed to the resolver.

The process of adding a WINS lookup record is slightly different than adding other records even though the WINS record shows up just like any other resource record in DNS Manager. To add a WINS record follow this process.

FIGURE 7-14
WINS Lookup Dialog.

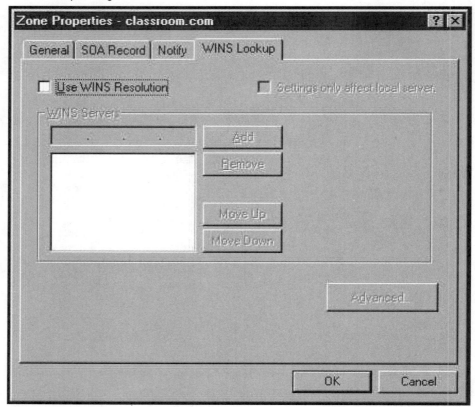

STEP 1—ACCESS THE WINS LOOKUP CONFIGURATION
Right-click on the zone name (in this example it is classroom.com). This will bring up a selection box. Highlight and select the Properties option. Then select the "WINS Lookup" Tab. You will be presented with the dialog shown in Figure 7-14.

STEP 2—CONFIGURE WINS LOOKUP
Once you have arrived at this tab, click the Use WINS Resolution checkbox. This will allow you to enter the IP address of your WINS server. Click on the Add button and enter the IP address. My WINS server is the same computer as my DNS server so I have entered its IP address of 10.216.5.250. When complete, your form will appear like that illustrated n Figure 7-15.

FIGURE 7-15
Entering IP Address of Your WINS Server.

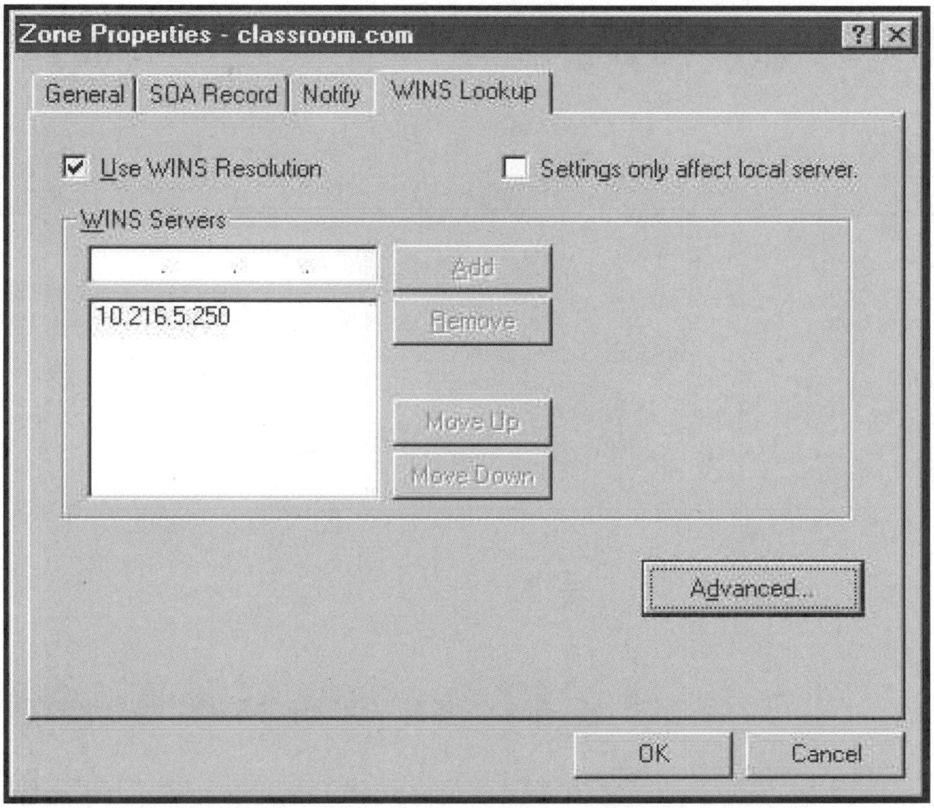

When you are done, click OK. Your WINS record will be added to the DNS zone. When complete, the DNS Manager zone properties will look something like Figure 7-16.

Congratulations! You have just added a WINS Lookup Record!

There is also a method of completing a reverse lookup using WINS. As outlined in the previous section, this requires another special record associated with the in-addr.arpa domain called a WINS-R record. The process for resolution is similar to that described above except that we will add the record using the in-addr.arpa domain instead of classroom.com. To add a reverse WINS lookup entry do the following.

FIGURE 7-16

DNS Manager Zone Properties After Adding IP Address.

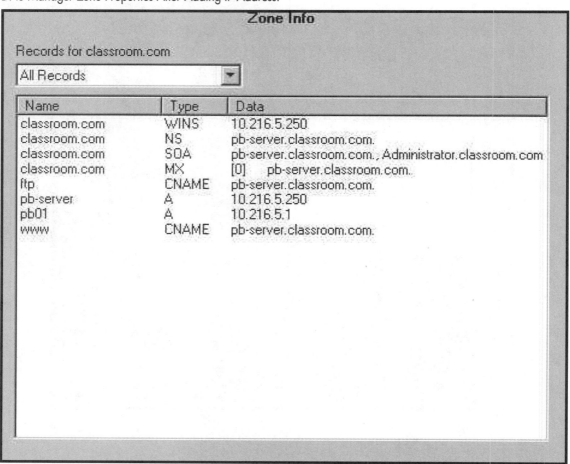

STEP 1—ACCESS THE REVERSE WINS LOOK-UP CONFIGURATION

Right-click on the in-addr.arpa zone name. This will bring up a selection box. Highlight and select the Properties option. Then select the WINS Reverse Lookup Tab. You will be presented with the dialog shown in Figure 7-17.

STEP 2—CONFIGURE REVERSE WINS LOOKUP

Once you have arrived at this tab, click the Use WINS Reverse Lookup checkbox. This will allow you to enter the DNS Host Domain. Enter the host domain of your DNS Server (In this case it is classroom.com). Click on the OK button when you are done. When complete, your form will appear as in Figure 7-18.

FIGURE 7-17
Accessing Reverse WINS Lookup Configuration.

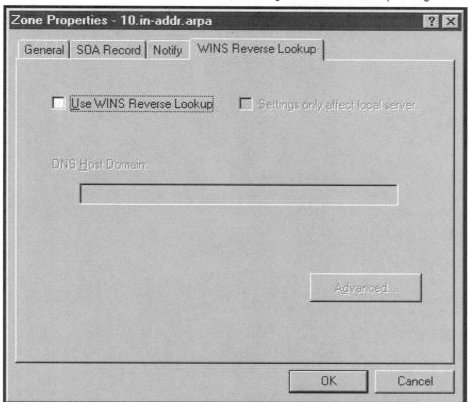

When you are done, click OK. Your WINS reverse lookup record will be added to the DNS zone. When complete, the DNS Manager zone properties for in-addr.arpa will look something like Figure 7-19.

Congratulations! You have just added a WINS reverse lookup record!

SETTING THE ZONE UPDATE NOTIFY PARAMETER

DNS servers are only as good as the information they contain. It is important that primary zone servers notify secondary zone servers periodically to update their entries to make sure they have the latest host and resource record information. By default, this will occur at a predetermined time. However,

FIGURE 7-18
Entering DNS Host Domain—Completed Form.

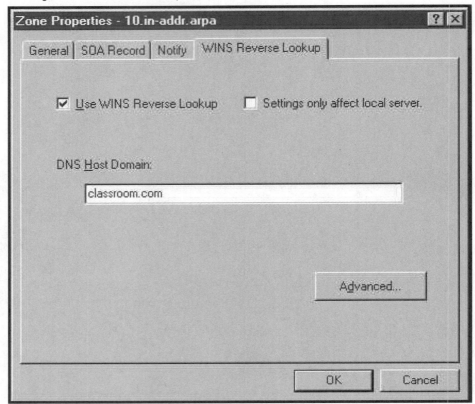

modifying the Notify tab will allow the secondary servers to initiate a zone transfer immediately upon receiving a "change notification message" from the primary zone. To configure this parameter, follow this process.

STEP 1—ACCESS THE NOTIFY TAB

Access the zone properties for classroom.com as described in the earlier example. Select the Notify tab. Your screen should look like Figure 7-20.

FIGURE 7-19
DNS Manager Zone Properties After WINS Reverse Lookup Record Added.

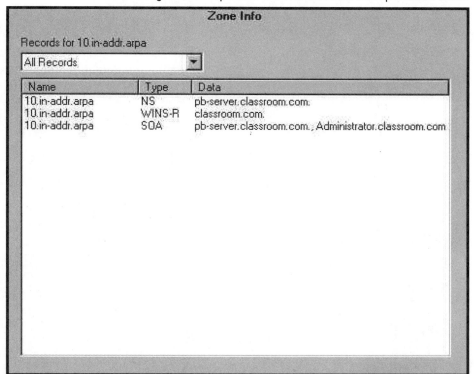

STEP 2—CONFIGURE THE NOTIFY TAB

Enter the IP addresses of secondary DNS servers you want to send change notification messages to. When complete, press the OK button.

That's it! Now, whenever a change is made to the primary zone, a message will be sent to all the secondary servers configured and they can initiate a zone transfer immediately. Of course, any secondary servers not listed will still receive their updates based on a predetermined timeframe.

That just about covers all the basic functionality you need to configure and set up a Microsoft DNS Server. Now that wasn't too bad at all, was it? The lab below will help you to practice configuring DNS.

FIGURE 7-20
The Notify Tab.

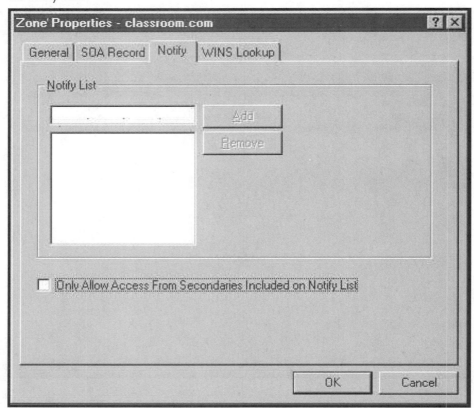

LAB

7.1

Installing and Configuring
Microsoft DNS Server

To complete this lab, you will need one Windows NT server and a client to test your configurations. This lab does not have diagrams associated with many of the instructions. Test your knowledge by trying to remember where to add and modify the options we discussed in the previous lesson. If you need help, refer to the previous lesson's demonstration.

On the NT Server

1. Validate that you have entered domain and host names for your server as well as the IP address of your server in the DNS Service Search Order. Your domain name should be "DomainX.com," where X is a number assigned by your instructor. Your host name should be the NetBIOS name of the server. The IP address should be the address of your server.

2. Make sure you are using a static IP configuration!

3. Add the Microsoft DNS Service using the appropriate TCP/IP protocol tab.

4. Restart the computer when prompted.

5. Reapply any Service Packs when your computer restarts.

6. Reboot the computer.

7. Log in as administrator and open the DNS Manager application.

8. Create a new DNS server if this has not already been configured by DNS by entering the IP address of your DNS server or domain name.

9. Create a new primary zone and name your zone domainx.com where x is a number assigned by your instructor. What records are automatically added when you create the zone?

10. Create the reverse lookup zone in-addr.arpa based on IP class parameters provided by your instructor.

11. Add an "A" record and its associated pointer record for the client computer.

12. Add a CNAME record for the client computer. Use the alias "cool."

13. Open a command window and PING cool.domainx.com. Did you get a response? What was the response?

14. Add a WINS lookup record to your domain. What is entered in the zone information panel?

15. Add a WINS reverse lookup record to the in-addr.arpa zone. What is entered in the zone information panel?

On the Workstation

1. Configure the TCP/IP DNS properties to use your partner's DNS server in the DNS Service Search Order. Restart your computer when prompted.

2. Log in as administrator and open a command window.

3. PING the DNS server using its fully qualified domain name of studentx.domainx.com. Did you receive a response? What was the response?

IF YOUR NT SERVER IS RUNNING DNS SERVER AND INTERNET INFORMATION SERVER

1. Configure a CNAME record pointing to the FQDN of the IIS/DNS server. Call the alias "www."

2. On the client, open Internet Explorer and type the URL www.domainx.com and record your results. Was a web page opened?

3. Configure another CNAME record pointing to the FQDN of the IIS/DNS server. Call the alias "ftp".

4. On the client, open Internet Explorer and type the URL ftp.domainx.com and record your results. Was the FTP site opened?

Congratulations! You have successfully installed and configured Microsoft DNS Server!

Lesson 7.8 Troubleshooting DNS and Name Resolution

General Name Resolution Troubleshooting

Host name resolution can present some interesting challenges for the network administrator. Because several methods are used together to resolve names, it is best to be very methodical in your troubleshooting approach. Listed below are a few tips as you try to isolate a name resolution problem.

1. Try pinging using the FQDN. If this doesn't work, try pinging a host using its IP address. If this works, then you definitely have some sort of FQDN name resolution problem.

2. Verify that other hosts can connect to the resource using the FQDN. If the problem is isolated, it may very well have something to do with the individual computer's configuration.

3. Use IPCONFIG to check the TCP/IP configuration settings.

4. If the client is DHCP enabled, be sure that the passed DNS entry is correct!

5. Check the DNS tab in TCP/IP to verify the DNS server is entered correctly.

6. Check DNS Manager to make sure there are entries for the hosts you are trying to ping.

7. Check to see if there is a problem in the local HOSTS file (if installed) on the client.

In general, try to eliminate as many variables from the problem as possible and narrow your hypothesis down. For more information on general troubleshooting technique, see chapter 10.

The NSLOOKUP Utility

NSLOOKUP is a Windows NT command line utility that allows you to interact with a DNS server. The command itself describes its function:

> NS = Name Server
> LOOKUP = Perform a DNS Lookup

NSLOOKUP is the primary tool used in diagnosing DNS server problems. The utility is installed as part of the base TCP/IP protocol. It displays resolution information from a specified DNS server. It can also use a remote server to see if the query process is working properly. The command works in two modes: interactive and noninteractive. The command line syntax is provided here along with a couple of examples:

nslookup [-option . . .] [computer-to-find | - [server]]

To show the current default DNS server of a computer, type the nslookup command at the prompt and you will receive the output shown in Figure 7-21 from NSLOOKUP.

FIGURE 7-21
The NSLOOKUP Utility.

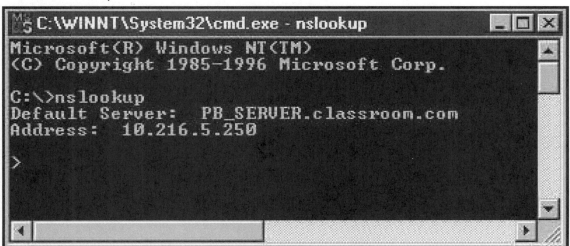

FIGURE 7-22
Performing a Lookup on a Host Name.

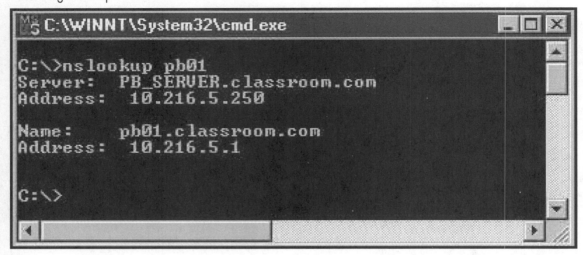

```
C:\WINNT\System32\cmd.exe                          _ □ ✕

C:\>nslookup pb01
Server:    PB_SERVER.classroom.com
Address:   10.216.5.250

Name:      pb01.classroom.com
Address:   10.216.5.1


C:\>
```

To exit NSLOOKUP type **Exit** at the > prompt or press Ctrl-C.

To perform a lookup on a host name, type the nslookup command and you will receive the output illustrated in Figure 7-22 from NSLOOKUP.

To receive help on NSLOOKUP at any > prompt type **?** and press Return.

As you can see, NSLOOKUP can be used to test and troubleshoot your DNS server entries from an individual computer configuration standpoint as well as from the entries made in Microsoft DNS Manager.

Summary

This chapter covered generic DNS, FQDN, and the Microsoft DNS Server Services. Throughout this chapter we learned the following.

- **History and DNS Terminology.** We reviewed DNS' origins and it link to the HOSTS file. We also looked at a large amount of terminology specifically related to implementation of a DNS name resolution service.

- **DNS Architecture.** We discussed how DNS is put together to provide scalable, extensible, and modular management of domains for the Internet.

- **DNS Server Types.** We discussed the three categories of DNS servers, their functions, limitations, and any uses in meeting business requirements.

- **Microsoft DNS Installation and Configuration.** We learned how to install and configure the Microsoft DNS Service, including addition of primary and reverse lookup zones, host records, and other important records in DNS.

- **FQDN/NBNS Integration.** We learned how to make DNS work with WINS to provide an additional layer of name resolution on Microsoft networks both from a standard and reverse lookup perspective.

- **Troubleshooting DNS Installations.** We learned a few key areas to focus on when attempting to troubleshoot DNS installations. We also looked at a useful utility called NSLOOKUP to help us in troubleshooting DNS Server problems.

● ● ● ● ● ● ● ● ● ● ● ● ● ●

1. *Select the best answer.* Mike is configuring an Intranet website at his company. He wants to allow all the clients on the network to access the site using a standard www URL. What type of DNS record should Mike add to his DNS zone?

   a. MX
   b. HINFO
   c. A
   d. SOA
   e. CNAME
   f. None of the above.

2. *Select the best answer.* Michelle has been asked to provide a extremely efficient and fast DNS solution for the far-side of a slow WAN link. She already has one DNS server configured as a primary zone. What is the best type of DNS server she can install to meet requirements?

   a. A second primary server.
   b. A secondary server.
   c. A caching server.
   d. A slave server.
   e. None of the above.

3. *Select the best answer.* Which DNS file contains all the root level Internet DNS server entries?

   a. Boot
   b. Reverse lookup
   c. Cache
   d. Master lookup
   e. None of the above.

4. *Select the best answer.* Drew installed Microsoft Exchange Server on a Windows NT server computer with the host name, exchange.corporate.com. Jake configures SMTP on his mail server to process Internet mail services. He wants users to be able to use this mail server for all their internal and external mail. Which resource record type must Jake add to his DNS zone?

   a. WINS Lookup
   b. CNAME
   c. A
   d. MX
   e. MINFO

5. *Select the two best answers.* Mark wants to install DNS servers in the company's two remote locations. A T3 line connects both offices. He wants to implement a redundant DNS server configuration while minimizing DNS traffic across the WAN link. How can do Mark do this?

   a. Configure a primary DNS server in the main office.
   b. Configure a secondary DNS server at the second office.
   c. Configure a cache server at the second location.
   d. Configure a secondary server at the main office.

6. *Select the best answer.* Which of the following HOSTS file entries will allow a computer to connect to the padev resource having the IP Address 68.112.45.98?

   a. 68.112.45.98 #padev #PA Development Server
   b. 98.45.112.68 PaDev # PA Development Server
   c. 68.112.45.98 PADEV
   d. 68.112.45.102 padev
   e. None of these entries will work.

7. *Select the best answer.* Randy wants to retrieve files from a Windows NT IIS server using ftp and a FQDN. His Windows NT workstation computer is *not* configured to use DNS. Which of the following components need to be installed on the workstation?

   a. HOSTS file
   b. LMHOSTS file
   c. DNS Manager
   d. WINS Manager
   e. This cannot be accomplished.

8. *Select the best answer.* Mary wants to assure that her secondary zone servers get updates almost immediately from their primary DNS server. What should Mary enable and configure to accomplish this?

   a. Configure the WINS lookup on both servers.
   b. Configure DNS push replication on the primary DNS server.
   c. Configure the Notify Parameter on the primary DNS server.
   d. Configure WINS reverse lookup on both servers.

9. *Select the best answer.* A user on a Windows 98 computer cannot connect to the resource, relay.mail.corp.com. However, all other users do not report any problems. The user has *both* a HOSTS file and a DNS server in use. What is the most likely cause of the problem?

   a. The DNS server has an incorrect entry.
   b. The HOSTS file has an incorrect entry.
   c. WINS lookup using DNS is not enabled.
   d. The subnet mask on the computer is incorrect.

10. *Select the best answer.* Paul has installed a redundant DNS server configuration, however, his two servers seem to be having slow response time. Paul needs to install a third server to load balance his DNS server configuration but does not want any additional zone transfer traffic to be generated. What is the best type of DNS server to implement?

   a. Another primary server
   b. A caching server
   c. A slave server
   d. A secondary server
   e. A forwarding server

11. *Select the best answer.* Sally manages a network that uses DNS for FQDN name resolution. Her network is connected to the Internet. Sally discovers that some of her clients can use FQDNs to access the Internet but others cannot. Everyone can use an IP address to access the Internet. What is the best tool that would help Sally to analyze the problem computers? What is the best way to troubleshoot this problem?

   a. NSLOOKUP
   b. PING
   c. IPCONFIG
   d. ARP
   e. Network Monitor

12. *Select the best answer.* Josh's DNS configuration is comprised of five DNS and WINS servers. The clients using this network are all Microsoft based. Josh wants to assure that even if a PTR record doesn't exist for a host, name resolution can still occur for the clients. What type of record needs to be added to the zone to accomplish this?

   a. WINS master lookup
   b. WINS reverse lookup
   c. DNS reverse lookup
   d. in-addr.arpa reverse lookup
   e. This cannot be done without a PTR record.

13. *Select the best answer.* Mary wants to streamline the administration of her UNIX and Macintosh clients by providing centralized name resolution. What service should she install?

   a. WINS
   b. HOSTS
   c. LMHOSTS
   d. DNS
   e. IP forwarding

14. *Select all that apply.* Which of the following resource records must be present when a primary zone is created?

   a. SOA
   b. MX
   c. HINFO
   d. NS
   e. CNAME

15. *Select all that apply.* Angie is troubleshooting a client workstation. She is able to PING by IP address to any computer on any subnet. However, she is unable to PING by either NetBIOS name or FQDN and is returned the message, Bad IP Address. Which of the following are the most likely causes of the problem?

   a. The HOSTS and LMHOSTS files are not configured correctly.
   b. DNS and WINS servers are incorrect in the TCP/IP configuration.
   c. DNS is not configured to do a WINS lookup.
   d. The WINS and DNS services have not been started.
   e. This is perfectly normal.

MICROSOFT DHCP SERVER AND DHCP RELAY AGENT

OBJECTIVES

By the end of this chapter, you should be able to:

- Define the importance of DHCP in managing a TCP/IP installation.

- Describe the benefits of automatic lease management.

- Describe the DHCP client/server leasing process.

- Install and configure the Microsoft DHCP Service.

- Manage DHCP fault tolerance.

- Install and configure the Microsoft DHCP Relay Agent service.

Introduction

DHCP is the Dynamic Host Configuration Protocol. This utility is one of the most useful to the network administrator in terms of reducing support and logistics of managing of a TCP/IP network. DHCP automates the TCP/IP management process, providing clients with IP addresses and other important configuration information automatically with a low degree of administrative overhead. This chapter explores the Microsoft DHCP Server service as well as the utility service used to allow multiple subnets access to a DHCP server—the Microsoft DHCP Relay Agent.

Lesson 8.1 DHCP Overview

This lesson provides a detailed overview of the Microsoft DHCP Server application. Within this lesson, we will take a look at the origins of DHCP, its uses, benefits, and the process a client and server go through to initialize a lease.

What Is DHCP?

DHCP, as you will recall from earlier chapters, is the Dynamic Host Configuration Protocol. DHCP provides a mechanism to automatically manage IP addresses in a TCP/IP network. In Windows NT, the DHCP server is an additional service provided with the operating system. Microsoft DHCP Server is a fully functional IP lease management tool that is easy to use and very powerful in managing an organization's TCP/IP configuration.

Why Use DHCP?

Before DHCP was introduced, all client computers had to be configured for TCP/IP statically. Statically is another word for manually. Manual TCP/IP configuration can be an administrative nightmare in a large organization. By now you know that each client must have a unique IP address and subnet mask to communicate on a TCP/IP network. Static installations of TCP/IP usually involved a manually updated spreadsheet to keep track of who had what address. This time-consuming process was also error-prone. It was (and still is) easy to make a mistake when entering this information. Each workstation would need a minimum of an IP address and subnet mask. In a routed network they would also need a default gateway. Further, if the computer was using FQDN or WINS name resolution methods, these options would also need to be configured. Manual configuration forced the administrator to physically seat themselves at each client workstation and enter this information. It was *very* time-consuming!

DHCP was introduced to solve these manual configuration problems. DHCP is actually a database like WINS and DNS. It allows an administrator to enter all types of information about a TCP/IP configuration in one place (the DHCP server). All client computers on the network can then "lease" their configuration from the server. This eliminates the manual configuration, automates the process, and reduces configuration errors significantly. DHCP is the answer to a particularly challenging problem of managing TCP/IP client configurations across an organization.

ARCHITECTURE AND TERMINOLOGY

Microsoft DHCP Server is a service in Windows NT server. It is provided at no extra charge with the operating system. In terms of architecture, DHCP works using a dynamic database. This means the process of acquiring a lease is completely automated once the service is properly configured. DHCP is founded on a very basic tenet that we can all understand: leasing. If you do not own your house, you would most likely rent or lease time in an apartment. The DHCP process works under this same premise. When you are running DHCP, you are "renting" or "leasing" an IP address from the server. DHCP manages the lease and renewal process of all types of TCP/IP configuration information. In terms of communications between client and server, DHCP always uses UDP ports 67 and 68 for transport and receipt of information.

Before we dig too far into the detail of how all this occurs, it will be helpful to define in a little more detail some of the terminology we will be using throughout this chapter.

Client Lease. When a client computer is configured to use DHCP, no information is entered for the TCP/IP configuration. All the information is leased from the DHCP server. As is the case in the rental of an apartment, leases have terms at which point you can renew or move to a new location. This same type of activity is in effect on a DHCP server. The client asks for an IP address and the DHCP server "leases" it to the client for a predetermined period of time. The lease period is determined by the administrator during the setup of the DHCP server.

DHCP Scope. The DHCP scope is simply a range of IP addresses that are available for lease. The administrator configures the scope as part of the initial installation of the server. Think of the scope as a range of "apartment numbers for rent." Of course, the "apartment numbers" are actually IP addresses. DHCP Server allows you to create multiple scopes for different subnets on one machine. All the information for a TCP/IP inter-network can be entered in one place, one time, and used throughout an organization. This is very powerful.

Client Reservation. Not all TCP/IP clients have the ability to automatically lease IP addresses using DHCP. This can be due to an operating system limitation, or in other cases, some computers require a statically configured address (like DHCP servers). These machines still need to be statically configured with TCP/IP information. In this case, we can manually enter a reservation for a client's address. By doing this, DHCP knows not to lease the address to any other clients. It is a "reserved" address for a particular computer.

Address Pool. An address pool is a range of IP addresses available to the client computers. The address pool makes up a large component of the DHCP scope. In DHCP, a range of IP addresses is provided to the server. The range of addresses is all-inclusive unless a client reservation is specified. What we mean by this is that all IP addresses, unless excluded, will be available for a client to use.

DYNAMIC DATABASE

DHCP uses a dynamic database to manage the leasing process. Once configured, the service pretty much runs in an automated fashion with little or no involvement from the administrator. As you will recall, a dynamic database is one that automatically updates itself. It requires no manual intervention whatsoever. We will see a bit later in the chapter how to restore and manage the DHCP database, but in general, once DHCP is configured, there is little administration required to keep the service running.

RENEWAL/RELEASE PROCESS

The DHCP leasing process is completely automated and requires no user intervention when the service is properly configured. As is the case with all we have learned up to this point, DHCP clients and servers follow a standard process to acquire and manage the lease process. Leasing occurs for any number of reasons but the most common are these.

■ This is the first time a machine has been on the network and it needs an IP address.

■ The client has lost its lease and needs a new one.

■ The client released its lease and now requires a new one

■ The server cancelled the current lease and now the client needs another.

The following process is used for a client to request and receive an IP address from a DHCP server.

Step 1—Client Asks for Lease. When a computer is first booting, one of the things that happens if DHCP is enabled is the client makes a broadcast on the network asking for an IP lease. The request is known as a **DHCPDISCOVER** broadcast. This broadcast is directed to any and all DHCP servers who live on the network.

Step 2—DHCP Servers Offer A Lease. Upon receipt of a client request, all DHCP servers on the network respond to the client offering a lease (if they have one available). This broadcast message is known as a **DHCPOFFER.** This offer message contains necessary configuration information for the client like who the DHCP server is, how long its lease will be, the IP address and subnet mask it will use, and the client's own MAC address.

Step 3—Client Selects DHCP Server. The client is not picky about which DHCP server it selects! The first one who is lucky enough to be processed by the client is selected. Once the DHCP server is selected, the client sends another broadcast back to the server requesting IP configuration information. This broadcast is sent in a **DHCPREQUEST** message.

Step 4—Client gets TCP/IP Configuration Information and Acknowledges. The DHCP server responds to the client providing configuration information. At the same time, all other DHCP servers withdraw their offers. This broadcast message is known as a **DHCPACK.**

As with all communications on the network, this process happens very quickly. Of course, there are a couple of situations where things might not go as planned.

WHAT HAPPENS IF I DON'T GET A LEASE?

There are several key dependencies in the four-step process outlined earlier. Any of the following will occur if a glitch occurs in the process.

DHCP Server Not Available. We must have a DHCP server on the network for this process to work! If a server is unavailable, the client will try to send the DHCPREQUEST message several times hoping to get a response from a DHCP server. Obviously, if it does not receive a response, TCP/IP will not be configured. However, the DHCPREQUEST process will continue to occur at predetermined intervals (once every five minutes) after a failed attempt until such time that a server is found and the interface can be configured.

DHCP Server Is Available but Cannot Lease Address. In the event that a client requests a lease and the server cannot comply, a special message is broadcast to the client called a DHCPNACK. This is not necessarily a fatal problem for the client, it simply means that there are no addresses currently available in the DHCP server's pool (they've all been used) or the current lease the client has is being used by another computer. The client will attempt to get a lease again following the same process after a predetermined period of time.

Lesson 8.2 Installing DHCP

This lesson leads you through the process of installing the Microsoft DHCP Server service. You will use the content in this lesson to install the software as part of an included lab exercise. Please note that to successfully complete this lab you need a Windows NT server machine. DHCP is only available on Windows NT server.

Installing DHCP Server is not all that difficult and is very much like every other service installation in Windows NT. All our work will be done in the Network Control Panel. Before we actually begin the process though, there are a few requirements that must be met:

Windows NT Installation Requirements

To install Microsoft DHCP Server, the following requirements must be met:

1. The Windows NT server must have a statically configured TCP/IP interface. You must specify at least an IP address and subnet mask. You may need to specify other information as well. A DHCP Server cannot be a client of itself!

2. At least one DHCP scope must be configured once the service is installed. Otherwise, clients would be unable to get a lease!

3. Because DHCP uses broadcast transmissions, there may need to be a separate server on each subnet. You will recall that broadcast transmissions do not cross routers. This can be avoided if you use the Microsoft DHCP Relay Agent (discussed later in this chapter) or your router supports BOOTP broadcast transmissions. Of course, this feature has to be turned on at the router for this to work!

We will assume that all these requirements are in place. Let's install the service!

LAB

8.1

Installing Microsoft DHCP Server

● ●

This lab allows you to install the Microsoft DHCP Server service on a Windows NT server. Follow all directions carefully and if you have any questions, be sure to consult with the instructor!

BEFORE YOU BEGIN THE INSTALLATION PROCESS

Check your TCP/IP settings to make sure you have a static IP address configured on the machine. At a minimum, you must have a unique IP address and the correct subnet mask. Consult your instructor for an IP address and subnet mask if this is not the case.

ON THE WINDOWS NT SERVER

1. Open the Network Control Panel applet. Your screen should look something like Figure 8-1.

2. Click on the Services Tab. Your screen should look something like Figure 8-2.

3. Click the Add button.

4. Select Microsoft DHCP Server from the list. Your screen should look like Figure 8-3.

5. Click OK.

6. Provide the installation path if you have not already done so.

7. Restart the computer when prompted.

8. Re-apply Service Pack 3 when you log on.

9. Restart the computer one more time. That's all there is to it!

10. Now you are ready to configure the DHCP service.

Well, that was pretty easy. Now let's dig into DHCP server and configure the server so we can implement automatic address management in our TCP/IP environment.

FIGURE 8-1
The Network Control Panel.

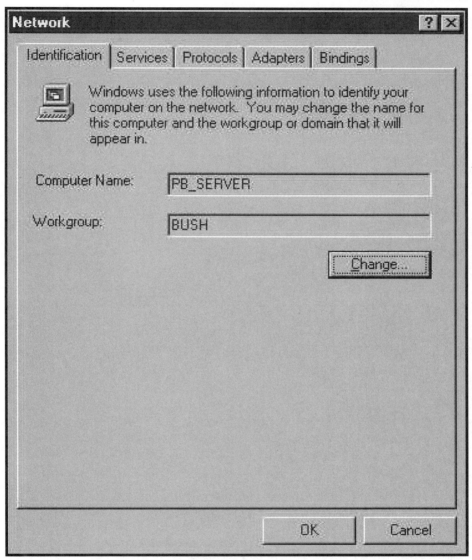

FIGURE 8-2
Network Control Panel Services Tab.

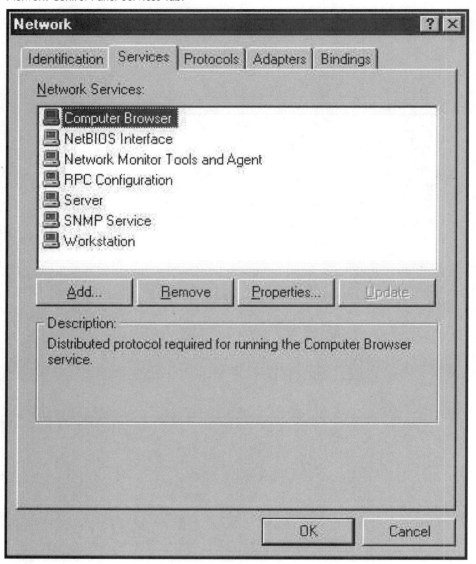

FIGURE 8-3
Add DHCP Server Service.

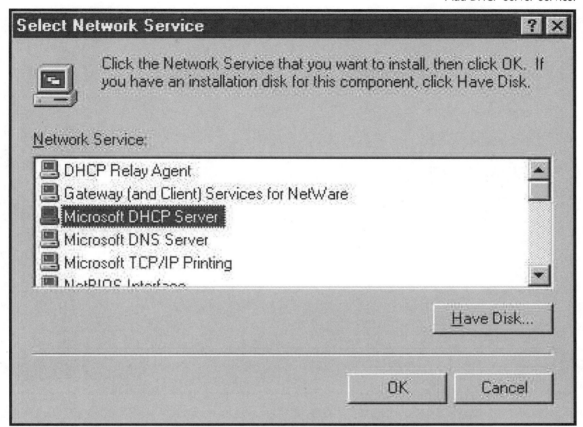

Lesson 8.3 Configuring Microsoft DHCP Server

This lesson covers the details of configuring a Microsoft DHCP Server. There will be many new terms and screens you may not have seen before. We will approach this topic like all the others in the book: one step at a time. DHCP server is really not hard to configure as long as you understand some basic terminology and the requirements of the software. To do this, let's take a look in a little more detail at some of the important concepts related to a DHCP server.

The DHCP Server Service

Just like DNS and WINS, the Microsoft DHCP Server is a service. The service can be accessed through the Control Panel Services applet. Once

FIGURE 8-4
Control Panel Services Applet.

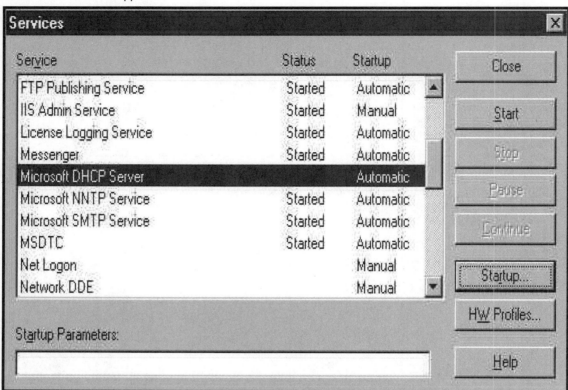

installed, it will appear in the list of services and will be started automatically when you boot Windows NT server. If you should ever need to stop the service, you can use this applet to do so. To stop and start the service complete the following procedure.

1. Open the Services applet logged in as an Administrator and scroll down to the Microsoft DHCP Server entry. This entry should be highlighted. Your screen should look something like Figure 8-4.

2. To start the Service click on the Start button. To stop the service click on the Stop button and to pause the service click on the Pause button.

3. If you need to configure how DHCP server starts on boot-up, click on the Startup button. Your screen will look like Figure 8-5.

NOTE: *Generally, you should not modify this screen unless instructed to do so. Making a change here can cause problems!*

FIGURE 8-5
Startup Dialog.

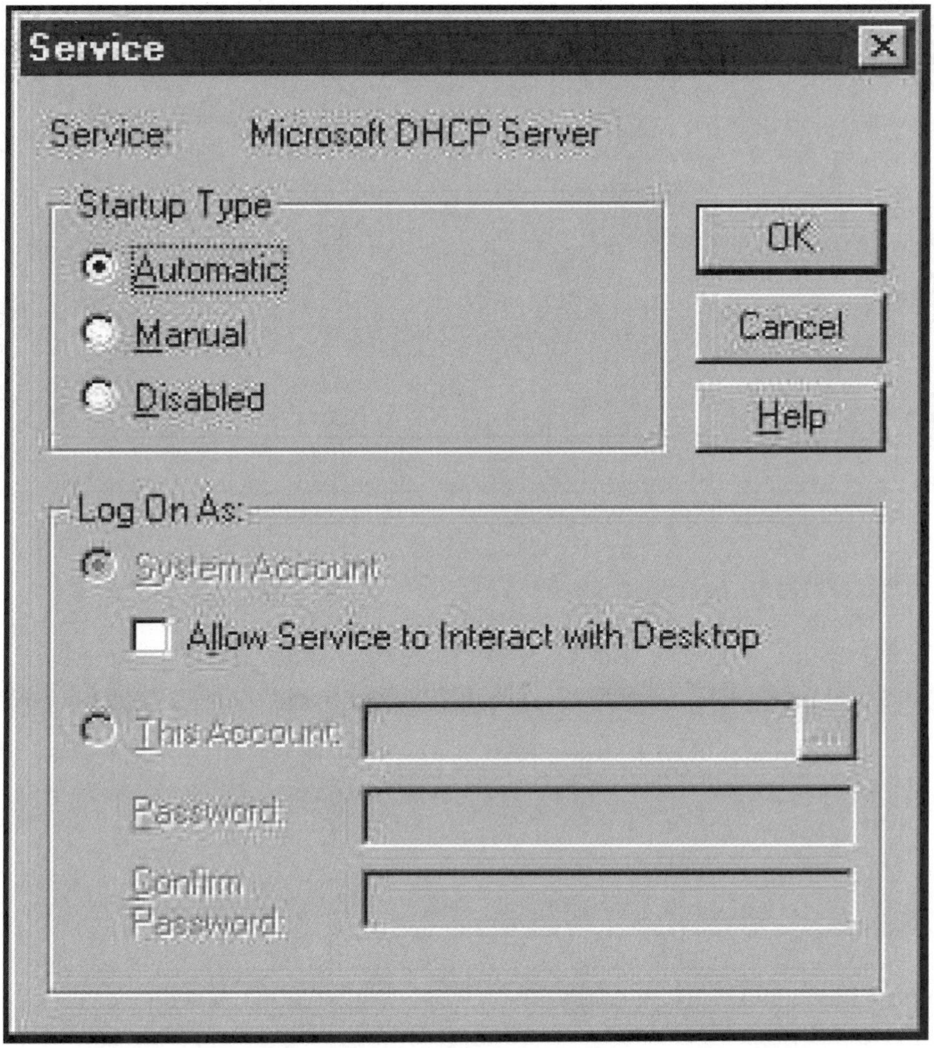

An alternate method of starting and stopping the service can be accomplished using a Windows NT command prompt. To start and stop Microsoft DHCP server from the command prompt type the following command:

To *stop* the service, type: **NET STOP DHCPSERVER**

To *start* the service, type: **NET START DHCPSERVER**

The results of these commands are provided in Figure 8-6.

FIGURE 8-6
NET START/STOP commands.

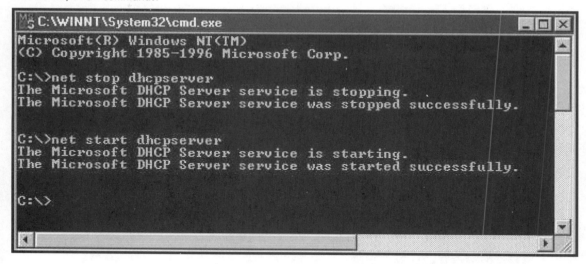

```
C:\WINNT\System32\cmd.exe                                    _ □ ×
Microsoft(R) Windows NT(TM)
(C) Copyright 1985-1996 Microsoft Corp.

C:\>net stop dhcpserver
The Microsoft DHCP Server service is stopping.
The Microsoft DHCP Server service was stopped successfully.

C:\>net start dhcpserver
The Microsoft DHCP Server service is starting.
The Microsoft DHCP Server service was started successfully.

C:\>
```

Opening Microsoft DHCP Server

Now that the service is installed and operational, let's open the DHCP manager application. To do this, click the Start button, select Administrative Tools, and then DHCP Manager. The application should look like the diagram in Figure 8-7.

Even though DHCP is installed, there is still some configuration we must complete to get the server ready for use. One of the first things we must do is create a scope. Before we do that though it will be helpful to understand a little about how DHCP deals with scopes.

Global Options versus Local Scopes

The second concept we must be aware of is the difference between a local scope and a global option. We already learned what a scope was in the last lesson. Now we must take a look at how DHCP handles the scopes and options.

DHCP server can have multiple scopes defined on a single server. For instance, you might have two scopes configured for separate subnets on your network. Each individually configured scope is called a **local scope**. They are completely separate and can be managed as such. Local scopes can have completely different parameters that are isolated within themselves.

In certain instances, there may be parameters that are applicable across all the local scopes installed on a DHCP server. When this occurs, there is a special type of configuration called a **Global option** that can be used. When you configure the Global Option, all the settings you specify are available to the local scopes on that particular server.

FIGURE 8-7
The DHCP Manager Application.

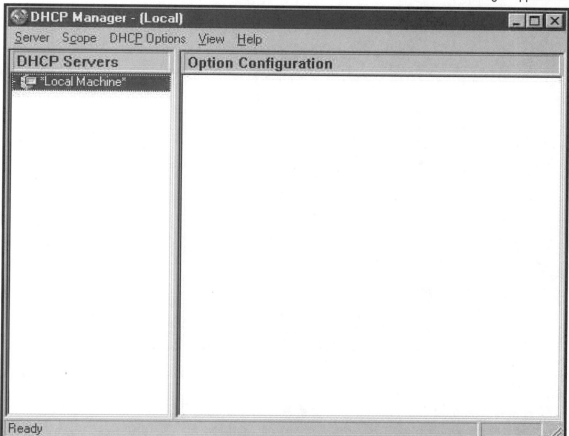

For example, even though the local scopes might have different IP ranges and gateways, they might use the same DNS and WINS servers. If this were the case, you could configure the WINS and DNS entries in the global options and these values would be made available to all the local scopes installed on the DHCP server. This allows a great deal of flexibility and easier administration of the server. We will see how to configure options using both these options in just a little bit.

Configuring a Local Scope

First and foremost, even though we have successfully installed the DHCP Service, we cannot have clients begin to use it until we have configured a scope. As you recall, the scope contains all the pertinent information for DHCP to lease an address to a client. To configure a scope we have to enter some mandatory information.

FIGURE 8-8
Creating a DHCP Scope.

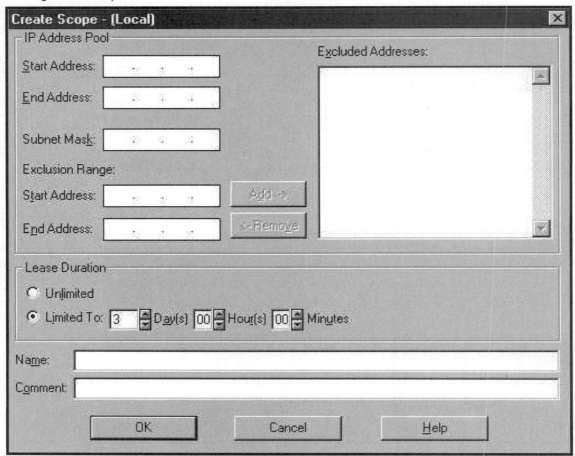

At a bare minimum, we must specify an IP address range and subnet address for the scope. To do this, we must create a new scope. To accomplish this task you click on the Scope menu option and then Create. When you do this you will be presented with a screen similar to the one provided in Figure 8-8.

Let's dissect this screen capture so we understand what we need to configure here:

IP Address Pool. This is the "pool" or group of addresses we wish to lease. This is normally limited to a particular subnet. The rule is typically one address pool per subnet. You must enter a valid IP address range using the Start Address and End Address entry points. *This is a mandatory entry.*

Subnet Mask. Enter the correct subnet mask in this field. *This is a mandatory entry.*

Exclusion Range. Setting an exclusion range allows you to remove certain IP addresses from the range you specified using the IP address pool. You might exclude a range of addresses for servers and workstations that require static IP mappings (like your DHCP Server). You can add multiple entries here and specify a range of addresses to exclude. Once you begin entering information in this section, the Add and Remove buttons will become active. *Setting exclusion ranges are optional to the creation of the scope.*

Lease Duration. This setting controls how long a client will have a lease. A general rule of thumb is to set this parameter to 1–3 days. The reason for this is that if you ever make changes to your DHCP configuration, you want clients to receive the changes in a timely fashion. If you selected an unlimited lease, the client would never be forced to renew and any changes that you made would never be reflected on the workstation. Typically, a window of one to three days is acceptable. Another reason you might have a short lease duration deals with effective address management of a small number of IP addresses. Remember, once a client has a lease, no one else can have that IP address. Setting a short lease allows more clients access to the available IP addresses. DHCP server defaults to renewal once every three days. This value can be changed to suit your individual needs. *A lease duration value is mandatory to configure the scope.*

Name. This allows you to enter an understandable name for the scope. You can enter any alphanumeric information in this field. *This is an optional field.*

Comment. As it implies, you can enter a little more information about the scope. *This is an optional field.*

Once you have entered the appropriate information, click the OK button. You will be asked if you wish to activate the scope. When scopes are active in DHCP Manager, they have a yellow light bulb icon next to them.

When the scope is created and activated your DHCP Manager application will look like Figure 8-9.

FIGURE 8-9
DHCP Active Scope.

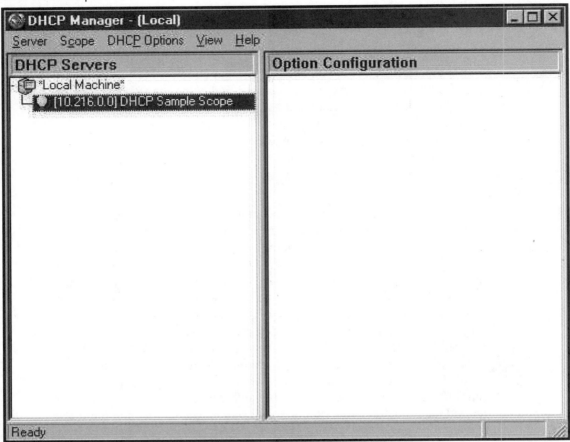

Adding Other Options to the Scope

Now that we have configured a basic DHCP scope, we can add additional information to the configuration. This information will be provided along with the lease to the client. To add additional options to be leased with the DHCP scope, select the DHCP Options menu and then pick the Scope option. When you do this, you will receive a dialog box like the one in Figure 8-10.

You will notice there are many different information options that can be passed to the client from this panel. We will not be using many of these, but there are several that are very common that we will use on a regular basis. These options are listed here.

003—Router. This is the address of the default gateway(s) for the client. Obviously, this is a heavily used option and one you will configure on a regular basis.

006—DNS Servers. This option allows you to configure the addresses of DNS servers on your network.

FIGURE 8-10
DHCP Options: Scope Dialog.

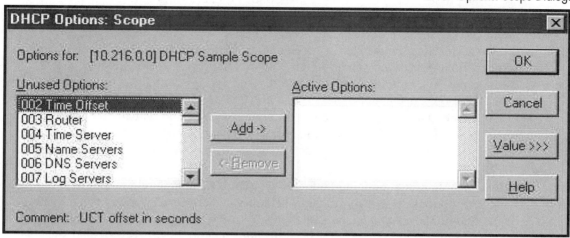

044—WINS/NBNS Servers. This option allows you to configure WINS server addresses on the client. To use this option, you must also include the 046 Option (WINS node type).

046—WINS/NBT Node Type. This option works in conjunction with the 044 option. It allows you to set the type of broadcast transmission sent by the client. We will always use the 0×8 "H" (Hybrid) node type. For more information on these node types see Chapter 6 on WINS.

To configure these options follow this outlined process.

1. Highlight the Option in the left-hand column.

2. Click the Add button. The option will be moved to the left-hand column.

3. Click the Value button.

4. Enter the correct IP address or configuration information requested. The required information will vary from option to option.

5. Click OK.

If you need to remove an option, highlight the option in the right-hand column and click the Remove button.

NOTE: *These options are for the individual scope. If you need to configure options for all scopes on the DHCP server, you use the Options menu option Global selection.*

Configuring Global Scope Options

The process for configuring global options is exactly the same as for local scope options except that you use a different option from the DHCP Options menu choice. To configure global options (those values which will apply to *All* the scopes installed on the DHCP server), select the Global menu selection. The screen will appear exactly as in Figure 8-10 and the configuration process will be the same. The only difference will be that the options configured will apply to *All* the scopes installed on the server.

Be sure that the settings you use for your global options actually do apply to all the local scopes! If they do not, erratic behavior can occur—some clients will be successful in performing functions while others will not!

Configuring Default Scope Values

This options allows you to enter default values for each option available in the Scope and Global menu selections. You may, of course, change these options on an individual basis for customized scope options. It is provided so that you can ease your configuration process. Enter a default value here and it will appear as the initial Value entry for a particular entry. You can edit as many of these as required. A good example of when to use this is with the Node Type entry. All the WINS node type entries should be set to an H-Type node. So, configure this as **0×8** in the Default Values section, and every time you use this option in a scope, it will be automatically entered for you.

Client Leases

Some clients cannot be DHCP-enabled. In this case, you may still wish to use DHCP as your primary address management tool and account for these computers as well. There is a special configuration option available in Microsoft DHCP Server to allow this to occur. This section covers the process of Adding a Client Reservation.

RESERVING LEASES

A Client Reservation is nothing more than a static IP address mapping to a particular host. For computers that are unable to use DHCP as an address management method, this is the preferred way of configuring their addresses while still using DHCP for all your other clients. To assign a Client Reservation, follow the outlined process here.

1. Select the Scope menu option and highlight the Add Reservations selection.

2. You will be presented with a dialog screen as in Figure 8-11.

    Let's take a look at these fields—the configuration here will be somewhat different than what you might expect.

    IP Address. Enter the IP address of the client in this field. Notice that this applies to the particular scope you are working on now. *Client reservations only apply to a specific scope/subnet!*

Add Reserved Clients

IP Address: 10 . 216 . | .

Unique Identifier:

Client Name:

Client Comment:

[Add] [Close] [Help] [Options...]

Unique Identifier. You must enter the MAC address of the client in this field. You can use the PING/ARP method to determine the remote host's address or use IPCONFIG/ALL if you are working locally on a machine to get the MAC address. The MAC address is entered in one long string. There are no hyphens between hex numbers for this entry. If you enter an incorrect MAC address, the client will be assigned any available IP address from your pool. Double-check your work on this field!

Client Name. This is the client NetBIOS name of the computer. It is used for information purposes only. All resolution is performed using the MAC address. Enter the NetBIOS name of the computer in this field.

Client Comment. This field is an optional additional information field. It is used to further define some basic information on the particular client.

3. Once you have entered the appropriate information, click the Add button. This will add the client reservation to your individual scope configuration.

An alternate method for reserving leases is to exclude a range of IP addresses from your scope that apply to non-DHCP clients. In this manner, the excluded addresses can be manually configured on the client and assure DHCP Manager will never attempt to allocate those IP addresses to another DHCP client since they are not included in the active scope.

A FINAL WORD ON CLIENT LEASES

As is the case with all protocols, leases are based on some basic rules. The process of lease renewal and assignment works in the following manner.

1. When a client receives its lease from the DHCP server, an entry is made when that lease will expire.

2. When the time period reaches approximately 50% of the lease value, the client will attempt to renew its lease with the original DHCP server. If it is successful, the lease will be renewed, the lease period will be reset, new configuration data will be updated, and the client will continue with its current IP address information. If not, the lease will still be in effect for the remaining 50% of its current lease.

3. When the time period reaches 85% of the lease duration, the client will begin attempting to renew its lease at regular intervals with any DHCP server on the network using the process outlined earlier in this chapter. If the lease is not renewed by the date specified, the client will lose its lease and attempt to get a new one from any DHCP server on the network.

4. If the client is unable to receive a lease, communications using TCP/IP will be halted until such time as it is successful.

DHCP and IPCONFIG

When using DHCP, your primary tool in troubleshooting and information gathering will be IPCONFIG on a Windows NT computer. In Windows 95 and 98, the tool is known as WINIPCFG. These two tools provide the same information. The NT version is command prompt-based, the 95/98 versions are GUI-based.

IPCONFIG can tell you whether your client received a lease, what that lease is, what information was leased, and lease duration information. In addition, you can use the tool to release and renew the address using the /Release and /Renew switches.

Signs of trouble are IP addresses and subnet mask values of 0.0.0.0. This means your client has not received its lease. Try a manual renew first. If this doesn't work, then try checking cables and a static IP entry to test the overall installation of TCP/IP. Follow standard troubleshooting procedure if you are still unsuccessful.

LAB

8.2

Configuring DHCP in a Single Subnet

● ●

In this lab exercise you will install and configure a DHCP server and client using the procedures outlined in this lesson. Your instructor will provide you with a range of IP addresses to configure your initial DHCP scope and all the parameters. Follow all the directions below and answer questions as appropriate. When you have completed the lab, share your results with the instructor. Please note if you are working with multiple DHCP servers, it is quite possible you will receive a lease from another machine in the classroom. This is to be expected and is perfectly normal. Remember, the first DHCP server that responds to the client request typically grants the lease. This may be your DHCP server machine or it may be another!

NOTE: *Complete Lab 8.1 on a Windows NT Server.*

ON THE WINDOWS NT WORKSTATION

1. Open the Networking Control Panel, Protocols Tab, and modify the properties of the TCP/IP protocol.

2. Configure TCP/IP to obtain an IP Address from a DHCP Server.

3. Click OK.

4. Restart your computer.

5. Use IPCONFIG/ALL to see if your workstation received an IP address.

6. What was the IP address and subnet mask you received?

7. What DHCP server gave you the lease?

8. Share your results with the instructor.

Lesson 8.4 DHCP Advanced Configuration

This lesson looks at some of the more advanced features available in the Microsoft DHCP Server. In this lesson, we will learn a few governing rules of implementing fault tolerance in a DHCP environment, how to configure multiple scopes on a single DHCP Server, and some considerations we must take when planning our DHCP implementation across routers.

Multiple Scopes

As we stated earlier, it is possible to configure more than one scope on a DHCP Server. There are many reasons we might want to do this, but in general we are usually trying to accomplish one of two objectives.

1. We want completely centralized IP management across an organization with multiple subnets.

2. We want a degree of fault tolerance with our DHCP management scheme.

Both of these instances require us to create multiple scopes on a server. The process for creating multiple scopes on a DHCP server is the same as creating a single scope except we add more than one scope to the server. Every setting we have looked at previously works with multiple scopes too.

One important concept to remember about multiple scopes is the following:

Each scope is limited to one subnet.

The balance of this lesson describes methods for configuring multiple scopes and obtaining fault tolerance in a DHCP configuration.

Multiple DHCP Servers and Fault Tolerance

Fault tolerance in any hardware or network configuration implies there must be more than one component or device located on hardware devices or a network. In terms of DHCP fault tolerance, two basic rules apply.

Rule 1—We need more than one DHCP server to create a fault-tolerant configuration for a particular network.

Rule 2—Different DHCP servers must have multiple subnet scopes configured with nonoverlapping IP address ranges.

Rule 1 seems pretty easy to understand, but Rule 2 probably needs just a little more explanation. What we mean when we say "multiple subnet scopes" is that the DHCP servers are primarily servicing a particular subnet and that if they are to be fault-tolerant, they must also be able to cover the other DHCP server's scope range as well as its own. The "nonoverlapping IP address range" component of the rule simply means that no matter who is servicing whom, we need to make sure that only one unique IP address can ever be assigned to any client, regardless of what DHCP server they get their address from.

It will help to explain this fault-tolerant configuration with a simple example:

TYPICAL SITUATION

John manages a TCP/IP with two subnets. He uses DHCP to manage IP addresses on each subnet. There is a DHCP server located on each subnet.

He wishes to implement a fault-tolerant configuration for his DHCP servers. How might he accomplish this?

SOLUTION

If we refer to our rules, John already has two DHCP servers installed so he has met Rule 1. To configure his network for DHCP fault tolerance, he needs to add a new scope on each of the DHCP servers. The first server (Server 1) needs to have a nonoverlapping range of IP addresses for the second server's (Server 2) client address pool. Likewise, Server 2 needs to have a nonoverlapping range of IP addresses for Server 1 clients. This will assure that if either DHCP server fails, clients from either subnet will still be able to lease addresses.

The only hitch in this process is that a DHCP relay agent must be installed on the servers *or* the router you are using must support a function like Boot P (more on this later).

The general rule of thumb for configuring fault-tolerant scopes up is as follows:

NOTE: *The primary DHCP server scope servicing a subnet should have approximately 75% of the available addresses available for clients on their primary subnet. The remaining 25% of the available addresses would be configured on the* other *DHCP server's address pool.*

In our example, Server 1's primary pool of addresses would consist of 75% of subnet A's address pool and 25% of subnet B's address pool. Server 2's address pool would have 75% of subnet B's address pool and 25% of subnet A's address pool. In this manner, we are providing fault tolerance across the subnets.

Managing the DHCP Database

In most cases, you will not need to backup, restore, tune, or optimize the Microsoft DHCP server's database. This was not the case with earlier releases of Windows NT server (version 3.5X and earlier). Version 4.0 handles this automatically for you—your database will be backed up once every hour. If DHCP detects a corrupted database, it will automatically restore the last version without your intervention. But, just in case . . .

DHCP databases are stored in several different locations depending on their type. They can always be found by searching for files with the extension .MDB. Microsoft DHCP databases are located in the following directories of a Windows NT server:

Main Files: \WINNT\System32\DHCP subdirectory

Backup Files: \WINNT\System32\DHCP\Backup\Jet subdirectory

If you know anything about Microsoft Access, you will also realize that the MDB file extension designates an Access database. It is possible to view the DHCP database using Microsoft Access (although Microsoft does not recommend *any* tampering with the files). The files DHCP Manager uses are as follows:

DHCP.MDB—This database contains all the information on client leases.

SYSTEM.MDB—This database contains the structure information of the DHCP database.

DHCP.TMP—This is a temporary "working" database that DHCP uses when the service is running.

JET*.LOG—These are transaction logging files for the databases showing all types of information on what has been occurring with the DHCP databases.

In the unlikely event that you must restore a damaged or corrupted database manually, there are two procedures you can follow.

PROCEDURE 1—COPYING BACKUP DHCP DATABASES (PREFERRED)

1. Stop the DHCP Server Service if it has not already been stopped automatically. Use the **NET STOP DHCPSERVER** command discussed earlier in the chapter.

2. Copy the contents of the . . . \Backup\Jet directory to the \WINNT\ System32\DHCP directory.

3. Restart the DHCP Server Service using the **NET START DHCPSERVER** command.

4. DHCP Server will restore the database automatically.

PROCEDURE 2—SETTING THE RESTORE FLAG IN THE REGISTRY

1. Stop the DHCP Server Service if it has not already been stopped automatically. Use the **NET STOP DHCPSERVER** command discussed earlier in the chapter.

2. Open REGEDT32 and open the key:

    HKEY_LOCAL_MACHINE\SYSTEM\CurrentControlSet\Services\ DHCPServer\Parameters

3. Set the RestoreFlag Key value to **1.**

4. Save the entry.

5. Restart the DHCP Server Service using the **NET START DHCPSERVER** command.

6. The value will automatically be reset to 0 (zero) once the database has been successfully restored.

NOTE: *Making changes using the Registry Editor can cause all sorts of problems! Use the registry editor only when no other method exists to make a required change!*

LAB

8.3 Configuring DHCP Multiple Parameters and Scopes (Optional)

• •

This lab is not required and is optional. The lab allows you to configure two scopes using DHCP Server. In addition, you will add additional parameters to each local scope and a global setting for both scopes. To perform this lab, you must have a routed network with at least two subnets and a router capable of DHCP broadcasts (or DHCP Relay Agent installed on an NT Server located on the subnet where there is none). If you have the appropriate configuration, you will be able to test your installation. If you do not, you can still set up the scopes and parameters, you will, however, be unable to test the configuration. Consult with your instructor to see if you have the necessary configuration in place to complete the testing component of this lab. Answer all questions and follow the directions below. When complete share your results with the instructor.

ON THE DHCP SERVER

1. Create two scopes using the DHCP Manager application. One of the scopes is for subnet A and the other is for subnet B. Assign a small range of addresses to the pools of each scope as specified by your instructor.

2. Configure the local scope options for subnets A and B with the router IP address of the individual routers on each subnet. This is the 004 Router value. These values will be different for each individual scope so you will enter the information using the Scope option as outlined earlier in the chapter.

3. Configure the NBNS and NBNS node type entries (This is the WINS server information—options 044 and 046) as global options so the WINS server addresses are the same for both scopes.

4. Activate both scopes.

ON THE WINDOWS NT CLIENTS

1. Assure the clients are setup to receive their addresses automatically from a DHCP server using the process outlined earlier in this chapter.

2. If required, restart your client workstation.

TESTING THE CONFIGURATION

1. Once the clients on both subnets successfully boot, log in to the computers.

2. Open a Command Window.

3. Type **IPCONFIG/ALL.**

4. Did your machines receive their lease information from the DHCP server?

5. If they did, record the information for each subnet client.

6. Were all the parameters passed correctly?

7. Try PINGING by NetBIOS name. Did you get a reply?

8. Close the NT Command Window.

9. Congratulations! You successfully completed setting up and implementing multiple scopes using DHCP Server.

If you run into problems with the configuration or testing, ask your instructor for assistance. There's much to do in the configuration process. I have purposely not provided step-by-step instructions so you can test how much you remember about our previous lessons!

Lesson 8.5 DHCP Relay Agent

This lesson describes the Microsoft DHCP Relay Agent and how to use it to allow multiple subnet clients to successfully lease addresses across remotely located DHCP servers.

What Is a Relay Agent?

You are probably well grounded in the concept of a relay race. DHCP Relay Agent functions very similarly to the concept of a relay race. In essence, when a client needs to get an IP address from a remote subnet, its request is relayed, or forwarded, to a relay agent, which then passes its request to a specified server on the remote subnet. This process has been established because DHCP transmissions are typically limited on the local subnet where they originated. The relay agent allows the transmission to be passed to a remote server. That's really all there is to the concept.

Why Do We Need DHCP Relay Agent?

DHCP, like WINS, uses broadcast transmissions to send its messages to and from clients and servers. This presents a problem in routed networks since broadcasts typically do not cross routers. Some routers support DHCP broadcasts and almost all need to have this feature enabled. If the router you are using does not support DHCP broadcasts as defined in RFC 1542 and you need to use a DHCP server to allow clients on multiple subnets to procure IP configurations, you will use DHCP Relay Agent to accomplish this task.

How DHCP Relay Agent Works

Any Windows NT server can function as a DHCP relay agent. The DHCP Service *does not* have to be installed for a Windows NT server to act as a relay agent. Once you have installed the Relay Agent software, it must be configured to point at the correct DHCP server on the network. The server can reside on any subnet accessible by the NT server.

DHCP Relay forwards DHCP requests to the DHCP server configured in the Relay Agent Service. You can specify several different DHCP servers as part of the process. The entire relaying process is seamless to the end user. When the client makes its initial request for an IP address, the request is picked up and processed by the DHCP Relay Agent computer and forwarded to the DHCP server. The DHCP server then sends its information back to the relay agent, which then passes it along to the client. Basically, the agent is the middle-man in the process serving as an intermediary between the client and the remotely located server.

Installing and Configuring DHCP Relay Agent

DHCP Relay Agent is a service that can be installed using the Network Control Panel; Services Tab. Installing the service is like installing any other Network Service in Windows NT. To install and configure DHCP Relay Agent, follow this outlined procedure.

ON THE WINDOWS NT SERVER

1. Open the Network Control Panel applet. Your screen should look something like Figure 8-12.

2. Click on the Services Tab. Your screen should look something like figure 8-13.

3. Click the Add button.

FIGURE 8-12
The Network Control Panel.

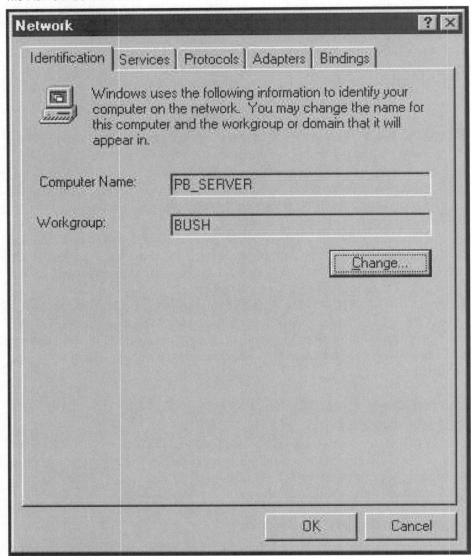

FIGURE 8-13
Network Control Panel Services Tab.

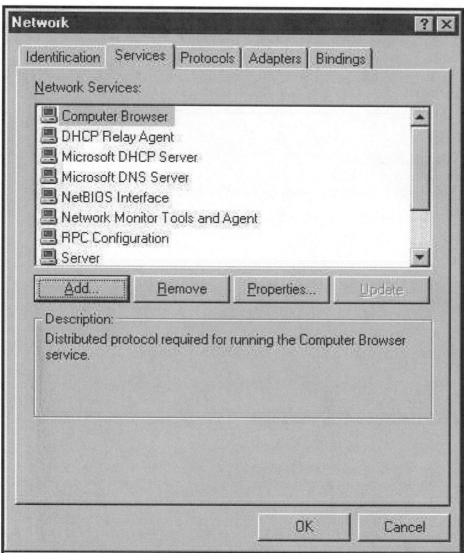

FIGURE 8-14
Network Control Panel Add Services Dialog.

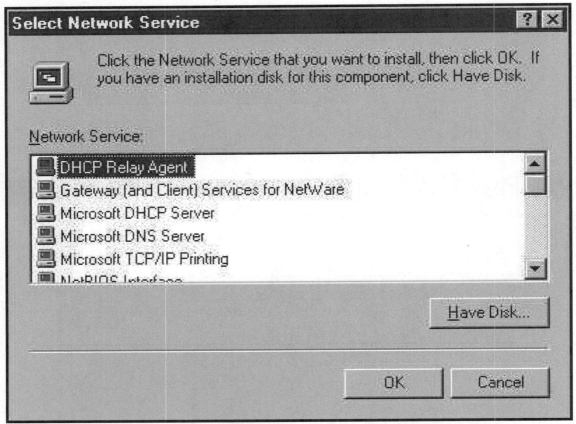

4. Select Microsoft DHCP Relay Agent from the list. Your screen should look like Figure 8-14.

5. Click OK

6. Provide the installation path if you have not already done so. Setup will copy several files. You will also be informed that the service requires at least one DHCP server's address to start. For this exercise *do not* enter the address. All we want to do is install the service at this point. We will configure it in the next exercise.

7. Restart the computer when prompted.

8. Re-apply Service Pack 3 when you log on.

9. Restart the computer one more time. That's all there is to it!

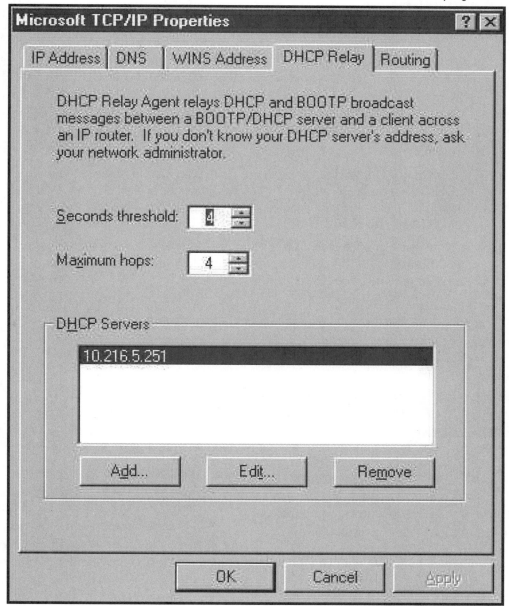

Now you are ready to configure the DHCP Relay Agent Service. To configure the service, follow the procedure outlined here.

1. Open the Control Panel Network applet. Click on the Protocols Tab, select the TCP/IP Protocol and then select the DHCP Relay Agent Tab. Your screen should look something like Figure 8-15.

2. Click the Add button to add the IP address of the DHCP server with whom you will relay messages.

3. Click OK when you are complete.

That's all there is to it! While we are looking at this screen, let's take a quick look at the other options that you can configure for your DHCP Relay Agent.

Seconds Threshold. This value determines the number of seconds before a request is sent to the DHCP server. This value's default setting is 4 and normally should not be changed.

Maximum Hops. This value determines the maximum number of hops a DHCP Relay Agent will make before discarding a packet. The default value is 4 and normally should not be changed. The maximum value for this field is 16.

Now that you understand the concept of a relay agent and how to configure the Microsoft DHCP Relay Agent, complete the following lab using all the information provided throughout this lesson.

LAB 8.4 Installing and Configuring DHCP Relay Agent

• •

This lab allows you to install and configure the DHCP Relay Agent. To complete this lab, you should have one DHCP server located on a remote subnet from the relay agent computer. Follow all directions and answer all questions completely. When you have completed the lab, share your results with the instructor.

IN GENERAL

1. Make sure there is only one DHCP server on the network and that it is functional. The server should be located on a remote subnet.

ON THE DHCP RELAY AGENT COMPUTER

1. Install the DHCP Relay Agent on an NT server computer on the local subnet you are working on. When prompted, provide the IP address of the DHCP server located on the remote subnet.

2. Click OK and restart your computer when prompted.

3. Upon reboot, reinstall Service Pack 3.

ON THE WINDOWS NT WORKSTATION CLIENT LOCATED ON THE REMOTE SUBNET FROM THE DHCP SERVER

1. Assure the workstation is setup to use DHCP.

2. Reboot if required.

3. Once the clients successfully boot, log in to the computer.

4. Open a Command Windows.

5. Type **IPCONFIG/ALL.**

6. Did your machines receive their lease information from the DHCP server?

7. If they did, record the information for each subnet client.

8. Close the NT Command Window.

9. Congratulations! You successfully completed setting up and implementing the Microsoft DHCP Relay Agent.

Lesson 8.6 Troubleshooting Microsoft DHCP Server Implementations

This lesson describes some basic troubleshooting techniques for managing a DHCP installation. Since DHCP must be enabled on both the client and server, these are two areas we will be focusing on in this lesson, server-based and workstation-based troubleshooting.

SERVER-BASED TROUBLESHOOTING

Here are some things to check:

■ Make sure the TCP/IP configuration on the server is installed properly.

■ Check all your network cables and assure you are appropriately connected to the network!

■ Assure you can PING hosts on local and remote subnets.

■ Make sure the DHCP server has a statically assigned IP address, subnet mask, and default gateway. This is required for the service to start and run.

■ Check event viewer for any networking issues related to DHCP. Note that a seemingly unimportant dependent service failure can cause the DHCP Manager to not initialize.

- Check the Services Applet in Control Panel to make sure the service has started. Some folks configure manual startup of certain services. If this is the case, start the DHCP Service. If the service fails to start, check event viewer for the error message.

- If the database appears to be corrupted and will not automatically restore itself, follow the instructions in this chapter to perform a manual restore of the database using one of the two methods listed.

- When all else fails, remove the DHCP Server Service and reinstall it. If you are running any Service Packs, be sure to reinstall them!

WORKSTATION-BASED TROUBLESHOOTING

Here are some things to check:

- Make sure the TCP/IP configuration on the workstation is set to use DHCP and not a static IP configuration.

- Check all your network cables and assure you are appropriately connected to the network! You would be surprised how many problems can be traced to a bad or incorrectly attached cable or port!

- Check event viewer for any networking issues related to TCP/IP networking. Note that a seemingly unimportant dependent service failure can cause TCP/IP to not initialize.

- Use IPCONFIG to see the configured TCP/IP parameters and see if they match what should be provided by the DHCP server.

- Check all the TCP/IP tabs for erroneous entries. This is the most common problem with DHCP client configurations. Even if a client is configured to use DHCP, if the user has entered values for DNS, WINS, or Default Gateway settings, this information will take precedence over what DHCP will provide to the client. When troubleshooting DHCP problems on a client, make sure there are no entries that conflict with the DHCP server settings being passed as either local or global options. One mechanism to manage this problem is to restrict access to the Network Control Panel using Windows NT System Policies.

Summary

This chapter covered the Microsoft DHCP Server and DHCP Relay Agent services. Throughout this chapter we learned the following.

■ **DHCP Benefits.** We discussed why DHCP is an important tool in managing TCP/IP installations across an organization and how automatic lease management can reduce the administrative overhead of managing a TCP/IP network.

■ **DHCP Leasing Process.** We learned how DHCP clients and servers work together to secure, maintain, and renew an IP lease. We also learned that DHCP can be used to provide many other TCP/IP configuration components, including default gateways, WINS server, and DNS server addresses

■ **Installation and Configuration of DHCP.** We learned how to install and configure the Microsoft DHCP Service including how to set up multiple scopes, pass global and local variables to clients, reserve client leases, and how to restore the DHCP database in the event of corruption.

■ **Manage DHCP Fault Tolerance.** We discussed strategies and methods for creating a fault tolerant DHCP configuration for an organization.

■ **Install and Configure the Microsoft DHCP Relay Agent Service.** We learned what DHCP Relay Agent is, what it is for, and how to configure this service to allow clients to access remotely located DHCP servers across routers.

■ **Troubleshooting DHCP Installations.** We learned a few key areas to focus on when attempting to troubleshoot DHCP installations. These areas focused on server- and workstation-based troubleshooting tips and techniques.

● ● ● ● ● ● ● ● ● ● ● ● ● ●

Q & A

1. *Select two.* John wants to configure DHCP to assign the IP address of the WINS server to all client computers. What does John have to do in order to allow client computers to use WINS?

   a. Specify the NetBIOS resolution mode on the DHCP server.
   b. Enter the NetBIOS name type on every client.
   c. Enter the IP address of the DHCP server on every client.
   d. Specify the NBNS server in the scope options of the DHCP server.

2. *Select the best answer.* Mary recently made a change in her DHCP Server scope options for an additional DNS server. She wants to see if this configuration has been updated on her machine. How would Mary view this information?

   a. ARP
   b. IPCONFIG/ALL
   c. IPCONFIG
   d. NETSTAT
   e. PING –c

3. *Select the best answer.* Mark wants DHCP to assign IP addresses to all Microsoft Windows-based client computers on his network. However, he wants to include Windows NT server computers serving as WINS and DNS servers to be assured they will receive the same IP address. The servers have noncontiguous IP addresses. What should Mark do to implement this?

   a. Exclude a range of IP addresses that will be assigned to the servers.
   b. Create a separate scope for each server that consists of only that server's IP address.
   c. Implement client reservations for all the servers.
   d. Specify unlimited lease periods for all the servers.

4. *Select all that apply.* You are the administrator of a large TCP/IP network consisting of 500 Windows 95 and Windows NT-based computers. The network has been segmented into nine subnets. Many users have laptop computers that run Windows 95. You want to automatically assign IP addresses and manage NetBIOS name resolution to all workstations on the network. Which services must you install?

   a. DHCP
   b. DNS
   c. LMHOSTS
   d. HOSTS
   e. WINS

5. *Select all that apply.* Hilda uses DNS, WINS, and DHCP to administer her TCP/IP network. She wants to assure that the IP addresses of her UNIX and statically configured NT servers

always receive the same IP addresses. What information must Hilda have when reserving these servers in DHCP Manager?

a. Hardware addresses
b. IP addresses
c. Lease durations
d. Subnet masks

6. *Select the best answer.* Gus administers a network with five subnets. He wants to implement DHCP on the entire network but only wants to use one DHCP server for the enterprise. The routers on Gus's network do not support DHCP message relay. Gus has installed his DHCP server on subnet 1. Where does Gus need to position DHCP Relay Agents?

a. On all subnets.
b. Install the Relay Agent on selected Windows NT server machines located on all subnets except subnet 1.
c. DHCP Relay Agent is not required for Gus to achieve his objective.
d. Install the Relay Agent on the router.
e. Install the Relay Agent on selected Windows NT workstation machines located on all subnets except subnet 1.
f. None of these configurations will work.

7. *Select the best answer.* Molly is troubleshooting a DHCP installation that uses both local and global options to provide host information to her clients. Users on the network appear to be functioning properly except for two folks located in different subnets. The subnets also support users who are reporting no problems. These users report they can connect to remote hosts using IP addresses but not NetBIOS names. What would be the most probable cause for these difficulties?

a. The client computer has manually configured an incorrect IP address and subnet mask and disabled DHCP address management.
b. The Client Reservation is not configured properly.
c. The local scope WINS option is incorrectly defined and conflicts with the global option.
d. The user's computer is still a DHCP client, but the WINS server options have been manually set by the user.

8. *Select all that apply.* Max has two multi-homed Windows NT server computers functioning as routers on his network. He wants to configure automatic updates of the tables and packet transfers on these servers with the least amount of administrative effort possible. What should Max do?

a. Install DHCP Relay Agent on a Windows NT server computer.
b. Install RIP for IP on each multi-homed computer.
c. Install DHCP Manager on each multi-homed computer.
d. Enable IP forwarding on each multi-homed computer.
e. Enable multiple gateways on each multi-homed computer.

9. *Select the best answer.* You have determined that you must configure a DHCP Relay Agent on a Windows NT machine. What is the mandatory piece of information required to configure the service?

   a. DHCP NetBIOS name.
   b. Maximum number of hops.
   c. DHCP server IP address.
   d. Threshold limit for DHCP transmissions.
   e. No information is required to implement DHCP Relay Agent. It is self-configuring.

10. *Select the best answer.* Ron moves a Windows NT server computer originally configured as a DHCP client from one subnet to another. When he reboots the computer on the new subnet, he can connect to all local resources on its new subnet but is unable to connect to any remote hosts. What is a possible cause of the problem?

    a. The default gateway address on the server has been manually set.
    b. Windows NT servers cannot be DHCP clients.
    c. The TCP/IP interface is statically configured.
    d. There is a conflict between the global and local scope options between the different subnet scopes.
    e. None of these situations are causing the problem.

11. *Select the best answer.* Mary is unable to start her DHCP Server Service on a dedicated Windows NT Server. She needs to restore the original DHCP database manually. What is the recommended method for Mary to accomplish this task?

    a. Modify the registry key.
    b. Copy the contents of the DHCP Backup directory to the DHCP Directory.
    c. Copy the contents of the DHCP Jet directory to the DHCP Directory.
    d. Reinstall DHCP Server.
    e. Force a restore using the Jetpack utility.

12. *Select the best answers.* John has two DHCP servers installed on his TCP/IP network. The network consists of two subnets. He would like to implement fault tolerance between these servers. His routers support relay of DHCP information. What is the correct configuration for John to implement to achieve a measure of fault tolerance on his network?

    a. On the first DHCP server, configure one scope with both ranges of IP addresses.
    b. On the second DHCP server, configure one scope with both ranges of IP addresses.
    c. On the first DHCP server, configure two scopes; the first being the primary for the DHCP server's home subnet with approximately 25% of the available addresses. The second scope will consist of 75% of the remote DHCP server's address pool.
    d. On the second DHCP server, configure two scopes; the first being the primary for the DHCP server's home subnet with approximately 25% of the available addresses. The second scope will consist of 75% of the remote DHCP server's address pool.

e. On the first DHCP server, configure two scopes; the first being the primary for the DHCP server's home subnet with approximately 75% of the available addresses. The second scope will consist of 25% of the remote DHCP server's address pool.

f. On the second DHCP server, configure two scopes; the first being the primary for the DHCP server's home subnet with approximately 75% of the available addresses. The second scope will consist of 25% of the remote DHCP server's address pool.

13. *Select the best answer.* Jack must install a DHCP server on a TCP/IP network with four subnets. The network has ten Windows NT server computers supporting 300 Windows NT workstation computers. The servers are all located on one subnet. Jack needs to isolate a group of addresses for non-DHCP UNIX hosts that exist on each of the subnets. All these UNIX workstations have contiguous addresses on each subnet and are statically configured. How should Jack configure the DHCP scopes?

a. Create one DHCP scope for all the subnets. Implement client reservations for all the UNIX hosts.

b. Create two DHCP scopes, one for the UNIX workstations and one for all the DHCP-enabled clients. Create a client reservation for each UNIX host.

c. Create four DHCP scopes, one for each remote subnet address range. For each subnet, exclude the range of addresses for the statically configured UNIX hosts.

d. Create four DHCP scopes, one for each remote subnet address range. For each subnet, create individual client reservations for the statically configured UNIX hosts.

e. Microsoft DHCP Server cannot manage this configuration.

14. *Select the best answer.* Sara has successfully installed a DHCP Server Service and the DHCP Relay Agent on her network with three subnets. All clients are successfully leasing their addresses and can access all other servers. One of the subnets is constantly changing WINS and DNS servers due to a pending migration. Sara needs to be able to make changes on her DHCP server and allow clients on the one subnet to receive the new configuration data for WINS and DNS. The other two subnets remain relatively constant in their configurations and only need to receive updates once a month. How can Sara allow subnet 3 to receive daily updates from the DHCP server?

a. Do nothing on subnet 3. The default value for renewal is 24 hours. Change subnet 1 and 2 to a 30-day lease period by modifying the local scopes that service these subnets.

b. Change the global option for lease renewal to 1 day and apply the change to subnet 3.

c. Set the local scope renewal period on subnet 3 to 24 hours. Change subnet 1 and 2 renewal to 30 days.

d. This cannot be done using Microsoft DHCP Server Service.

15. Suppose the following situation exists:

Mike administers a TCP/IP network of computers on two subnets. He wants to install two DHCP servers, that will automatically assign IP addresses and various configuration options to the client computers. Mike has been informed that his network does not support DHCP broadcasts and he must allow for fault tolerance in his configuration.

Required result:

■ The DHCP configuration must be fault tolerant.

■ All computers must be able to receive addresses from the remote subnets.

Optional desired results:

■ DHCP should provide the DNS Server address to the clients.

■ DHCP should assign the IP addresses of the WINS server to all DHCP clients.

Proposed solution:

■ On each subnet, install and configure a DHCP Relay Agent to point at the remote DHCP server.

■ For each Windows NT server computer, create a client reservation.

■ On both DHCP servers, define a DHCP scope for each subnet as well as the remote subnet it will have to support. In each scope, define approximately 75% of the IP addresses in the local range. Assign the remaining 25% of the available IP addresses on the remote DHCP server.

■ For each scope on all DHCP computers, enable and configure a local option to apply the 44 WINS/NBNS servers, and the 46 WINS/NBT Node Type options.

Which results does the proposed solution produce (select the best answer)?

a. The proposed solution produces the required result and all of the optional desired results.
b. The proposed solution produces the required result and one of the optional desired results.
c. The proposed solution produces the required result, but does not produce any of the optional desired results.
d. The proposed solution does not produce the required result nor any optional results.

MULTI-SYSTEM CONNECTIVITY

OBJECTIVES

By the end of this chapter, you should be able to:

- Identify, configure, and use network device management tools (SNMP).

- Identify, configure, and use file transfer and management utilities (FTP and Telnet).

- Identify remote management utilities (Finger, RSH, and RXEC).

- Identify, configure, and use the various components of heterogeneous TCP/IP printing (LPR, LPQ, and LPD).

- Explore other BackOffice products that provide heterogeneous connectivity.

Introduction

This chapter discusses several other utilities that allow TCP/IP to communicate with a variety of different operating systems. In this chapter we will look at methods of remotely accessing resources, printing, file transfer, and network management. Microsoft TCP/IP provides full functionality in these areas, allowing users to communicate using any number of different platforms. Throughout this chapter we will look at function as it applies to the UNIX operating system. While the tools provided will work with many other implementations of TCP/IP, it is most common that you will use the utilities provided in this chapter to communicate with UNIX hosts.

Lesson 9.1 Cross-Platform Connectivity

Microsoft TCP/IP provides functionality allowing hosts to communicate across many different platforms. This connectivity is often referred to *heterogeneous* communications. Microsoft TCP/IP cross-platform connectivity is based on adherence of other TCP/IP protocol standards to the de facto UNIX standard. If a particular platform supports UNIX connectivity (using the tools described in this chapter), then Microsoft TCP/IP will also work within this environment. To keep things simple, we will be focusing on the generic implementation of these cross-platform tools; not the specific.

Cross-platform connectivity can be broken into three main areas. Each of these areas is discussed below, covering a specific cross-platform connectivity function.

Network Device Monitoring and Management. In the world of TCP/IP, network device management is typically controlled by SNMP. SNMP, as you recall, is an acronym for the *Simple Network Management Protocol.* We will be looking at the features, configuration, and function of SNMP in the Microsoft Windows NT environment.

File Transfer and Remote System Management. Connectivity utilities included with Microsoft TCP/IP allow users and administrators to remotely manage, copy files, and interact with different systems. These functions are accessed through the FTP (File Transfer Protocol), Telnet (Telecommunications across a network), Finger (a remote administrative tool) and RXEC (Remote Execution) utilities. We will define all these protocols and actually use FTP and Telnet to communicate with remote systems.

Printer Access and Administration. Windows NT also provides the ability to serve a UNIX print client/server. This allows UNIX print devices located on a network to be accessed by both Windows NT and UNIX systems. We will be looking at the main components of the TCP/IP printing subsystem, where each of the components must reside, and how they work together. TCP/IP printing consists of the LPD (Line Printer Daemon), LPQ (Line Printer Queue), and LPR (Line Printer Request) utilities.

Using these tools correctly provides a full-featured set of utilities for communication between different operating systems. We will be looking at each of these areas closely throughout this chapter.

Lesson 9.2 The Nuts-and-Bolts of Cross-Platform Connectivity

We have closely looked at how Microsoft hosts communicate using TCP/IP throughout this book. This lesson will take a look at how we can configure Windows NT to allow other operating system clients to use resources on our servers. For the purposes of this discussion, we will be focusing on UNIX hosts connecting to Windows NT resources.

What Resources Are We Trying to Use?

Predominantly, we will be dealing with the whole reason we started networking in the first place: File and Printer Sharing! Every operating system uses a different kind of file system to arrange data on a hard disk. Likewise, they also have different mechanisms for managing printers. The ability for us to seamlessly integrate these systems together is very important if we are to have a group of happy users! In this section, we will look at, compare, and describe methods for accessing data and printers from a UNIX client. Before we begin though, let's review a couple of basic rules:

Rule Number 1—Like Equals Like. From the very beginning of our networking education we have seen that everybody has to be talking the same language to communicate. This is true of network protocols as well as printer and file subsystems. For example, a Windows NT NTFS or FAT volume is unreadable by a UNIX client because UNIX expects to get data from a hard disk in a certain way using its file system—NFS. The same holds true for printers and network protocols. So, our axiom will be that to communicate we must talk the same "languages." This is, of course, no different than how humans communicate. If you do not speak Spanish, you will never understand a person fluent in that language!

Rule Number 2—Access Depends! Now what am I talking about? Well, what I mean by this rule is that different versions of operating systems come with varying degrees of connectivity between different systems. For instance, Windows NT can use both the FAT and NTFS files systems but not FAT32. UNIX, on the other hand, uses NFS for file system access and that's basically it! Out of the box, certain access features and functions will be considered part of the operating system. Windows NT provides a fairly high degree of interoperability with other TCP/IP systems right out of the box—and at no additional charge. It is important for you to look at the different features and functions of *both* operating systems before settling in on a connectivity method. It is totally possible that a printer or file system will only need to be configured on one server!

Rule Number 3—There's Only So Many Ways to Connect! We have only three scenarios for connectivity with any system. No matter what we are trying to access (network, files, printers) on any system, access will always fall into one of the following categories:

- **You Have to Connect to Them.** We need to connect to UNIX resources and use them.

- **They Have to Communicate with Us.** We need to allow UNIX access to a particular resource on our system.

- **We Have to Talk Together.** We have to share information between the operating systems.

Everything we learn about connectivity in general, and specifically in this chapter, will fall into one of these categories. Now that we have that out of the way, let's look at a couple of examples of cross-platform connectivity between Windows NT and UNIX. The examples below discuss differences in file and print mechanisms between the two operating systems.

FILE SYSTEMS

Windows NT uses the FAT (File Allocation Table) and NTFS (Windows NT New Technology File System) to arrange its files. Natively, a UNIX host cannot access data on these file systems. UNIX uses the NFS (Network File System) for disk access and management. For us to access Windows NT data, we must install a NFS service on the NT machine that makes the UNIX client think its working with NFS and still allow all our Microsoft clients to access files using FAT and NTFS. Windows NT does not come with this feature built-in, so if you need to use a Windows NT machine as a UNIX file server, you will have to find a third-party NFS file management system.

PRINTING

UNIX natively uses three services to print. LPR (Line Printer Request) and LPQ (Line Printer Queue) run on the client. LPD (Line Printer Daemon) runs on the server. Windows NT supports UNIX printing right out of the box! We can install these services (and will do so in this chapter) to enable a UNIX host to use a Windows NT printer resource. However, if you do not install these services, the UNIX host can't see or use the NT printers since Windows has a totally different printer subsystem for its clients.

Lesson 9.3 Cross-Platform TCP/IP Utilities

This lesson defines and provides some more detailed information on the actual utilities we will use to implement a heterogeneous TCP/IP platform. At a high level, the following table shows the utilities we will be discussing in this chapter:

TABLE 9-1 TCP/IP CROSS-PLATFORM CONNECTIVITY UTILITIES

TCP/IP UTILITY	CONNECTION USE	USED TO
FTP	File Transport	User/Password Guaranteed Transport
RXEC	Run Process	Remotely executes a process on a UNIX host.
LPD	Printer	The UNIX Printer Service
LPQ	Printer	The UNIX Printer Queue
LPR	Printer	The Client Print Director
Finger	Administration	Remotely run UNIX processes.
SNMP	Device Management	Monitors physical network devices and server performance.
TelNet	Remote Access	Access a remote UNIX host (terminal emulation).
RCP	File Transport	File copies with no user validation.
RSH	Administration	Run UNIX commands with no user validation.
HTTP	Web Browsing	Display, manipulate, and view data through a browser.

Let's break these tools apart and provide a description of their purpose and command syntax:

TCP/IP Printing Commands

TCP/IP printing is actually simpler in function than the Windows NT printing subsystem. A diagram of this process is provided in Figure 9-1.

FIGURE 9-1
The TCP/IP Printing Process.

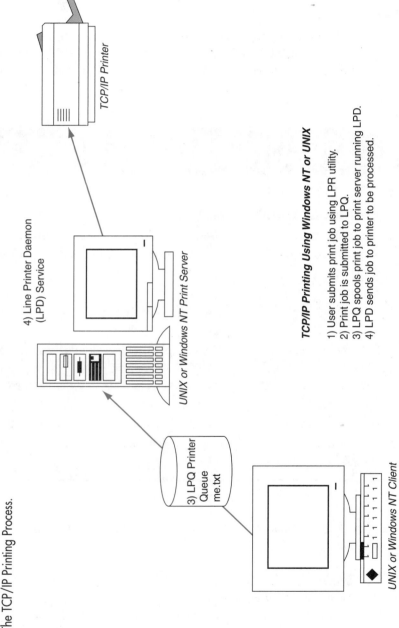

TCP/IP Printer

4) Line Printer Daemon
(LPD) Service

UNIX or Windows NT Print Server

3) LPQ Printer
Queue
me.txt

UNIX or Windows NT Client

1–2) C> lpr-S 10.215.5.250 -P HP_LJ4 me.txt

TCP/IP Printing Using Windows NT or UNIX

1) User submits print job using LPR utility.
2) Print job is submitted to LPQ.
3) LPQ spools print job to print server running LPD.
4) LPD sends job to printer to be processed.

Notice that there is no print queue on the server itself. This is very different from the way that NT Printing works—where there are spoolers on both the client and server. Here's what the commands and utilities actually do.

LPD. This is the *Line Printer Daemon.* If you are wondering where that funny name came from, not all demons are bad. We usually think of demons as things that go bump in the dark and that are evil. A daemon is a "good spirit" by definition. Daemons equate to processes or services on a Windows NT machine. LPD comes from UNIX (where every process is known as a Daemon). LPD is the process that manages printing on a UNIX machine. Under NT, it serves the same purpose—management of TCP/IP print jobs. Adding LPD to a Windows NT machine makes it look like a UNIX print server, allowing UNIX and Microsoft clients to print to a Windows NT TCP/IP print device. LPD always runs on a NT server. LPD has no command syntax. It is simply a service that runs on the UNIX or Windows NT print server.

LPQ. This is the *Line Printer Queue.* The queue serves a similar function to the Windows NT Print Queue. It stores print jobs until they can be processed by the print server. LPQ resides on the client machines with LPR. LPQ also allows the user to view the status of a print job. LPQ is a Windows NT Command Line utility. Using LPQ to view the status of a print job is simple. Here's the command syntax:

LPQ -S <IP address of Printer> -P <Printer Name> -l

NOTE: *Remember that UNIX commands are case-sensitive. Since LPR is natively a UNIX command, you must type this command exactly as above. Lowercase* s *and* p *have very different meanings to this LPR!*

LPR. This is the *Line Print Request* program. This is a client side program that allows a Windows NT client to print to a UNIX print server (whether this is being managed by a Windows NT server or UNIX server is irrelevant). UNIX clients will have their own LPR utility native to the particular implementation of the operating system. Windows NT clients use the LPR program provided as part of the Microsoft TCP/IP Printing Service. LPR initiates the print job and sends it to LPQ. LPQ "spools" the job to the LPD service, where it is processed on the NT or UNIX server. Using LPR to initiate a print job is simple. Here's the command syntax:

LPR -S <IP address of Printer> -P <Printer Name> <Filename>

NOTE: *Remember that UNIX commands are case-sensitive. Since LPR is natively a UNIX command, you must type this command exactly as above. Lowercase* s *and* p *have very different meanings to this LPR!*

FIGURE 9-2
The Service Add Screen.

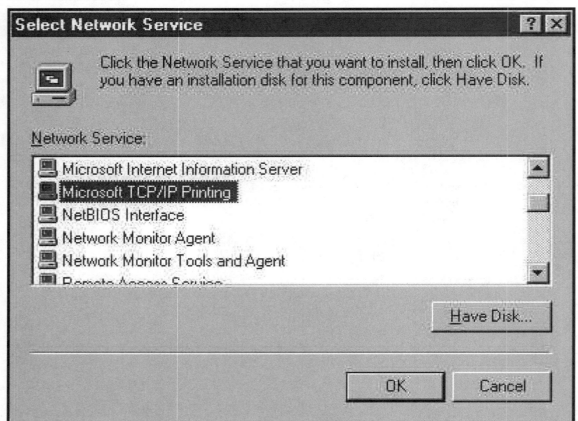

LAB

9.1 Configuring and Using TCP/IP Printing Services

To complete this lab, you must have at least one NT server, NT workstation, and a shared print device. Follow all directions and report your results to the instructor when complete:

1. Install the Microsoft TCP/IP Printing Services on the Windows NT server and workstation computers. Installing this service is similar to all other installations we have performed throughout

the book. A graphic of the Service Add screen is provided in Figure 9-2.

2. Install the files as requested. When complete, restart your computer.

3. If your print device is network-enabled using a HP JetDirect card, be sure it has an IP address configured.

FIGURE 9-3
Adding a New Printer.

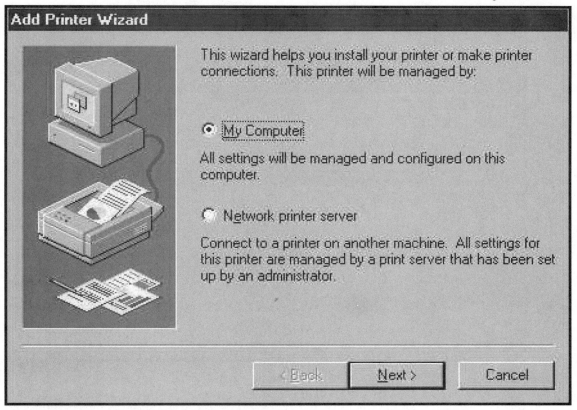

4. Configure a new printer on the Windows NT server using the Add Printer applet. (See Figure 9-3.) When asked for a port, select the LPR Port. Your screen should look like Figure 9-4.

5. Configure the port, answering the questions required. For this exercise, you will be adding a port to print from. So click on the Add Port button and select the LPR Port option. Your screen will look like Figure 9-5.

   Click the New Port button and configure the TCP/IP Printing port by providing the IP address of the NT server (unless the printer is physically attached to the network—then enter the IP address of the printer), and the printer name. Your screen will appear as follows in Figure 9-5.

   Remember to enter the correct IP address and printer name for your configuration. The figure above is for my computer!

6. Once the port is configured, it will appear in the list of ports for you to select. Pick the newly created LPR port, select the correct printer model, share the printer, and complete the New Printer configuration.

FIGURE 9-4
Selecting a Port.

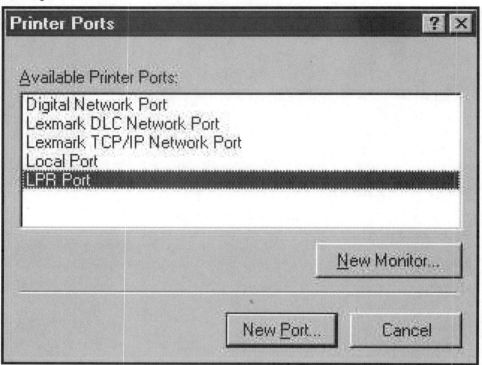

FIGURE 9-5
Adding a Port.

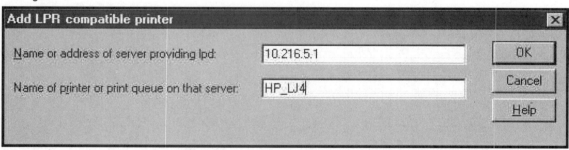

7. This completes the server side installation.

8. On the workstation, follow the same process as above to install the TCP/IP Printing Services. This will give you the LPR and LPQ command so you can test the printing.

9. Add the Network Printer you just specified on the server.

10. Create a NotePad text document and save it.

11. Try using the LPR and LPQ commands to send and monitor jobs printing to your TCP/IP printer (use the commands listed above to complete this process).

12. Were you successful? What information was returned from the LPQ command? The LPR command?

13. If you have problems, work with your instructor to resolve your printer configuration.

File Transfer, Remote Execution, and Terminal Emulation Utilities

The next set of utilities we will look at deals with the transport of data and execution of commands across a TCP/IP network. Some of the commands we have discussed in some depth earlier in the book, but it is helpful to understand more of how they all interact to provide cross-platform support in a heterogeneous TCP/IP network environment. The following utilities are broken out based on their general function. Some you will use regularly, others you may not use at all. It is still nice to know they exist!

FILE TRANSFER UTILITIES

FTP. The venerable FTP (File Transfer Protocol) utility has been around for years. It is still the predominant method for transferring data files across the internet. FTP, as you will recall, stands for the *File Transfer Protocol.* It uses TCP for reliable guaranteed connections with a host. FTP provides three basic methods of security: Anonymous, Clear-Text Password Validation, and Allow Anonymous Only connections. The problem with FTP is all validation information is sent in clear-text and it would be easy to hack network security with a packet sniffer. This is why most FTP sites allow only an anonymous user with no real password (except a user's mail address—and it can really be anything at all!) Once logged into the site, permissions to directories can be assigned using Windows NT NTFS and FTP combined security. This is a highly used utility today. If you plan on certifying in Internet Information Server, you will get a great deal of practice in configuring and administering a FTP site. Many GUI versions of FTP software are available for free download. Windows NT provides a FTP command line utility. If you need to connect and use FTP the command syntax is as follows:

FTP <command options> <IP Address or FQDN>

Once logged into a FTP server, you can receive command help by typing the following command at the FTP prompt:

ftp> ?

TFTP. TFTP (*Trivial File Transfer Protocol*) is also used for transport of data files. The main difference between TFTP and FTP is that TFTP uses UDP for transport and it is not nearly as robust in command structure as FTP. TFTP delivers and gets files but the connection is not guaranteed. Because of this fact, it is quite fast and efficient. You will most likely not use TFTP all that much in your day-to-day activities—FTP is far more common. But if you need to, the syntax is provided below:

TFTP –i <hostname> get <filename>

HTTP. HTTP is the *Hypertext Transfer Protocol.* It is the protocol used by browsers to communicate with Web servers. HTML (*Hypertext Markup Language*) is the actual code that provides a web-page format. Although primarily used for displaying text and graphics, HTTP can also be used to transport data files. If you can use a web-browser, you can use HTTP!

RCP. RCP is the *Remote Copy Protocol.* RCP provides file-copying capabilities between a Windows NT client and UNIX server running the RCP Daemon. It is fast but has no real security except a file that lives on the UNIX server that defines valid users—no password information is required. You will most likely not use RCP all that often in your day-to-day activities unless you work in a UNIX environment. However, the syntax to use the command is as follows:

RCP <Host.User:Sourcehost.User:Destination>

REMOTE EXECUTION UTILITIES

These commands are exclusively used to execute processes and commands on a UNIX server. All the commands listed below are installed with the default Windows NT TCP/IP protocol installation. They are all command line utilities. If you work in a heterogeneous environment where development occurs on UNIX servers or you need to retrieve information from a UNIX machine (like initiating mail transport), you may see the use of these commands.

RXEC. RXEC is the *Remote Execution Utility.* RXEC is used to run a command on a remote UNIX host. This command will prompt the initiator for a user id and password. If the user successfully enters this information, the command they pass in the utility will be executed. Once the command is complete, RXEC normally terminates. Should you need to use RXEC, the command syntax is as follows:

RXEC <TCP/IP hostname> <UNIX command>

RSH. RSH is the *Remote Shell* command. This command also allows a user to run a command on a UNIX host running the RSH Daemon. The major difference between RXEC and RSH is that is no password validation necessary to execute the command. Security is similar to that provided with RCP (see above). The most common use of this command is to initiate a program compile sequence. You will see this command in use mostly in UNIX development shops.

FINGER. The Finger command retrieves system information from a UNIX host running the Finger Daemon. Finger can be used to retrieve all sorts of information depending on how you use it. One common usage is to retrieve mail information from a mail exchange server. Finger's command syntax is as follows:

FINGER <your FQDN domain name>@<hostname>

TERMINAL EMULATION UTILITIES

Telnet. Telnet was, and is, a popular package for terminal emulation on UNIX hosts. Before PCs existed, all computers used dumb terminals to communicate. Because these terminals expected certain characters and formats, they were pretty much usable only on the system they were designed for. A good example of this would be a DEC VT-100 terminal. This terminal is used to communicate with a DEC/VAX host and was dedicated to that purpose. When PCs arrived on the scene, it was necessary to still work on these backend systems. This is when terminal emulators entered the picture.

In essence, a terminal emulator "acts" just like a dumb terminal and sends the character sets required for communication with the host. Telnet is just such a utility. In Windows NT, it is a GUI utility and is located in the \WINNT directory. The Telnet application provided with Windows NT is for basic connectivity. Other emulators from different third party manufacturers will more closely map to an actual dumb terminal from DEC, HP, IBM, or UNIX, complete with function keys and all sorts of extended characters and functions. However, the Windows NT version works just fine for basic connectivity and allows you to establish a connection with a remote UNIX host (or even routers and other systems that support the same character set) using DEC VT-100, ANSI, or TTY character sets. You can then run applications and configurations as if you were seated at a dumb terminal.

Telnet uses TCP for transport and the remote host must be running a Telnet Daemon for you to connect.

LAB

9.2 Using FTP

• •

To complete this lab, your instructor will install Internet Information Server on his machine and provide you with an IP address. Follow all directions and review your results with the instructor.

1. Create a NotePad text file on your computer and save it in the Root directory of your hard drive.

2. Open a Windows NT Command Window.

FIGURE 9-6
FTP Login.

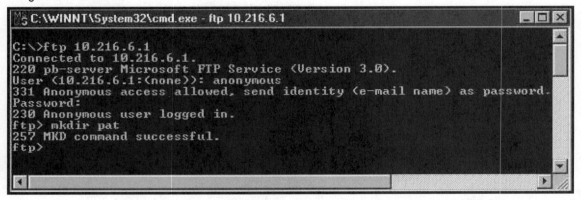

```
C:\WINNT\System32\cmd.exe - ftp 10.216.6.1

C:\>ftp 10.216.6.1
Connected to 10.216.6.1.
220 pb-server Microsoft FTP Service (Version 3.0).
User (10.216.6.1:(none)): anonymous
331 Anonymous access allowed, send identity (e-mail name) as password.
Password:
230 Anonymous user logged in.
ftp>
```

FIGURE 9-7
Using mkdir Command.

```
C:\WINNT\System32\cmd.exe - ftp 10.216.6.1

C:\>ftp 10.216.6.1
Connected to 10.216.6.1.
220 pb-server Microsoft FTP Service (Version 3.0).
User (10.216.6.1:(none)): anonymous
331 Anonymous access allowed, send identity (e-mail name) as password.
Password:
230 Anonymous user logged in.
ftp> mkdir pat
257 MKD command successful.
ftp>
```

3. Type **FTP <IP Address of Instructor computer>** and press Return.

4. Log in as an Anonymous user with a password of <your first name>.

5. You should get a response something like that shown in Figure 9-6.

6. Type **?** and press Return. These are the commands available in FTP. How many can you name the function of?

7. Make a directory using the mkdir command. Name the directory using your first name. Press Return. Your screen should look something like Figure 9-7 after the command has completed.

8. List the contents of the FTP site by typing **dir** and pressing the Return key. What directories have been created? Your screen will look something like Figure 9-8.

9. Change Directories to the directory you created using the **cd** command. Your screen should look something like Figure 9-9.

FIGURE 9-8
Using dir Command.

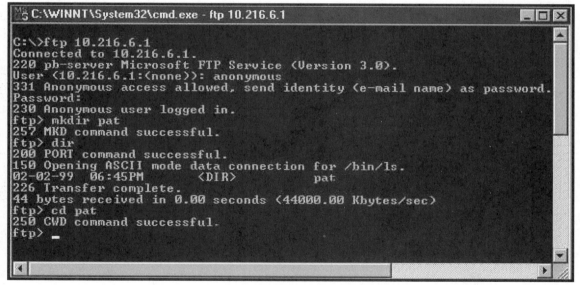

```
MS C:\WINNT\System32\cmd.exe - ftp 10.216.6.1                    _ □ ✕

C:\>ftp 10.216.6.1
Connected to 10.216.6.1.
220 pb-server Microsoft FTP Service (Version 3.0).
User (10.216.6.1:(none)): anonymous
331 Anonymous access allowed, send identity (e-mail name) as password.
Password:
230 Anonymous user logged in.
ftp> mkdir pat
257 MKD command successful.
ftp> dir
200 PORT command successful.
150 Opening ASCII mode data connection for /bin/ls.
02-02-99  06:45PM        <DIR>          pat
226 Transfer complete.
44 bytes received in 0.00 seconds (44000.00 Kbytes/sec)
ftp>
```

FIGURE 9-9
Using cd Command.

```
MS C:\WINNT\System32\cmd.exe - ftp 10.216.6.1                    _ □ ✕

C:\>ftp 10.216.6.1
Connected to 10.216.6.1.
220 pb-server Microsoft FTP Service (Version 3.0).
User (10.216.6.1:(none)): anonymous
331 Anonymous access allowed, send identity (e-mail name) as password.
Password:
230 Anonymous user logged in.
ftp> mkdir pat
257 MKD command successful.
ftp> dir
200 PORT command successful.
150 Opening ASCII mode data connection for /bin/ls.
02-02-99  06:45PM        <DIR>          pat
226 Transfer complete.
44 bytes received in 0.00 seconds (44000.00 Kbytes/sec)
ftp> cd pat
250 CWD command successful.
ftp> _
```

FIGURE 9-10
Using put Command.

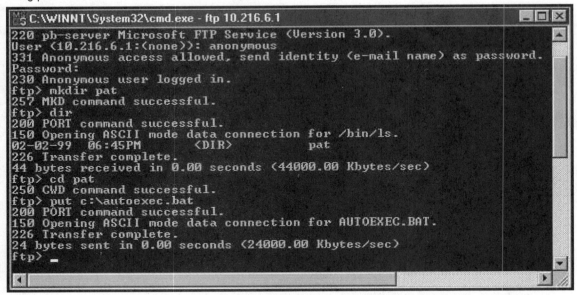

```
C:\WINNT\System32\cmd.exe - ftp 10.216.6.1

220 pb-server Microsoft FTP Service (Version 3.0).
User (10.216.6.1:(none)): anonymous
331 Anonymous access allowed, send identity (e-mail name) as password.
Password:
230 Anonymous user logged in.
ftp> mkdir pat
257 MKD command successful.
ftp> dir
200 PORT command successful.
150 Opening ASCII mode data connection for /bin/ls.
02-02-99  06:45PM        <DIR>          pat
226 Transfer complete.
44 bytes received in 0.00 seconds (44000.00 Kbytes/sec)
ftp> cd pat
250 CWD command successful.
ftp> put c:\autoexec.bat
200 PORT command successful.
150 Opening ASCII mode data connection for AUTOEXEC.BAT.
226 Transfer complete.
24 bytes sent in 0.00 seconds (24000.00 Kbytes/sec)
ftp> _
```

10. Copy the file you created in Notepad to your directory using the **put** command. Command output will look like Figure 9-10.

11. List the contents of the directory using the **dir** command. Did your file copy? Share your results with the instructor.

12. Type **bye** to exit FTP.

13. Close the Command Window.

Lesson 9.4 Network and Local Server Management Utilities

Administering TCP/IP does not stop at a UNIX or Windows NT computer. This lesson discusses management of other devices (predominantly network hardware like routers) that use TCP/IP for communications and management. We will also look at some Windows NT utilities that provide network management capabilities like Performance Monitor and Network Monitor. With the tools provided in this lesson, you can remotely monitor, analyze, and even predict performance in your network.

Three tools are covered in this lesson. The first is known as SNMP. As you will recall from earlier chapters, SNMP is the protocol that allows us to monitor performance information on network devices. Our second tool is called Network Monitor. This is a Microsoft-provided tool that allows us to monitor detailed information on the data and performance of our network. Finally, we will look at the Microsoft Performance Monitor and see that we will be able to monitor, maintain, and optimize our TCP/IP workstations and servers for optimal performance.

SNMP—The Simple Network Management Protocol

SNMP is the *Simple Network Management Protocol*. It is a tool that was designed as part of the TCP/IP suite of protocols to provide a mechanism for monitoring network device performance. SNMP uses UDP for transport so the connections are not guaranteed. However, with SNMP, you can monitor not only physical network devices like routers and bridges but computers and peripherals as well. They must, of course, have the protocol loaded for you to do this. In this section we will be discussing SNMP, some unique terminology associated with it, and how to configure the protocol.

SNMP TERMINOLOGY AND ARCHITECTURE OVERVIEW

First and foremost, there are two types of SNMP devices. The first is known as an **SNMP Agent**. SNMP Agents can be any physical device located on a network, including routers, bridges, "smart hubs," switches, computers, and network-attached peripherals. SNMP Agents send their information to the second type of device: the **SNMP Manager.**

SNMP Managers are typically computer workstations of some type. They have a special piece of software installed that allows them to collect and analyze SNMP Agent information.

NOTE: *Windows NT does not ship with SNMP management software. A Windows NT machine can only function as an SNMP Agent out of the box. It is possible to configure Windows NT as a management station, but you must purchase a piece of third-party software.*

It is possible for a computer workstation to be *both* a SNMP Agent and Management device, assuming the correct software is installed and the hardware supports it. The diagram in Figure 9-11 illustrates the relationship between the agent and management components:

SNMP TERMINOLOGY

We have already introduced two new terms in the prior section. In this section we will continue to describe the terminology most commonly associated with the SNMP protocol.

MIB. Every SNMP Agent has a MIB. A MIB is an acronym for *Management Information Base.* The MIB contents vary from device to device but essentially these databases contain all the performance and statistics for a

FIGURE 9-11
SNMP Architecture.

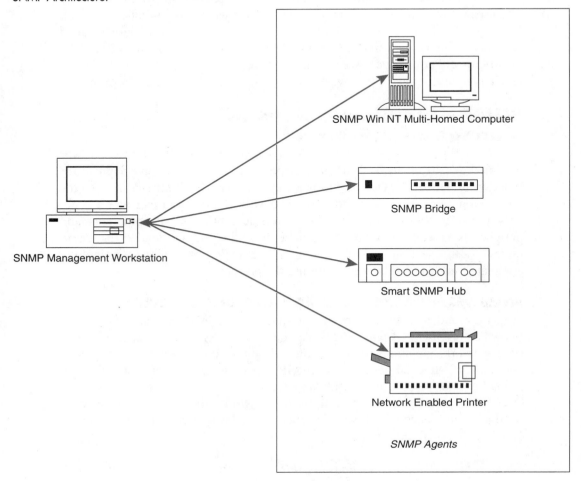

SNMP Win NT Multi-Homed Computer

SNMP Bridge

Smart SNMP Hub

Network Enabled Printer

SNMP Management Workstation

SNMP Agents

particular type of network device. Windows NT has several MIBs for various services. For example, the WINS MIB has over forty statistics that are captured. All SNMP Management machines understand these different MIBS, can collect and analyze data from them, and provide support because of their common universal format.

SNMP Namespace. SNMP uses a hierarchical tree similar to that of DNS to group different MIBs together. Organizations (like Microsoft) are assigned a MIB range (which sort of is like an IP range) and they manage creation of MIBs in that *namespace*. This namespace is completely separate from DNS! If you would like to understand more about how this namespace is created and managed, consult RFC 1212.

Community. In SNMP, a grouping of devices that logically fit together are known as a *Community*. Communities provide a basic level of security and additional organization of network devices in a given situation. There can be multiple communities in an organization and it is quite possible that one SNMP agent belongs to multiple communities. As you will see later, this can be configured in the Windows NT SNMP Service. There are two types of communities in SNMP: Public and Private. The default (and most common community) type is Public.

Trap. A trap is analogous to an alert. Basically, when a device reaches a threshold value, an alert is sent to a predefined SNMP Manager provided the manager belongs to the appropriate community. Traps are also configured within the SNMP Service.

SNMP Manager Commands. Not all of SNMP is about crisis management. The Trap function alerts us about particular negative conditions of a device. However, SNMP Managers can also request regular updates of information from various SNMP agents. Several commands are used to complete this function and they are described here:

- **SET.** The SET command allows you to modify a value in a MIB. This command can rarely be used because most MIBS are configured as "read-only". The manufacturer defines performance parameters for a particular device—and most times you wouldn't want to modify the values. If you are able to change the value and had a need to do so, then you would use the SET command.

- **GET.** As you may have surmised, the GET command retrieves information from a SNMP agent. This information is usually a very specific value contained within a device's MIB. For example, a router might contain many fields related to packet performance, but the GET command might only retrieve information on a field like "Number of Packets Discarded."

- **GET-NEXT.** This command allows you to work down a particular value tree and retrieve the next piece of data related to the object (field) you previously selected.

Configuring SNMP in Windows NT

Now that we have some idea how SNMP operates, we can look at the process for installing the service in Windows NT. One important thing to remember before we get started though—You must install SNMP to gain access to the TCP/IP Performance Monitor counters! If you are planning on monitoring TCP/IP local and network performance, you will have to install the service!

SNMP SERVICE INSTALLATION

We have been installing Windows NT Services throughout this book. SNMP is no different from an installation perspective. As usual, we install SNMP using the Network Control Panel Services Tab. To install SNMP complete the following steps.

1. Install the Microsoft SNMP Service on the Windows NT server or work-station computer. Installing this service is similar to all other installations we have performed throughout the book. A graphic of the Service Add screen is provided in Figure 9-12.

2. Install the files as requested. At this point, you will receive the SNMP Properties dialog. We have to configure SNMP with some basic information to successfully set the service up. A graphic of this dialog box is provided in Figure 9-13.

FIGURE 9-12
Service Add Screen.

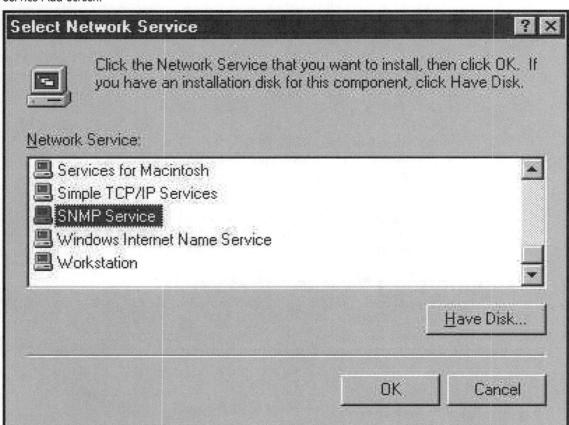

FIGURE 9-13
SNMP Properties Dialog.

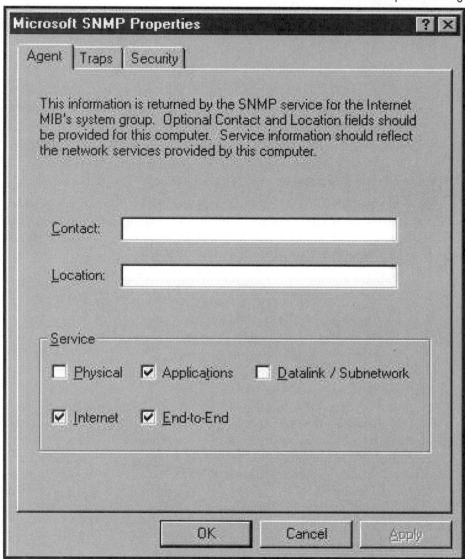

Notice that the default tab we receive is the Agent. The checkboxes in the services refer to those components this particular agent manages. By default, the Applications, Internet, and End-to-End services are selected. Following is a description of each and when it is appropriate to select a particular agent service option.

- **Physical.** If your agent is managing or acting as a physical device like a repeater, you would select this option.

- **Internet.** If the computer is acting as a router (a multi-homed Windows NT computer), you would select this service.

- **Applications.** If the computers use any applications that use TCP/IP, you would select this option. This option should always be selected since you already are using TCP/IP utilities!

- **End-to-End.** If your computer acts as a TCP/IP client (host), which it must be if you have the protocol installed, this service is selected. As in the case with the Applications service, this option should always be selected.

- **DataLink/Subnetwork.** If your Windows NT computer is managing a sub-networking device like a bridge, you select this option.

- **Contact and Location Fields.** These fields provide information to SNMP on who to contact in the event of a trap. Usually the contact is the machine's administrator and their location is exactly that: where the machine is located!

1. Let's take a look at the Traps Tab in Figure 9-14. When you click on this tab, it is a tabula rasa, or blank slate. No information is provided. It is here that we specify the community the agent belongs to and the computer we will send trap information. In most cases, the community name is defined as public, although it is possible for you to define this field with any name you wish so long as the management station belongs to the same group. The Trap Destinations field allows you to specify either an IP address or computer name. However, be sure you have name resolution functioning correctly if you use a computer name!

2. Next, let's take look at Figure 9-15 to see the Security Tab. This tab configures various security options for the SNMP service. The following paragraphs describe the function of each of the two main areas in this dialog.

- **Send Authentication Trap.** By default, this check box will be selected. This configuration option allows an SNMP agent to send an authentication trap, or alert, to a management station when another station from a different community or accepted host attempts to use the agent's MIB. Information you configured on the Trap tab is automatically entered into the Accepted Community Names field. Anyone not in this list will generate a trap. You would select this box if you wished to monitor who is attempting to access a particular agent.

FIGURE 9-14
The Traps Tab.

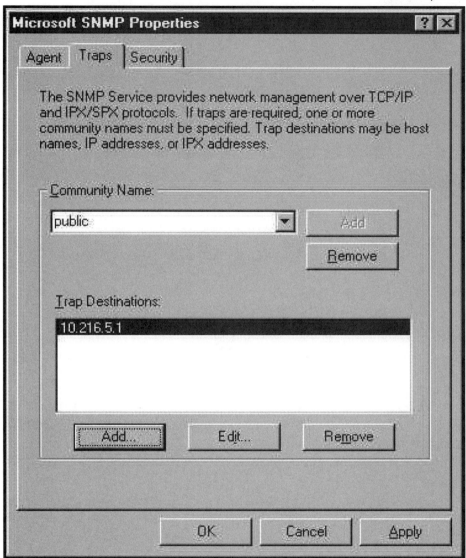

FIGURE 9-15
The Security Tab.

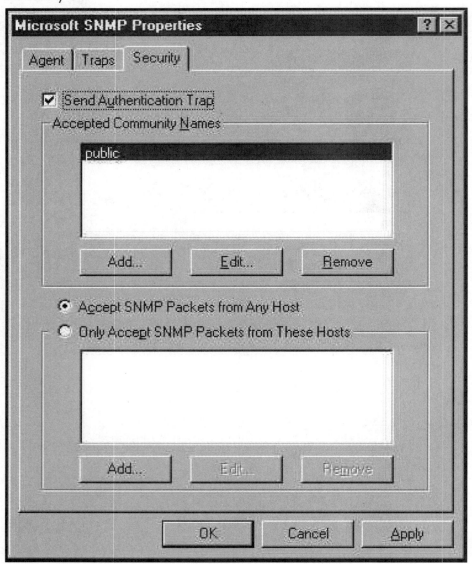

- **SNMP Packet Acceptance.** This radio-button option determines if you will limit requests to a certain group of management workstations. If you select the Only Accept Packets from These Hosts radio button, you will be required to enter the IP address of the hosts. If not, SNMP will receive packets from all hosts. By default, the SNMP service accepts packets from all hosts.

3. Once you have entered all the values to configure the service, click OK. You will be prompted to restart your computer.

4. Once Windows NT has restarted, check Event Viewer to assure the SNMP service has successfully started.

LAB

9.3 Installing and Testing the SNMP Service (Optional)

To complete this lab, you will need to install and use a special Windows NT test utility called SNMPUTIL to test your configuration. SNMPUTIL is a test utility that ships with Windows NT Server Resource Kit. If you do not have this utility, complete the installation of SNMP and check its status in Event Viewer. If you do have the utility, you may complete the test. SNMPUTIL allows you to issue GET and GETNEXT commands to a Windows NT SNMP Agent. The agent will return information to SNMPUTIL and it will be displayed on your screen.

TO INSTALL SNMP

1. Follow the steps outlined in Lesson 9.4 to install SNMP with the following values.

SNMP CONFIGURATION OPTIONS		
SNMP TAB	**FIELD**	**VALUE**
Agent	Name	Your Name
Agent	Location	Classroom
Agent	Services	Check Applications, Internet, End-to-End
Trap	Community	Public
Trap	Trap Destination	IP Address of Instructor Computer
Security	Send Authentication Trap	Checked
Security	Accept SNMP Packets	Select "Accept from any Host" radio button

2. Restart your computer when prompted.

3. Check Event Viewer. Did SNMP start correctly?

TO TEST YOUR SNMP INSTALLATION (OPTIONAL)
1. Open a Windows NT Command Prompt.

2. Type and run the following command:

SNMPUTIL getnext <Your IP Address> public .1.3.6.1.4.1.311.1.3.2.1.1.1

This command should return values stored in your DHCP server on how many IP addresses have been leased from your machine.

3. What values did you receive? Verify this number by checking your DHCP scope. Share the results with your instructor.

4. Close the Windows NT Command Window.

Lesson 9.5 Performance Manager and Network Monitor

Two GUI-based monitoring tools that are very useful in managing and reporting information on your local computer and network are Performance Manager and Network Monitor. This lesson assumes that you already understand the basic features of these tools and you have used them extensively with Windows NT in previous courses. What we will look at in this section are those features that are specific to TCP/IP in monitoring your local machine and network.

Network Monitor. The version of Network Monitor shipped with Windows NT Server allows you to gather network and protocol metrics/data for your local machine. You can easily see important information on packets received, transmitted, and overall bandwidth of your system using this tool. If you need to monitor machines other than your own, you will need to install the full version of Network Monitor. This full Network Monitor package is included with Microsoft Systems Management Server (SMS).

WHAT TYPES OF DATA WOULD I USE NETWORK MONITOR TO TRACK?

You would use Network Monitor to track and report statistics on anything having to do with packet or protocol information on a particular computer.

Network monitor will show you exactly where the data is arriving from, being sent to, and it even enables you to open and inspect the contents of captured packets that your machine has transmitted or received. One of the nicest features is a bar graph of your network performance that is displayed in the tool. If you recall, consistent bandwidth measurements above 80% usually mean the network is "saturated" and should probably be either segmented (into a subnet) or optimized. Network Monitor captures this data and stores it in a file. The file can be used to sort, analyze, and report network metrics to management.

HOW DO I INSTALL NETWORK MONITOR?

Network Monitor is not installed by default when you initially install Windows NT Server. To install the package, you must go to the Network Control Panel, Services Tab. Once there you select the Network Monitor Program and Agent and install the service. Once the program and agent are installed, you can begin capturing data about your computer's protocol and local network segment information.

A sample of the type of information provided by Network Monitor is provided in Figure 9-16.

FIGURE 9-16
Network Monitor Sample Capture Screen.

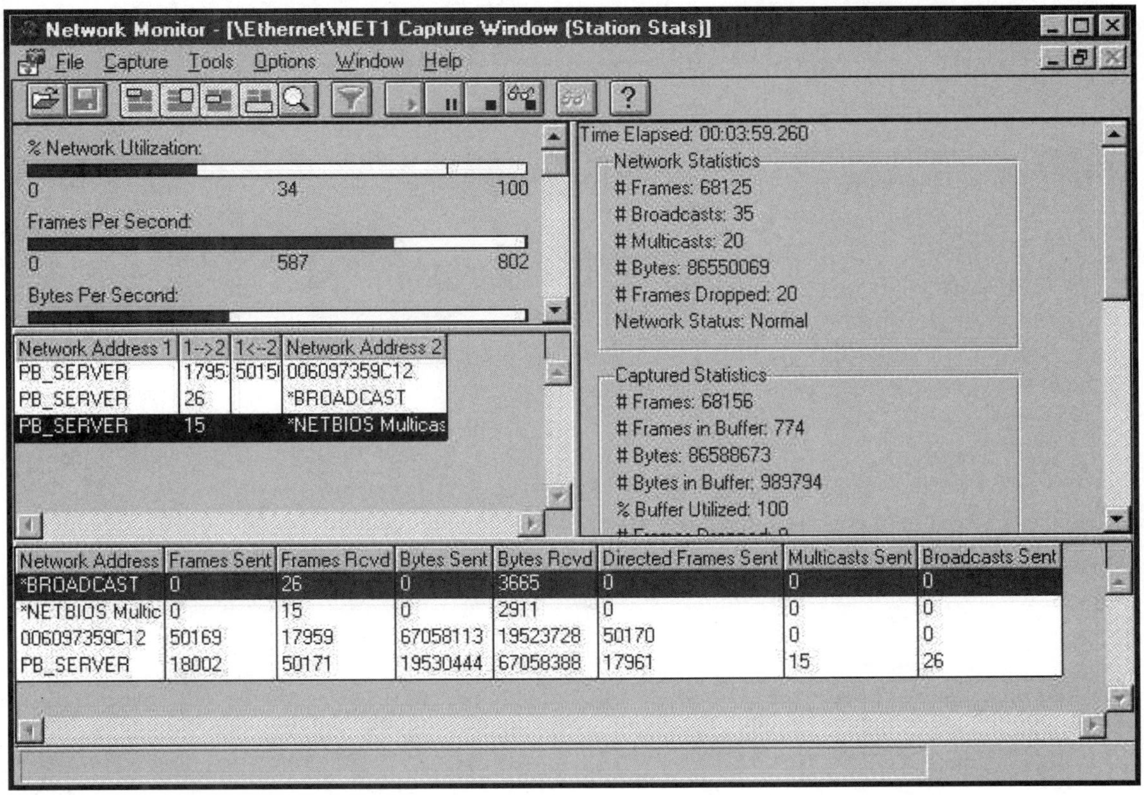

FIGURE 9-17
Network Monitor Detail Capture View.

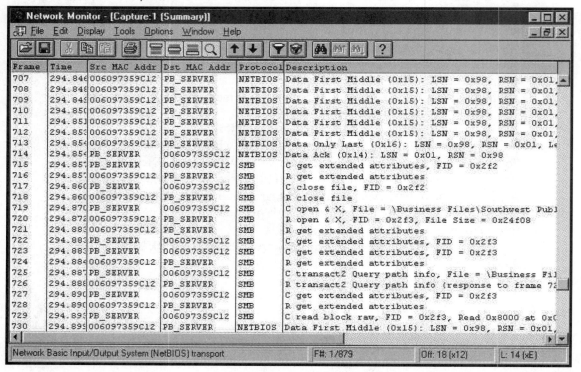

Figure 9-16 shows summary level information. There is also a detail view if you needed to view the actual packet metrics. A sample of this view is provided in Figure 9-17.

As you can see, I was performing a file copy using Windows Explorer Microsoft Networking. You will see that SMB and NETBIOS are the two predominant protocols that are used for this action. Network Monitor also allows you to capture packets based on criteria (also known as filtering). So, it is very possible for me to capture any particular protocol in almost any situation between two network devices. This is very useful in troubleshooting problems on a network.

It is possible for me to drill down even further and actually view the contents of a packet as well. In Figure 9-18, I PINGED another computer on my network and have opened up the ARP/RARP packet that was returned. Figure 9-18 shows what the display looks like.

FIGURE 9-18
Network Monitor Packet Detail.

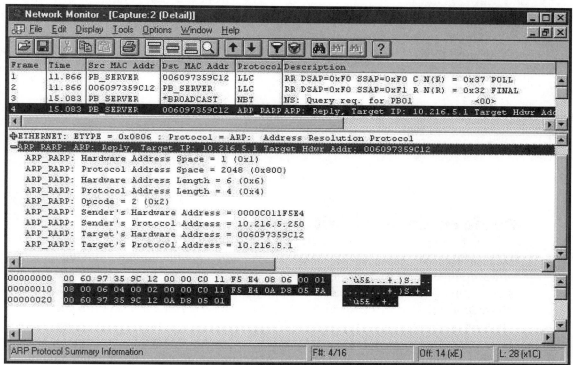

LAB

9.5

Capturing and Viewing Packets Using Network Monitor

This lab allows you to install and explore some of the features of Network Monitor. In this lab, you will install Network Monitor, capture some data, and view the results. Follow all instructions and review the results of your capture with the instructor when complete.

1. Install Network Monitor using the procedures provided in this lesson.

2. Restart the computer when prompted.

3. Click Start-Administrative Tools-Network Monitor to open the application.

4. On the Capture Menu, select Start Capture.

5. Open a Windows NT Command Window.

6. PING your partner and the instructor's computer.

7. On the Capture Menu, select Stop and View.

8. On the Capture Menu, select Display All Captured Data.

9. Double-click on an ARP or ICMP entry.

10. Explore the contents of the packet and document the results. Was the PING successful? How do you know from the data gathered in Network Monitor?

11. Close Network Monitor, do not save your work.

12. Share your results with the instructor.

Performance Monitor

Performance Monitor is installed automatically when Windows NT is initially configured. Many useful counters are installed with the base product. However, in terms of TCP/IP, no counters are installed unless the SNMP service is configured. You can use Performance Monitor to view all kinds of TCP/IP information relevant to the local workstation or server. You can also do some minor inbound/outbound network traffic analysis. However, you cannot monitor the overall status of a network—you can only monitor a specific machine (or group of machines remotely) to see what is transpiring. Some useful counters to watch when analyzing TCP/IP performance on a computer are described here.

TCP COUNTERS

These counters are used to display TCP statistics on a host computer. Consider using this following counters when analyzing TCP traffic.

Segments Received

Segments Transmitted

Segments per Second

UDP COUNTERS

These counters are used to display UDP statistics on a host computer. Consider using the following counters when analyzing UDP traffic.

Datagrams Sent

Datagrams Received

Datagrams/Sec

IP COUNTERS

These counters are used to display IP statistics on a host computer. Consider using the following counters when analyzing IP traffic.

Datagrams Sent

Datagrams Received

Datagrams/Sec

NETWORK SEGMENT

These counters are used to display general network statistics for a host computer's home subnet. Consider using the following counters when analyzing general traffic on a computer's local subnet.

% Network Utilization

% Broadcast Frames

Total Bytes Received/Second

Total Frames Received/Second

NETWORK INTERFACE (NIC CARD)

These counters are used to display Network Card statistics on a host computer. Consider using the following counters when trying to determine the throughput of a NIC or whether there is a problem with the physical card itself.

Bytes Received/Sec

Bytes Sent/Sec

Bytes Total/Sec

There is much that can be gleaned from Performance Monitor and there are literally thousands of counters you can track. The counters listed above are some of the useful ones when looking at a TCP/IP network. However, there are many more! If you are interested in using more Performance Monitor counters, check out *Optimizing Windows NT* by Russ Blake. It is the authoritative description of Performance Monitor functions and counters (Russ wrote the product for Microsoft). This book is part of the Windows NT Server 3.51 Resource Kit.

Lesson 9.6 TCP/IP Connectivity Using BackOffice Products

Microsoft is committed to Internet connectivity and produces several products that are used specifically for this goal. Along with the utilities and applications we have already looked at (WINS, DNS, and DHCP), Microsoft also makes additional products that are used extensively in TCP/IP networks. In this lesson we will take a quick overview of two major Internet Connectivity applications that are part of the BackOffice Suite: Microsoft Internet Information Server and Microsoft Proxy Server.

Microsoft Internet Information Server

Also known as IIS, this BackOffice product ships with Windows NT Server. IIS is used to create and manage a website and the associated services. With IIS, you can configure, setup, and manage an Internet website. IIS is part of the BackOffice suite of applications and is closely integrated within the Windows NT Server environment. It offers integrated and highly secure environment for full control over a website, including such features as Virtual Servers, FTP, Gopher, and WWW-based services. It also allows for remote administration of the site via a HTML-based web management interface.

When Windows NT Server 4.0 was released, it shipped with the then-current version of IIS (Version 2.0). When you install NT, you have the option of installing this service. With the release of Service Pack 3, IIS was upgraded to Version 3.0. If you have IIS 2.0 installed on your machine, it is automatically upgraded to Version 3 as part of the Service Pack Installation. The newest version of IIS is shipped with the Windows NT Option Pack (available free from Microsoft to registered users of Windows NT Server). IIS 4.0 introduces a new interface—the Microsoft Management Console (MMC) and a huge amount of additional function in the product, including full integration of FrontPage 98 Web Publishing, SMTP, NNTP, and Transaction Server.

A scaled-down version of the software ships with NT Workstation and Windows 98. The scaled-down versions are known as "Peer Web Server" on Windows NT Workstation and "Personal Web Server" in Windows 98. These versions can only accept a maximum of ten simultaneous inbound connections but are very useful for publishing web-based Intranet information to your colleagues. These servers can also be used to extensively test web page applications and sites.

Microsoft Proxy Server

Microsoft Proxy Server is a firewall and caching server product for Internet connectivity. If you recall from our discussions in WINS, the concept of a proxy is that it is a "go-between" two things. A Proxy Server usually sits between a dedicated Internet connection and a company's internal network. The proxy can process, filter, accept, or reject inbound and outbound traffic to and from the Internet and provides a high degree of network security when properly configured.

Another major feature of Proxy Server is its ability to cache commonly accessed websites, providing increased performance for internal Internet browser users. Further, these servers can filter sites as configured by an administrator. They can also provide IP re-mapping services limiting the need for InterNIC dedicated internal IP addresses, using something called a Logical Address Table or LAT. This allows network administrators to be very flexible in configuring subnets and assigning addresses in their internal networks.

Microsoft Proxy Server is currently in Release Version 2.0. Like IIS, security is integrated within the Windows NT and the Proxy service itself is managed from the common interface used by IIS. To install Proxy Server 2.0, you must have a NTFS partition for caching and be running Service Pack 3.

Summary

This chapter explores the topic of UNIX connectivity in TCP/IP. In this chapter, we discussed several different types of connectivity methods including:

■ How to configure and use network device management tools SNMP, Network Monitor, and Performance Monitor.

■ How to configure and use file transfer and management utilities like FTP and Telnet.

■ The definition and basic command syntax for remote management utilities like Finger, RSH, and RXEC.

■ How to interoperate with TCP/IP Printing Systems thought the identification, configuration, and various components of the Microsoft TCP/IP Printing Tools LPR, LPQ, and LPD.

■ Exploration of two other commonly used BackOffice products for heterogeneous connectivity: Microsoft Internet Information Server and Microsoft Proxy Server.

● ● ● ● ● ● ● ● ● ● ● ● ●

1. *Select the best answer.* Installing TCP/IP counters requires what other service to be installed on a Windows NT server?

   a. WINS
   b. DNS
   c. DHCP
   d. SNMP
   e. Simple TCP/IP services

2. *Select the best answer.* Which of the following tools can capture TCP/IP frames from a network?

   a. SNMP
   b. Network Monitor
   c. Performance Monitor
   d. LPQ

3. *Select the best answer.* Mike runs a local intranet site and wants to allow his users to access and download company phone lists to their local machines. Which of the following TCP/IP connectivity utilities is best suited to allow users to complete this task?

   a. FTP
   b. RSH
   c. TELNET
   d. RXEC
   e. RCP

4. *Select two.* A UNIX workstation needs to be able to print to a Windows NT Print Device. The printer has already been configured with an IP address. What steps would you complete to allow the UNIX client to use Windows NT TCP/IP Printing Services?

   a. Assign an IP address to the printer port in Windows NT Print Manager.
   b. Install the TCP/IP Printing service on the server.
   c. Install the TCP/IP Printing service on the UNIX computers.
   d. Share the printer on the server.

5. *Select two.* Harriet works on a Windows NT Workstation and wants to send a text file to a UNIX-based TCP/IP printer. What utility and command must she install/run before she can successfully print?

   a. SNMP
   b. LPQ
   c. LPR
   d. Simple TCP/IP Print Services
   e. TCP/IP printing

6. From her Windows NT Workstation computer, Sam wants to administer a UNIX server located on her network without installing any additional software. Which TCP/IP utility will allow Sam to accomplish her task?

    a. Finger
    b. Telnet
    c. RXEC
    d. RSH
    e. None of the above.

7. From your Windows NT Server computer you want to use Performance Monitor to see TCP/IP protocol statistics for that server. What additional service must you configure?

    a. Network Monitor agent
    b. RIP for IP
    c. TCP/IP
    d. SNMP service
    e. No additional service is required.

8. *Select the best answer.* Mary wishes to see the status of several documents she sent to a TCP/IP printer through her Windows NT Workstation. Which utility will allow her to accomplish her objective?

    a. LPD
    b. HTTP
    c. LPR
    d. LPQ
    e. Telnet
    f. None of the above.

9. *Select the best answer.* After installing TCP/IP on her Windows NT Workstation on his computer, Michelle needs to test her connectivity to a remote host. Which TCP/IP utility will provide the fastest method to assuring connectivity?

    a. ARP
    b. TRACERT
    c. SNMP Management Agent
    d. SNMP Workstation Agent
    e. PING
    f. Network Monitor

10. How would Jerry enable security to only allow certain SNMP management workstations to access his MIB?

    a. Assign a user ID and password to the SNMP community.
    b. Designate the server to be a trap security destination.
    c. Enable integrated Windows NT security on the MIB file packets and grant access to the appropriate user accounts.
    d. Enable the Only Accept SNMP Packets From These Hosts option on the server.
    e. Enable the Restrict Access to These Hosts Option on the server.

11. *Select the best answer.* Molly wishes to enable Windows users to print to a printer connected to a HP-9000 UNIX server. She has installed the LPD service on the UNIX server. What else must she do on the Windows NT Workstation computer to allow her to print to this device?

    a. Create a printer share on the UNIX server.
    b. Install the TCP/IP Printing service on the UNIX server.
    c. Enable the LPQ queuing feature on the workstation.
    d. Install the LPR utility on her workstation.

12. *Select the best answer.* Bill wants to gather TCP/IP statistics from several Windows NT Server computers and save them to a logging file for later analysis in an Microsoft Access database. What utility is best suited for this task?

    a. Telnet
    b. NETSTAT
    c. Network Monitor
    d. Performance Monitor
    e. SNMP Management Software

13. *Select the best answer.* Tim wants to use Performance Monitor on his Windows NT Workstation computer to compile the TCP/IP network statistics generated by several Windows NT Server computers. How can Tim accomplish this?

    a. Install the SNMP service on *each* Windows NT Server computer.
    b. Install the SNMP service on *only* his Windows NT Workstation computer.
    c. Set up each server to use the SNMP service.
    d. Use the SNMPUTIL utility to query each computer.
    e. This cannot be done. You must physically sit at each computer and run Performance Monitor.
    f. Nothing needs to be done. The computer will be able to monitor these statistics automatically.

14. *Select the best answer.* Jack needs to compile a program on a remote UNIX server. Which is the best utility for Jack to use?

    a. RSH
    b. RCP
    c. RXEC
    d. Telnet
    e. Finger

15. *Select the best answer.* Samantha needs to view MIB information from several different SNMP agents. What Windows NT service should she install?

    a. Network Monitor
    b. The SNMP Agent only.
    c. The SNMP Agent and Monitor
    d. Telnet
    e. This cannot be done using any Windows NT factory installed service or application.

TCP/IP TROUBLESHOOTING

10

OBJECTIVES

By the end of this chapter, you should be able to:

- Quickly classify TCP/IP problems into one of three categories.

- Define methods to define, address, and solve problems.

- Define tools used to assist you in different troubleshooting situations and scenarios.

Introduction

This chapter discusses common problems and troubleshooting techniques involved in TCP/IP implementations. By this point in our discussions, you have probably surmised that with all the configuration techniques and components in TCP/IP, troubleshooting installations can be (and is) one of the network administrator's biggest jobs. This job can be difficult in complex networks. However, if we apply a methodical approach similar to all the other topics we have covered, we will be able to eliminate, classify, approach, hypothesize, and eventually solve many TCP/IP problems. This chapter contains very important information as you prepare for the exam. The topic of troubleshooting is so important, an entire section of your TCP/IP test will be dedicated to this area. If you follow the steps outlined in this chapter, you should be able to troubleshoot most problems related to TCP/IP quickly and efficiently using the several tools discussed.

Lesson 10.1 TCP/IP Troubleshooting at a Glance

TCP/IP troubleshooting can be a long and sometimes frustrating process of elimination if you are not well-versed in good general troubleshooting technique. This protocol suite can be difficult to troubleshoot mostly because there are so many components and pieces that could possibly be causing a problem. However, despair not! If we look at the entire protocol suite, we can broadly categorize problems into three main areas. If we understand the symptoms of each type of problem, and its most probable resolution, it will be possible for us to narrow our scope and focus on the most probable root causes. The three main areas we will be troubleshooting in this chapter are:

Configuration. Configuration problems have to do with the internal TCP/IP configuration of either a client or a server. When we are troubleshooting these areas of TCP/IP we are predominantly concerned with the services and protocols that are installed on a particular workstation or server.

Connectivity. Connectivity troubleshooting encompasses some configuration issues but is most commonly associated with problems related to connecting hosts in an inter-network. As you may have guessed, we will be focusing on issues surrounding correct configuration of subnet masks, routers, permissions, and various connection-oriented problems due to network saturation.

Name Resolution. As this title hints, this area involves connectivity and configuration problems surrounding FQDN and NetBIOS name resolution. It is here that we are focusing on topics such as WINS, LMHOSTS, HOSTS, and DNS configurations.

For each of these areas, there are methods and tools for us to quickly assess a particular situation and recommend a possible solution. These techniques and tools are the topic of this chapter.

Lesson 10.2 Generic Troubleshooting Technique

Much has been written regarding effective troubleshooting techniques. If you have made it this far in your certification, then you are probably well-versed in some of the basic tenets we will review in this section. What we describe in this section is applicable to all troubleshooting and is not specific to TCP/IP. As a matter of fact, it is highly reminiscent of the scientific method you have most likely studied in science classes throughout your years in school. However, application of these basic principles will greatly assist you as you attempt to solve a TCP/IP problem. Figure 10-1 illustrates the basic steps you will follow.

General troubleshooting can be broken down into the following areas:

Problem Assessment. Of all the steps in troubleshooting, this is the most important. It is here that you gather problem information, determine the problem type, and begin the process of developing a basic hypothesis on what has caused the problem. In the network administration environment we are usually speaking with the end-user, looking at their configuration, and beginning the process of narrowing the scope of an issue.

Research Possible Scenarios. If we have not encountered a problem like this before and we do not know the answer, we begin the research process to help define the problem further. Researching networking problems usually means consultation with fellow employees, a great deal of "book work", contacting the vendor, and ancillary research methods like Microsoft Technet and web-based search tools. By the time we complete this process, we should have a few targeted ideas of what our problem actually is. Although we may not know the exact answer, we are well on our way to developing one or more solutions to the problem.

Formulation of a Hypothesis. In this step, we look at our possible problems and try to come up with methods for resolving the issue. This may require further investigation and discussion before anything becomes apparent. When we have completed this process, we have a probable protocol (steps to solve a problem)

FIGURE 10-1
The Problem Solving Method.

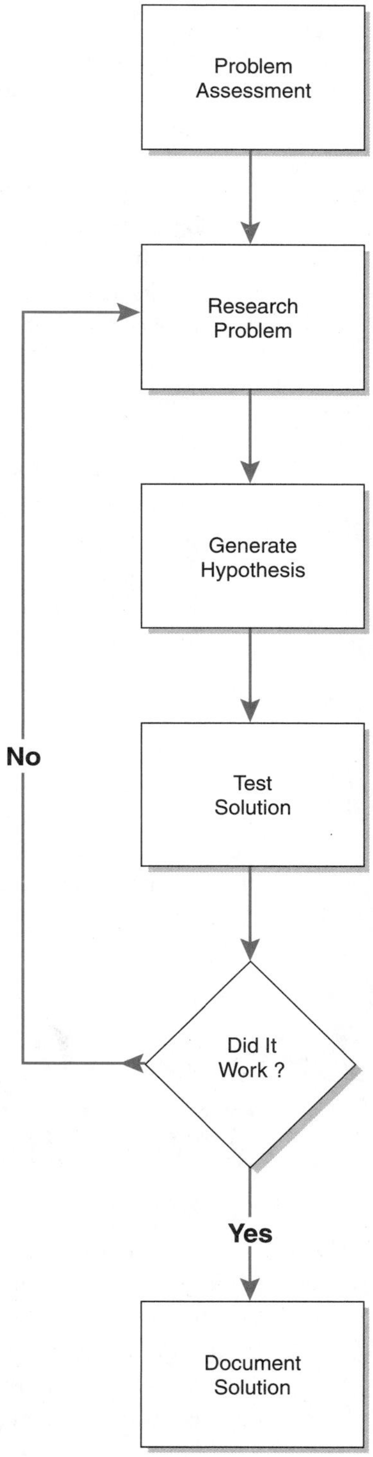

and are ready to test the solution. Oftentimes, a hypothesis will have both the statement of the problem and the steps you believe must be taken to resolve it.

Testing the Hypothesis. This is the "go for it" step. Here, we try to implement the solution we have developed and test it. If it works, we then document our resolution for poor unfortunate souls who encounter similar situations. If our solution does not work, we go back to the drawing board and try to develop another hypothesis. It is important to note that simply because your current hypothesis failed, does not mean it might not have validity. Remember that many problems may not have just one solution. It could be that you have solved a piece of the puzzle but the piece is not the root of the problem. Hold onto your initial hypothesis—it may be required to solve the balance of the problem!

Documentation. Assuming your hypothesis works, your next step is to document what the exact situation was and the steps you used to remedy the situation. Oftentimes, problems repeat themselves. If you do not have documentation, you (or someone else) will have to go through the entire process again. Trust me, if you don't write it down, you will probably forget what it was that you did! The process of developing a troubleshooting log will eventually result in something we call a "knowledge base". The knowledge base, when implemented properly, is the summation of all the support personnel's combined knowledge and experience. This can be an extremely powerful tool in resolving problems.

Not surprisingly, this technique is used throughout all the sciences to resolve problems. At a basic level, all medical and scientific research follows this process. What we actually are doing is narrowing scope, and applying a methodical trial-and-error method to problem resolution. In TCP/IP troubleshooting, we will always be completing these four steps regardless of the problem type.

Lesson 10.3 TCP/IP Troubleshooting Tools

When attempting to ascertain the nature of a TCP/IP problem, we usually look for some high-level indicators of where the problem actually lies. Our first step is to determine whether the problem lies within the internal configuration, connection, or name resolution areas. To gather this information, we use several tools and utilities. This section takes a look at the tools we have at our disposal to gather information from a reported problem.

TABLE 10-1 TCP/IP TROUBLESHOOTING TOOLS

TCP/IP TROUBLESHOOTING TOOL	USED TO
PING	Test TCP/IP Configuration and Connectivity
IPCONFIG	View the Client TCP/IP Configuration
ARP	View MAC to IP Address Mapping Cache
NETSTAT	View Client TCP/IP Network Information
NBTSTAT	View and Edit NetBIOS Client Connections
ROUTE	View and Edit Route Table Entries
SNMP	Install TCP/IP Counters; Send SNMP Traps
Network Monitor	Monitor Network Packets and Performance
Performance Monitor	Monitor Client Performance
TRACERT	Trace a Route to Destination Computer
Event Viewer	View System Errors and Status of Internal TCP/IP Configuration
NSLOOKUP	View and Receive DNS Name Entries

Configuration Tools

Our primary tools for configuration are Event Viewer, PING, and IPCONFIG. As you recall, these two tools allow us to test, display, and report any errors for the internal configuration of a TCP/IP host. With these tools you can gather almost everything you need to solve ninety percent of the problems you will encounter on a day-to-day basis.

PING. PING is used to test both the internal TCP/IP configuration as well as connectivity between local and remote subnet hosts. Of all the tools in your bag, this one is probably the most heavily used. A ping failure is indicative of a configuration, connectivity, or name resolution problem. It usually leads to the use of IPCONFIG to gather further information.

IPCONFIG. IPCONFIG is used to display a local machine's TCP/IP configuration. The information reported from IPCONFIG is very complete and provides a one-stop snapshot of a TCP/IP configuration. Many problems in TCP/IP can be identified and resolved through the use of IPCONFIG data.

Connectivity Tools

Tools we use in this area include Network Monitor, Performance Monitor, SNMP, ARP, TRACERT, ROUTE, and NETSTAT. These tools and their roles in troubleshooting are briefly described here.

ARP. ARP allows us to view the IP to MAC address resolution cache on a Windows NT host. Remember that if there is no mapping, communications will be unable to successfully complete. The way to use ARP in troubleshooting is to PING a host and then see if the ARP cache has been updated. On a successful PING, an entry will be placed in the ARP cache.

TRACERT. TRACERT is used to determine the path and connection metrics between two hosts. Small TTL (*Time-to-Live*) values to a remote host are indicative of excessive network traffic and slow connections. A time-out across a particular router may indicate either a dead gateway condition or excessive traffic.

ROUTE. ROUTE is used to display the internal route tables of Windows NT computers (both standalone and multi-homed). It is possible to see configured routes and identify problems related to local and remote connectivity by viewing and making modifications using this utility.

Network Monitor. Network Monitor is a Microsoft tool provided with Windows NT Server. NetMon (as it is affectionately known) allows you to capture packets to a particular computer. It is useful in determining what is being transmitted to a particular host and identifying possible bottlenecks on the network.

SNMP. SNMP allows us to look at network devices and computers and assess various statistics and error states on these devices. SNMP is a very useful tool when assessing physical network devices such as routers, bridges, switches, and repeaters. SNMP is also very important in Windows NT because you must install this service protocol for Performance Monitor TCP/IP counters to be installed.

NETSTAT. NETSTAT is a Windows NT command line utility that allows the network administrator to view various statistics and information on connections for a particular TCP/IP host. NETSTAT shows ports used, connected users, transport mechanisms, and other useful information. Use NETSTAT if you are attempting to monitor and/or troubleshoot connected users to a particular Windows NT host.

Performance Monitor. In general, Performance Monitor allows you to view, track, and report various hardware and protocol statistic related to a local or remote host. In terms of TCP/IP, Performance Monitor can be used to evaluate various states of connections using the different transport and networking protocols as well as transmission statistics over time. It is very useful in determining performance bottlenecks on a particular machine due to inbound and outbound traffic. SNMP must be installed for TCP/IP counters to be enabled in Performance Monitor.

Name Resolution Tools

Name resolution tools available for our use include NBTSTAT, NSLOOKUP, and NotePad. As you might also guess, delving into the DNS and WINS manager applications are also places you might look for problems. These tools are briefly described below:

NotePad. NotePad, in and of itself, is simply a word processor. However, it is the tool of choice for viewing and editing information on the HOSTS and LMHOSTS files. These two files can wreak havoc in name resolution if they are improperly configured. As such, NotePad becomes a very useful utility for our name resolution troubleshooting.

NBTSTAT. NBTSTAT is a Windows NT command line utility that is used to display NetBIOS for TCP/IP information on a local TCP/IP host. All sorts of useful information is displayed here, including the state of current NetBIOS connections and determination of the NetBIOS scope (if used). It is also used to update the LMHOSTS cache.

NSLOOKUP. NSLOOKUP is a Windows NT command line utility that allows you to display name resolution information from a DNS server. The DNS server can be of any type. NSLOOKUP is a generic command for troubleshooting TCP/IP.

WINS Manager. A huge amount of information resides in the WINS manager application related to registered NetBIOS names, static address mapping, push/pull replication, and all things related to NetBIOS name resolution. When you need the definitive source of NetBIOS name resolution information in a dynamically configured Windows network, this is the place to go!

DNS Manager. Here again, if you believe there is a problem with a FQDN to IP address mapping, DNS is the place to check and repair this information. When NSLOOKUP fails and you can ping an IP address, the problem will likely reside in the DNS database. DNS entries are prone to error entries and even an out-of-sequence entry can cause name resolution problems.

Lesson 10.4 How to Troubleshoot TCP/IP

When a TCP/IP troubleshooting problem arises, you should work from the bottom-up to solve the issue. What we mean by this is that you should first try to assess the overall network configuration before working on higher level problems relating to network connectivity and name resolution. Obviously, if TCP/IP is not configured properly at a basic level, none of the other functions will work! So, let's see how we troubleshoot a basic configuration.

Troubleshooting TCP/IP Configurations

Troubleshooting TCP/IP configurations should always start by asking (and answering) a couple of key questions.

1. ***Is the remote computer accessible from other workstations?*** If other computers are able to communicate with the remote computer, it is most likely a problem on the local host. If other hosts cannot communicate with a remote host, it may be a problem on the destination computer. Depending on the nature of the problem, it might also be a problem with a physical device connecting the two networks.

2. ***Can the user's computer connect to anything else?*** When we answer this question, we are attempting to determine a basic configuration problem. Usually problems will arise in the following areas/combinations.

   - ***Computer is unable to communicate with itself.*** If the user is unable to communicate with itself (failed the loopback test), there is definitely a TCP/IP configuration problem. It could be the protocol is installed incorrectly or there is a problem with the Windows NT networking installation.

   - ***Computer can communicate on its own subnet but not with remote subnet hosts.*** If a computer is able to communicate with other local subnet hosts but unable to communicate with remote subnets, it could be an incorrect gateway address.

   - ***Computer can communicate with itself, but no other computers.*** If a computer passes its internal loopback test but is unable to communicate on either a local or remote subnet, this is an indicator that the subnet mask has been incorrectly specified.

To determine the nature of a connectivity problem, use PING. The following approach will assist you in troubleshooting problems of this nature:

Step 1—PING a Remote Host. Attempt to establish whether you can see a remote subnet by pinging another host you are sure is operational and configured properly. If this works, there is nothing wrong with the client and the problem lies with the remote host.

Step 2—PING the Far Side of the Router. Pinging the far side of a router will tell you that the router, subnet mask, and default gateway are properly configured. If you do not get a reply, the client's default gateway could be misconfigured or the router might be down.

Step 3—PING the Near Side of the Router. Pinging the near side of the router will let you know whether the router port is active. If you get a reply, you may have an incorrect default gateway specified on the client. If you do not, it could be your subnet mask or the router is down.

Step 4—PING a Local Subnet Host. If you can Ping a local host on the same subnet, this assures that the subnet mask is properly configured. If you are unable to do so, check the subnet mask.

Step 5—PING the Local Loopback Address. If none of the above situations are working, the problem may very well lie with the internal configuration of the TCP/IP client. Try Pinging the loopback address (127.0.0.1). If you get an error here, you definitely have a problem with the internal configuration of TCP/IP. Also, check Event Viewer at this point. If there is a problem with your network configuration, there will usually be several errors in the system log. This can help you identify the root cause of the problem.

If the host passes Test 1, it is implied that all the other tests will also be completed successfully. So try Test 1 first and then work your way down the list. These tests can be performed very quickly and will help you narrow the problem down in a matter of minutes. When one of these tests fail, it is time to pull IPCONFIG out of the toolbox.

Using IPCONFIG to Locate the Problem

OK, so we have a configuration problem. Our next step is to try to find the offending configuration entry. Based on your results from the tests above, you should have some idea where to look. All information related to configuration problems can be displayed using the IPCONFIG /ALL command. Some indicators of where a problem may lie are listed here.

Statically Configured TCP/IP Computers. Look at all the entries listed by IPCONFIG. It is easy to make a mistake manually entering information for TCP/IP. Based on the results from your PING tests, you should know what entries to focus on.

Dynamically Configured TCP/IP Computers. If the client is using DHCP for address leasing, look for an IP entry of 0.0.0.0. This is a sure sign that the client didn't get an IP address. Make sure the loopback test passes. This will verify that IP is correctly configured on the machine. Assuming that test passes, try renewing the lease using the IPCONFIG /RENEW. If that doesn't work, check all the cable connections. For testing purposes, you may wish to try a static configuration to isolate whether the problem is hardware related. If the client has a DHCP lease and information is configured for the client, review that information to make sure there are no incorrect entries on the DHCP scope for that subnet. Of course, if that is the issue, you will have many calls from your users and they will all be having the same problem!

Following this method will usually put you on the right track to problem resolution in a short time. The nice thing about this is that the process we use here is additive. This means that everything we have done up to this point will serve us well as we move onto the other types of problems.

Troubleshooting Connectivity Problems

Connectivity problems are usually related to either an overutilized network or an inappropriate router table configuration. Once we have eliminated the client configuration, we must look at the overall network to determine if this might be causing our problem. To do this, use the following procedure.

TRACERT to Another Host on the Remote Network. TRACERT will tell us if there is a congested link anywhere in the route path from source to destination network. If a packet is dropped or a TTL value decreases substantially (more than 4 or 5 values) at one router, it is an indicator that the router is either malfunctioning or there is a bucket of traffic trying to move across the link. If this is outside your control, the user may have to try accessing the resource later!

Use Network Monitor and Performance Monitor. These two tools will inform us if we have excessive network traffic on our LAN or WAN internetwork. Remember though that you must install the full version of Network Monitor (included with Microsoft SMS Server) to analyze other computers on the network. The version that ships with Windows NT can only monitor the server itself. Also, if you are using Performance Monitor, install SNMP to gain access to the TCP/IP performance monitor counters. Acceptable network performance varies, but usually a sustained throughput above 80% indicates a network performance problem.

Use NETSTAT. If things look good in terms of network utilization, use NETSTAT to look at a host's connection activity and traffic. If you get an error, or nothing is shown, you very likely have some sort of internal hardware or configuration-related problem.

Use ROUTE. Display the ROUTE table to see if anything looks awry. You may also need to do this on the router if you are unable to get across a gateway.

Use SNMP. If you work in an environment that uses SNMP for network management and you have a SNMP management station on your network, peruse the MIB information for the physical network devices to see if any traps have been generated related to poor performance or errors in hardware.

These type of connectivity problems can be very difficult to resolve and you may very well be using resources well outside your span of control. Prepare yourself for a series of calls and interaction with several groups when troubleshooting network connectivity issues. Typically, if things look good here, there is only one other type of problem we have to resolve.

Name Resolution Troubleshooting

Next to a basic configuration problem, this type of situation will rear its ugly head on a regular basis! Name resolution problems are most commonly associated with network browsing and FQDN/NetBIOS name resolution.

In these situations, you must first determine whether the problem resides with FQDN or NetBIOS name resolution. If you can ping using a NetBIOS name, this means NetBIOS name resolution is working fine. Likewise, if you can use a FQDN to ping to a host, DNS name resolution is working fine.

NOTE: *You should always determine whether the TCP/IP configuration is correct first by pinging a host using its IP address. If this works, then try pinging the host with its NetBIOS or FQDN. You will never be able to resolve a higher level name if the interface is configured incorrectly!*

For the purposes of this discussion, we will assume that you can ping using an IP address but not with a higher level name. Resolving name resolution problems requires that you again answer a few basic questions.

1. **Are you able to browse the local subnet?** If you are able to bring up a list of computers using Network Neighborhood on your local subnet but not on a remote subnet, this means browsing is working properly. If it is not, try "finding the computer" using the Start/Find Computer command. It is possible that the browse list on your local machine or a browse master has not been recently updated with the name of the computer you are looking for. Remember that there can be a time lag of up to 45 minutes due to the way browsing works. If this works, you should be able to connect to the machine. Also, browsing is broadcast-based and will typically not traverse a router (unless the feature is enabled) so if machines are not configured properly, you may only see computers on the local subnet. The problem here will require you have either a LMHOSTS file on each PDC and/or WINS servers with the addresses of other PDC servers on remote networks. The other option (and recommended) is to enable Push/Pull WINS replication across the WAN links.

2. **Are you using HOSTS or LMHOSTS files for name resolution?** If your network is using LMHOSTS and/or HOSTS files for name resolution, be sure the files are being replicated to the local machines and that they have valid and correct entries. Remember that if a network only uses this type of resolution, each client must have the files locally and they must be configured correctly. Use NotePad to check the file configurations. If you use both LMHOSTS and HOSTS file resolution in conjunction with DNS and WINS, make sure there are no conflicting entries!

3. **Are the correct IP addresses specified for the WINS and DNS servers?** If you are using WINS and DNS in a static configuration, the server addresses must be specified for name registration and resolution to occur in a timely fashion. Check these values! If you are using DHCP, assure they are appropriately configured and that there is a WINS broadcast entry for "H-Node" transmissions. Again, use IPCONFIG to view the current configuration and make modifications as necessary.

4. **Are the WINS and DNS servers online?** Now I know this sounds like a rather stupid thing to check, but you would be surprised how many name resolution problems can be resolved simply by assuring a server is up and running! This is particularly the case in smaller institutions where secondary servers are not used.

5. **Does the Internet application require NetBIOS names to connect even though they use a FQDN for name resolution?** This is a hybrid problem that causes big headaches when an application expects to connect to a resource using a computer name and regular name resolution only occurs using DNS. To get around this problem, you should enable a Domain Suffix in TCP/IP properties. This will in effect concatenate (add together) the NetBIOS name and the domain suffix, allowing the application to get what it needs and DNS to appropriately resolve its name. Some Microsoft products like RDS and Exchange require this type of configuration.

Name resolution troubleshooting really is not all that bad once you have determined it is the cause of the problem. Assuring that both the clients and their respective name resolution services are operational requires only a few checks and tests. Although annoying and sometimes difficult to troubleshoot, a name resolution problem is not necessarily a critical error. The TCP/IP installation will still be functional. It is important that you resolve the problem as quickly as possible though to stop a flood of potential support calls.

Lesson 10.5 Houston, We Have a Problem—Now What?

So you have a TCP/IP problem. . . . And no matter what you've tried, nothing works! Now what? It's time to "hit the books" and research your situation. There are a number of places for you to go. Listed below are some of the more common sources of information that will be useful as you attempt to solve a TCP/IP problem.

Windows NT Resource Kits. The Windows NT Workstation and Server resource kits have a wealth of detailed information on Windows NT generally and TCP/IP specifically. Many questions and problems can be answered using these books. They are well worth the investment both in the additional tools and content found in the texts. If you purchase a subscription to Microsoft TechNet, these manuals in electronic format are provided as part of your subscription.

Microsoft TechNet. This piece of software solves more problems on a regular basis than any other tool used by this support engineer. It contains the entire Microsoft Knowledge Base, resource kits for almost all products, and a host of patches, service packs, tools, and additional information. It has bailed me out of literally hundreds of difficult troubleshooting problems—all in a huge query-able database. Of all the resources available to you, this one will assist you the most. You must subscribe to TechNet to get the information. It currently costs $295.00 per year. If you solve just two problems over the year, the subscription has paid for itself. One Microsoft support call can easily cost that much!

Microsoft Support. When all else fails, and you have a real zinger, sometimes you have to go to the source. Microsoft support is excellent but expensive. If you just can't find the answer to a problem and have exhausted all other avenues, this is the place to go. Microsoft will help you and stay with the problem until it is resolved. But this is expensive! It depends on your organization's support arrangements but can cost in excess of $150.00 per call. So, try everything else before you contact them!

Microsoft Internet Knowledge Base. Microsoft provides an Internet-based version of their support knowledge-base. This is available free to everyone. You will need to register with the service, but you may use it to search through the same databases Microsoft support engineers use to troubleshoot problems. It is searchable on any product and provides all types of information that may be useful as you troubleshoot. The URL to gain access to the website is http://support.microsoft.com.

Books, Books and More Books. If you can't find information in Microsoft documentation, go to the local bookstore and see if any books have been written generally or specifically on the type of problem you are having. There are literally hundreds of third-party books on Microsoft BackOffice and networking topics. Chances are, one of these authors will answer your question. I have spent many an evening having a good cup of coffee, grabbing several texts, and pouring over books to locate a particular solution to a problem. If you go to one of the larger bookstores, you don't even have to buy the books! You can do your research, and then return them to the shelf—almost like a library.

Fellow Engineers. Talking through problems with other network administrators is a very valuable source of information. A person who is completely objective about a particular problem may see the obvious that you have missed. I always speak with my peers about problems. You'd be surprised how many issues can be solved by talking your way through a problem!

Summary

This chapter explored basic troubleshooting of TCP/IP networks. We discussed various methods and tools to use in identifying the source of a problem and providing a method of resolution. Within this chapter, we looked at the following processes and tools:

- **The Scientific Troubleshooting Method.** We learned how to methodically identify, research, hypothesize, and test a solution to a problem.

- **TCP/IP Problem Classification.** We looked at the three main types of troubleshooting problems you will encounter when working with a TCP/IP network: Configuration, Connectivity, and Name Resolution.

- **TCP/IP Troubleshooting Utilities.** We discussed potential situations where a particular tool would be used to troubleshoot a TCP/IP problem. Recommendations and possible resolutions were presented for many of the problems.

- **Sources of Information.** We took a quick look at some of the most common places you can look for information to assist in troubleshooting.

● ● ● ● ● ● ● ● ● ● ● ● ● ●

Q & A

1. *Select the best answer.* A Windows NT Workstation computer named CORP1 resides on a remote subnet. Keri has performed some basic troubleshooting and can successfully ping her default gateway address and other computers on the remote subnet. However, Keri cannot ping CORP1 using its IP address. What is the most likely cause of the problem?

   a. Keri's computer is set up with an incorrect IP address.
   b. Keri's computer is set up with an incorrect subnet mask.
   c. CORP1 is not DNS-enabled.
   d. The IP configuration on CORP1 is incorrect.
   e. The HOSTS file on Keri's computer has no entry for CORP1.

2. *Select the best answer.* Paul administers a TCP/IP network comprised of three Windows NT Server computers and 500 Windows-based computers. Network traffic is heavy and Paul wants to assess impact on the workstations and servers. What must he do to capture the necessary data?

   a. Run the full Network Monitor application from a server to monitor all systems.
   b. Run the standard Network Monitor on each server.
   c. Run the standard Network Monitor on each workstation.
   d. Run Performance Monitor on each computer.
   e. Run Performance Monitor on each server.

3. *Select all that apply.* You want to manage and monitor using SNMP. Which of the following do you need to install on your Windows NT machines to make this work?

   a. Performance Monitor.
   b. SNMP agent software on each server.
   c. Third-party SNMP manager software on any workstation or server.
   d. Network Monitor.
   e. TCP/IP and nothing else.

4. *Select the best answer.* Phil, a Windows NT Workstation user, is unable to access a Windows NT Server computer on a remote subnet. Using ping to troubleshoot the problem, he finds that every time he tries to connect to the server or any other workstation he gets a "Request Timed Out" reply. No other users on the TCP/IP network have trouble accessing the server or network. What is the most likely cause of Phil's problem?

   a. The workstation is not set up to use DNS.
   b. The workstation is not set up with a default gateway.
   c. The workstation is set up with a duplicate IP address.
   d. The workstation is set up with an incorrect subnet mask.
   e. None of the above.

5. *Select the best answer.* What ROUTE switch/command option enables a user to display route table entries for a host computer?

    a. ROUTE –p PRINT
    b. ROUTE PRINT
    c. ROUTE –f CHANGE
    d. ROUTE –p
    e. ROUTE VIEW

6. *Select the best answer.* Sally cannot connect to a remote UNIX computer via its IP address. She knows TCP/IP is properly installed on her computer. How should she check to see if the router is working correctly?

    a. PING the loopback address 127.0.0.1.
    b. PING another host on the same subnet.
    c. PING the far side of the router.
    d. PING a remote server on another subnet.
    e. PING the near side of the router.

7. *Select the best answer.* Barbara complains that she cannot connect to any other computers on your TCP/IP network. The network uses DHCP, DNS, and WINS servers as well as remote LMHOSTS and HOSTS files. You instruct her to ping the loopback address and get a "Request Timed Out" response. What is the most probable cause of the problem?

    a. TCP/IP is not properly installed on the workstation.
    b. The default gateway address on the workstation is incorrect.
    c. The subnet mask on the workstation is incorrect.
    d. The workstation is not set up for DHCP.
    e. The workstation is not set up for WINS.
    f. None of the above.

8. *Select the best answer.* Fred wants to see current inbound TCP/IP traffic on his Windows NT workstation. What command utility should he use?

    a. ARP
    b. NBTSTAT
    c. NETSTAT
    d. Network Monitor
    e. Performance Monitor
    f. SNMP
    g. None of the above.

9. *Select two.* Mark recently installed a Frame Relay connection between the Los Angeles and Atlanta offices. He needs to be able to allow users at each remote network to be able to browse computers on both subnets. What two methods would allow Mark to accomplish his objectives?

    a. Statically map the other WINS server IP address in the other's WINS database.
    b. Install LMHOSTS files for each remote subnet PDC consisting of the other PDC's address.
    c. Configure each WINS server as both a push partner and a pull partner of the other WINS server.
    d. Configure only the Atlanta office WINS server as a push partner.

10. *Select the best answer.* Which of the following entries in a LMHOSTS file residing on a Windows 95 computer will fail to connect to the NetBIOS machine SERVER40?

   a. #SERVER40 #corporate server
   b. SERVER40 #DOM:SUBNET2
   c. 208.257.45.98 SERVER40 #corporate server
   d. 208.202.98 SERVER40 #corporate server
   e. All these entries are valid.
   f. None of these entries are valid.

11. *Select the best answer.* Working at her Windows NT server computer, Paula wants to capture, view, and report information on ARP packet information for the server since she started it. What utility should she use?

   a. IPCONFIG
   b. PING
   c. NBTSTAT
   d. Network Monitor
   e. Performance Monitor
   f. SNMP

12. *Select the best answer.* Max uses his Windows NT workstation computer to access a UNIX-based server using Telnet. The UNIX computer is located on a remote subnet. Terry's workstation has a HOSTS file with the following entries:

   144.120.19.9 research.comp.com

   156.129.22.1 design.comp.dev.com

   When Max runs the command "telnet design.dev.comp.com," he receives the message "Bad IP address." However, when he runs the command "telnet 156.129.22.1," he connects to the UNIX computer. What is causing the problem?

   a. The Telnet command cannot be used with a hostname.
   b. The FQDN is incorrect.
   c. The hostname and the IP address are wrong in the HOSTS file.
   d. The workstation is set up to use DNS to resolve host names.

13. Mary is troubleshooting a Windows NT server computer on a TCP/IP network. The server is on a subnet with the network ID 150.128.0.0. Users on a remote subnet cannot access the server. Mary executes IPCONFIG /ALL and receives the following output:

   Windows NT IP Configuration:

   Host Name: PA_PDC
   DNS Servers: 150.128.4.1
   Node Type: hybrid
   NetBIOS Scope ID:
   IP Routing Enabled: No
   WINS Proxy Enable: Yes
   NetBIOS Resolution Uses DNS: Yes

Ethernet Adapter: NE2000 Adapter
Description: NE2000 Adapter
Physical Address: 00-FF-21-56-33-10
DHCP Enabled: No
IP Address: 150.128.2.226
Subnet Mask: 255.255.224.0
Default Gateway: 150.128.2.1
Primary WINS Server: 150.128.2.50

What is the most likely cause of the server's problem?

  a. DHCP is not enabled.
  b. The default gateway is incorrect.
  c. DNS is not configured properly.
  d. The subnet mask is incorrect.
  e. The MAC address is incorrect.

14. *Select all that apply.* What utilities are associated with testing connectivity in a TCP/IP network?

  a. PING
  b. NETSTAT
  c. TRACERT
  d. ROUTE
  e. All of the above.
  f. None of the above.

15. *Select the best answer.* Installing TCP/IP counters requires what other service to be installed on a Windows NT Server?

  a. WINS
  b. DNS
  c. DHCP
  d. SNMP
  e. Simple TCP/IP Services

and DHCP, 268

switches, 40

for troubleshooting, 329, 333

IPX/SPX, 2, 13

ISO/OSI model, 2, 4

ISOC (Internet Society), 4, 14, 15

Iterative queries, 209

K

KB (kilobytes), 84

Kernigan, Brian, 12

Kilobytes. See KB

L

LAN (local area network), 76, 94, 107, 128, 334

LAT (logical address table), 320

Layers of the OSI model, 67–68

LCD (least common denominator), 6

Leasing or renting IP addresses, 251–253

Least common denominator (LCD), 6

LMHOSTS (logical machine hosts) files, 52–53, 162, 166–171. See also NetBIOS; WINS

commands for, 168–170

and DNS files, 217–218

integrating WINS and LMHOSTS, 193

management and guidelines, 171

purpose of, 167

and TCP/IP use, 167–168

for troubleshooting, 331, 335

Load balancing, 213

Local area network. See LAN

Local scope options, 260–262

Logical address table. See LAT

LPD (line printer daemon), 290, 292, 295

LPQ (line printer queue), 290, 292, 295

LPR (line printer request), 290, 292, 295

M

MAC addresses, 44, 47, 107

Management information base. See MIB

Manager commands in SNMP, 307

Mapping to the OSI model, 68–71

Massachusetts Institute of Techonology (MIT), 12

Master browser, 165

Master name servers, 212

Maximum hops in DHCP relay agent, 280

MIB (management information base), 305–306

Microsoft Corporation, 53

Microsoft Internet Knowledge Base, 337

Microsoft Knowledge Base, 337

Microsoft NetBEUI, 6

Microsoft Proxy Server, 128

Microsoft support, 337

Microsoft TCP/IP 4.0 installation, 17–27. See also TCP/IP

default gateway, 18

DHCP installation, 19

IP address, 17–18

services and utilities installed, 20–21

static IP address installation, 19–20

static versus dynamic address management, 18–19

subnet mask, 18

Microsoft TCP/IP, 5. See also TCP/IP

features of, 7–10

handshaking, 83–84

IP forwarding, 77

multi-homed computers, 77

NT Server name resolution applications, 11

RAS (remote access server), 74–76

RIP (routing information protocol) for IP, 77–79

security, 80–83

sliding windows, 84

TCP windows and handshaking, 83–84

Microsoft TCP/IP implementation, 64–74. See also TCP/IP

layers of OSI, 67–68

mapping to the OSI model, 68–71

network architecture, 68–71

network model, 66–74

network transport overview, 65–66

OSI model, 66–68

U

UDP (user datagram protocol), 4–5, 66, 251

UNC (universal naming convention), 160. *See also* WINS

United States Department of Defense. *See* DOD

United States National Science Foundation, 4

Universal naming convention. *See* UNC

UNIX, 3
  case sensitivity, 13, 36, 295
  print client/server, 290
  shorthand notation, 13
  and TCP/IP, 12–13, 290

User datagram protocol. *See* UDP

User-defined ports, 71–72

Utilities for cross-platform connectivity, 293–304

V

Virtual Servers, 320

W

WAN (wide-area network), 3, 76, 189, 212–213

and forwarding servers, 214

and troubleshooting, 334, 335

Well-known ports, 71, 72

Wide-area network. *See* WAN

Windows 95, 7

Windows and handshaking, 83–84

Windows NT, 7
  installation of Microsoft TCP/IP 4.0, 17–27
  remote access server (RAS), 74–76
  test utilities, 34–50

Windows NT Resource Kits, 336

Windows NT Workstation, 7, 20, 21

WINIPCFG, 268

WINS (Windows Internet Naming Service), 4, 52, 171–174. *See also* LMHOSTS files; NetBIOS
  backing up the database, 197
  compressing the database, 198
  configuring a client, 180–182
  database maintenance, 197–198
  definition of, 172

and DNS, 217–218, 232–237

installation, 175–178

integrating WINS and LMHOSTS, 193

manager application, 182–184

name resolution, 172–174

NBT (NetBIOS for TCP/IP), 172

NBTSTAT utility, 195–197

non-WINS clients, 174

proxy, 174

registration parameter management, 184–187

replication, 188–193

restoring the database, 198

starting and stopping service, 178–180

static versus dynamic mappings, 172, 187–188

troubleshooting, 194–196, 331, 335, 336

WWW, 320

Z

Zone transfers, 212

Zone update notify parameter in DNS, 237–240

Zones in DNS domains, 211